# Modern County Government

# Modern County Government

**Herbert Sydney Duncombe**
Professor, Political Science
University of Idaho

**National Association of Counties**
Washington, D.C.

*To my parents Herbert S.
Duncombe and Frances Riker
Duncombe who provided me with
inspiration and an early interest in
local government.*

# Foreword

This book is a snapshot of our political system in evolution. Because the system is in constant flux, between the time Professor Herbert Sydney Duncombe has written the words and the time you actually read them, some American counties may be quite different in several respects from what he describes.

From the first days of European settlement, it has been necessary for Americans to invent governmental institutions to provide for public service and safety. We continue to do so. When we stop innovating, the vitality of our political system will be in serious question.

One of the most notable of American contributions to the evolution of political institutions was the ingenious provision in the Northwest Ordinance of 1785 providing for the establishment of states in unorganized territory once the population reached a certain level. Obviously, these states were too large to provide effective local government and so we settled upon a jurisdictional concept borrowed directly from our British heritage: the shire or county, a subdivision of the state.

The role of the county took several forms depending upon whether a state borrowed its concepts from Virginia, Massachusetts, or Pennsylvania. Virginia's system of strong counties with no towns became the southern model and perhaps it explains why today, given the strength of the southern county versus the municipality, it has proven easier to develop new forms of government in metropolitan areas of the South than in other areas of the country.

The New York model—a "supervisor" form of county government in which the county's governing body consists of a legislature of supervisors elected from towns or townships—spread across the nation's northern rim through Michigan, Illinois, and Wisconsin.

Pennsylvania's "commissioner" form is the commonly accepted model in most of the Midwest and Western states. Louisiana, given its unique history, borrowed from the French, however, and established parishes.

Now under the pressures of new conditions, we see these basic forms changing to meet new needs. The counties in many parts of the United States today are in flux. They are changing in their functional responsibilities, in their structures, in their methods of financing, and in their political behavior.

The reasons are not difficult to detect. In the past four or five decades, the conditions of settlement in our country have changed profoundly.

In the previous five decades, huge numbers of Americans moved out of our rural counties and into the cities and the suburbs. But now, in the 1970s, many are moving beyond the suburbs back into nonmetropolitan counties again. The nation is de-centralizing, its patterns of settlement dispersing away from the old concentrations which grew up in the late 1800s and early in the present century.

Today, the boundary distinctions between city, suburb, and rural area mean little in economic terms to 95 percent of all Americans. A family may live in a rural farmstead, but shop and work in the city. A suburbanite may not only commute in to the city to a job, he may also commute out to a plant in a rural community 50 miles away. Our way of life has changed, thanks mainly to the automobile and communications.

But the shape of our political jurisdictions has not changed correspondingly. Many local problems today are in reality boundary problems; the capabilities of municipal governments in the older urban areas no longer match the scale of demands placed upon them, the financial resources available to them, nor the territorial extent of the constituency to be served. There is little correlation any more between the functions of municipal government in many older metropolitan areas and the territory and finances it commands.

More and more attention is turning to the county as the jurisdictional solution to the problem in many of these areas.

We have been trying other approaches of course. In recent decades, the nation has experimented with regional councils, substate regions, and a variety of other intergovernmental devices intended to surmount the mismatch between boundaries and problems. Despite some outstanding successes, the overall experience has been less than satisfactory. They created another layer of government, usually without any real power.

In the coming decade and a half it seems quite probable that we will be forced to go beyond these efforts to more substantive reforms, more likely to restore jurisdictional and functional integrity to local governments. We seem less and less able or willing to accept cosmetic changes. We are beginning a search for substantive solutions to local government problems in both urban and sparsely populated rural regions.

It seems fair to guess that the changes the public is more likely to accept will not involve actual changes in physical boundaries of jurisdictions, but rather in the functions of existing jurisdictions. We are likely to see increased reliance on the use of general government to meet urban needs rather than further establishment of special purpose entities. The urban county, for example, may become a primary vehicle for services in the smaller metropolitan areas. In sparsely populated regions, the counties will be the basic mechanism for services and governance. Sydney Duncombe has captured in this book the direction of these changes.

The county, until recently, was considered to be one of the poor stepchildren of American politics, a simple subdivision of the state. But more and more, as the territorial patterns of our daily life expand, the county is growing into potentially the most useful instrumentality of local government to deal with the problems of a highly decentralized pattern of settlement and economic activity.

This book provides an ideal background for an informed discussion of the possibilities.

Ralph R. Widner, President
Academy for Contemporary Problems
Columbus, Ohio
May, 1977

# Preface

It has been sixty years since H.S. Gilbertson wrote one of the earliest (and best known) books on county government. At the time, sheriffs frequently pocketed fees for feeding prisoners, county employees commonly paid salary kickbacks to their bosses, county public works projects were often poorly planned and constructed, and most county alms houses and poor farms were a disgraceful means of caring for the elderly. Gilbertson was writing of an era of boss rule, a splintered county executive branch, and a lack of professionalism when he labeled county government as "the dark continent of American politics."

County government has come a long way since 1917, when Gilbertson's book was written. The evils described by Gilbertson have largely disappeared from county government. County home rule, recommended by Gilbertson, has spread to at least fifteen states. If he were alive today, Gilbertson would be amazed (and pleased) to find that, while there was not a single county with a county manager or elected county executive in 1917, more than half the people living in counties today have a council-elected executive or council-administrator form of county government.

The most significant change in county government in the past six decades has been the tremendous expansion and urbanization of county services. When Gilbertson wrote, the typical county provided about a dozen state-mandated services such as recording of deeds, property tax assessment and collection, law enforcement, judicial administration, poor relief, and road maintenance. Today, there are more than one hundred county services, and many of these (such as energy conservation, consumer protection, and growth management) did not exist as county functions sixty years ago. Counties have increasingly provided urban services such as planning, zoning, solid waste disposal, mass transit, parking, and recreation programs to both urban and rural residents. The accelerating change in county government and county services deserves to be described more fully than it has been in the past half century.

This book is written to meet the needs of instructors in local government for a textbook on the current status of the organization, functions, financing, politics, and intergovernmental relations of county government. The book is also intended to provide a useful reference source for county officials and to serve as a textbook for in-service county training courses. No single volume can adequately describe the subject, but it is hoped that this book will provide students with a useful summary of the progress of county government and its status in 1977. Further studies of county government are needed—particularly studies of county modernization, case studies of county politics, and behavioral studies of county officials and the county decision-making process.

The stress placed on county modernization deserves explanation. It is the author's contention that county modernization has been particularly rapid during the past decade and that this is reflected in the more extensive use of the council-elected executive and council-administrator forms of county government, the increase in the adoption of county charters, and the more widespread provision of modern, urban services by county governments. The author has developed a county modernization index in the concluding chapter of the book which he uses to relate modernization to county characteristics. Further research needs to be done to better understand the factors serving as catalysts for county modernization and change.

This book makes use of several sources of information on county government that were not available a decade ago. Comprehensive statistical studies of county services have appeared in recent editions of *The County Year Book* and have been used widely in this volume. The National Association of Counties has collected and made available to the public hundreds of descriptions of innovative county programs through its achievement award system and publication, *The Living Library*. Behavioral studies of county political organization and county officers have been made in the past decade, and their findings are included in this book.

The problem of describing more than three thousand diverse counties is enormous. To better understand the differences among county governments, the author drove from coast-to-coast interviewing county officials in nineteen states. In addition, the author interviewed officials from nearly fifty counties at two national conferences sponsored by the National Association of Counties in 1976 and obtained information from nearly one hundred county achievement awards. This book includes references to county organization, services, politics, or intergovernmental relations in more than one hundred and fifty counties.

The author is greatly indebted to the National Association of Counties for making available its case study files and statistics. The author is particularly indebted to Bernard F. Hillenbrand, Executive Director of the National Association of Counties, for his encouragement and support and to Thomas P. Bruderle of the NACo staff who thoroughly reviewed and edited the entire manuscript. Beth Denniston of NACo is to be thanked for her work in preparing the manuscript for publication. The author is appreciative of the suggestions made by other members of the NACo staff who reviewed parts of the manuscript.

The author is also indebted to the many county officials who supplied information for the book and reviewed the portions of the book describing their counties. The author is particularly appreciative of the time taken by: Daniel Lynch, Douglas County (Nebraska) Commissioner; Bernard Smith, Sioux County (Iowa) Supervisor; William Brennan, Rio Blanco County (Colorado) Commissioner; Joseph Torrence, Nashville-Davidson County (Tennessee) Finance Director; Alastair McArthur and Neal Potter, Coordinator of Intergovernmental Programs and County Councilman of Montgomery County (Maryland); Conrad Fowler, County Judge, Shelby County (Alabama); Richard Bryant, Parks Director, Montgomery County (Ohio) and County Executive Louis Mills

of Orange County (New York) and members of his staff.

The author has appreciated also the ideas, comments, and personal contact with a number of writers on county government and county services including: Ralph Widner, President of the Academy for Contemporary Problems, Professor John DeGrove of Florida Atlantic University, and Professor Clayne Jensen of Brigham Young University.

The author appreciates the assistance of Linda Fulton and Carol Matsui who spent many hours typing the later drafts of the manuscript. Finally, I am indebted to my wife, Mary Conklin Duncombe, for her typing of the first draft and her many hours of proof reading, and to my whole family for their patience, support and great understanding during the period this book was written.

# Table of Contents

# Chapter 1

# Three Thousand Counties

"It has come to pass that the city government with its legislative, executive and judicial branches, is of major concern to the city dwellers and the administration of the affairs of the county is of major concern to the rural dwellers."[1]

One of the enduring myths of American local government, carried over from a simpler past, is that county government is rural or non-urban government. Some people believe that counties begin outside the city limits; in fact, one city resident commented that he did not vote for county officials because their work affected only farmers.

Certainly ignorance on the part of an average citizen is understandable, but the position of the Texas Supreme Court, cited in the case above, reveals how this myth, as recently as 10 years ago, was sustained by even those who should have known better. The majority in the above case recognized that a county included both urban and rural areas, but argued that county services—such as roads, bridges, and property taxes—concern mainly rural residents. Most county of-ficials, therefore, should represent rural areas. The myth of the county as a rural unit of government rests on misconceptions about the characteristics of counties as well as a lack of knowledge about the type of services which they provide.

## THE COUNTY AS GEOGRAPHIC AREA

A large wall map of the United States will show state boundaries by thick lines and will often show, by thinner lines, the boundaries between the counties within each state. If a map is very large or very detailed, it may show the boundaries of cities, townships, boroughs, school districts, or special districts. In geographic terms, the basic subdivision of the state is the county or county area.

There were 3,146 county-type

areas in 1972 which covered the entire United States, according to the Bureau of the Census, including "boroughs" in Alaska and "parishes" in Louisiana which are similar to counties.[2] Not all county areas have county government, however. The states of Connecticut and Rhode Island are divided into geographic areas called counties but do not have county governments.

Recent figures published in the County Year Book show 3,104 county-type governments in the United States in 1976.[3] These include: 3,042 counties, 23 city-county consolidations, and 39 independent cities. City-county consolidations are mergers of the governments of the county and the largest city in the county. An independent city is a form of local government found mainly in Virginia performing both city and county functions. The National Association of Counties, the only national organization representing county government, has listed city-county consolidations and independent cities as county-type governments because, regardless of area, they all provide county services.

The number of county-type governments in each state varies from 254 in Texas to three in Delaware. The average number of county governments per state is 65, with southern and midwestern states generally exceeding the average and New England and many western states falling below the average.

Map 1-1
NUMBER OF COUNTY-TYPE GOVERNMENTS BY STATE

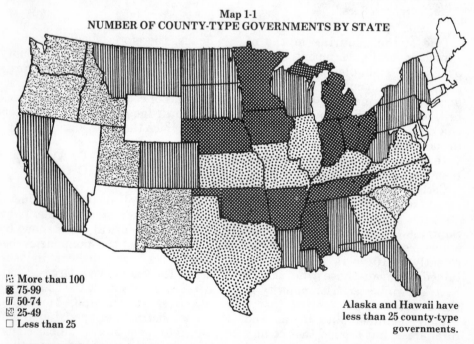

⠿ More than 100
▧ 75-99
⫼ 50-74
⬚ 25-49
☐ Less than 25

Alaska and Hawaii have
less than 25 county-type
governments.

SOURCE: The map was prepared from National Association of Counties and International City Management Association, *The County Year Book, 1976* (Washington: National Association of Counties and International City Management Association, 1976), Table 2.

The last four decades have seen very little change in the number of county governments or county-type governments. The National Association of Counties has been keeping statistics on the number of county-type governments since 1973, and the number has declined slightly from 3,106 to 3,104. The U.S. Bureau of the Census, which has been compiling statistics on the number of county governments for a much longer time, reports that the number of county governments declined from 3,053 in the 1930-33 base period to 3,042 in 1976.[4]

Since the 1930's, counties have been established in Hawaii, boroughs created and given county status in Alaska, county governments abolished in Connecticut, and some counties have become city-county consolidated governments. The last consolidation of two or more counties occurred in the 1930's when two rural counties near Atlanta, Georgia merged with Fulton County.[5] County consolidation and boundary changes have been made difficult by restrictive provisions of state constitutions and laws. In Idaho, for example, the state constitution requires a two-thirds or greater majority vote in each county to be consolidated.[6] It is very difficult to get such a majority in the county which would lose its county seat and the economic advantages of a county government payroll. Since the 1930's, there have been fewer changes in the numbers and boundaries of county governments than in any other unit of local government.

**Geographic Size.** America's counties differ greatly in area. San Bernardino County (California) has 20,117 square miles and is larger than the combined area of Massachusetts, Connecticut, Rhode Island, and Delaware. One of the boroughs of Alaska, Upper Yukon, has an area of 84,142 square miles and is larger than most states. In contrast, Arlington County (Virginia), with an area of 26 square miles, could be contained in a small corner of one of our larger counties. Table 1-1 shows that the predominant area covered by a county is 400-599 square miles. In counties of this size, a person can drive from nearly anywhere within it

Table 1-1
AREA IN SQUARE MILES OF SAMPLE COUNTIES

| Area | Percent |
| --- | --- |
| Less than 200 square miles | 3.3% |
| 200-399 square miles | 14.7% |
| 400-599 square miles | 29.3% |
| 600-799 square miles | 13.7% |
| 800-999 square miles | 11.7% |
| 1,000-1,499 square miles | 10.3% |
| 1,500-1,999 square miles | 6.3% |
| More than 2,000 square miles | 10.7% |
| | 100.0% |

SOURCE: The table was prepared from data in National Association of Counties and International City Management Association, *The County Yearbook, 1975* (Washington: National Association of Counties and International City Management Association, 1975), pp. 127-178. A ten per cent sample of counties was selected by random means.

to the county seat in less than an hour.

Almost all counties are larger than a typical city, village, town, or township. From a geographic point of view, this makes the county a middle sized area—smaller than a state, but larger than other general purpose units of local government.

According to Bernard F. Hillenbrand, Executive Director of The National Association of Counties, some of the advantages of the county as a middle level unit between state and local government include:[7]

"*(1) A broad tax base which insures financial stability.*

*(2) An areawide jurisdiction which enables it to administer and enforce important regulatory functions, such as housing codes and environmental programs.*

*(3) An economy of scale that is beyond the capacity of smaller jurisdictions.*

*(4) As a middle level of government, the county serves as an intermediary of governmental relations between the state and federal governments' programs and the nation's citizenry.*

*(5) Political accountability. The people who reside within the county elect their representatives and pay the county taxes. They are served by the county governing board.*"

**Population.** The populations of counties vary greatly. With a 1970 population of 7,036,887, Los Angeles County is the nation's most populous county. In contrast, Hinsdale County (Colorado) had a 1970 population of 202 and Loving Coun-

Table 1-2

NUMBER OF COUNTY GOVERNMENTS IN 1970
BY POPULATION GROUP

County Governments

| Population-Size Groups | Number | Percent | Percent of Population Served by County Governments |
|---|---|---|---|
| 250,000 or more | 127 | 4.2% | 48.2% |
| 100,000 to 249,999 | 185 | 6.1% | 16.3% |
| 50,000 to 99,999 | 326 | 10.7% | 12.6% |
| 25,000 to 49,999 | 566 | 18.6% | 11.0% |
| 10,000 to 24,999 | 997 | 32.8% | 9.1% |
| 5,000 to 9,999 | 538 | 17.7% | 2.2% |
| Less than 5,000 | 305 | 10.0% | 0.5% |
| | 3,044 | 100.0% | 100.0% |

SOURCE: U.S. Bureau of the Census, *Census of Governments, 1972, Vol. I. Governmental Organization* (Washington: U.S. Government Printing Office, 1973), p. 2. The 3,044 counties included in the table are just those having an organized county government in 1970. Not included were city-county consolidations and independent cities. In 1975 there were 3,043 counties. Detail may not exactly add to totals due to rounding.

ty (Texas) a population of 164. The density of population in American counties varies from two people in every ten square miles in a few parts of the West to more than five thousand people per square mile near the centers of a few northeastern and midwestern metropolitan areas. Two generalizations about county population can be drawn from Table 1-2, however.

The statistically average county has about 10,000 to 24,999 people who may or may not be concentrated in urban areas.

Secondly, most of the people in the nation live in counties of 100,000 or more population. The 312 counties with 100,000 or more population contain 64.5% of all people living in counties with county governments.

**Urban-Rural Characteristics.** The myth that most counties are rural should be examined closely. First, we need to define what we mean by urban and rural. The Bureau of the Census has an official definition of an urban area which includes:[8]

- *places of 2,500 or more inhabitants incorporated as cities, boroughs, villages, and (in some states) towns;*
- *unincorporated places of 2,500 or more inhabitants; and,*
- *the densely settled urban fringe, whether incorporated or unincorporated, of urbanized areas.*

Rural areas, in contrast, are the nonurban parts of the nation. They include cities of fewer than 2,500 people, subdivisions outside cities and their urban fringes, farm lands, forests, and wilderness areas.

Dividing our nation geographically, we find that 98½% of the land area in the United States is rural and only 1½% is urban.[9] More meaningful than this statistic, however, is the percentage of people residing in urban areas. Data from the 1970 census reveals that 73½% of the population of our nation is packed

Table 1-3

**PERCENT OF COUNTY POPULATION LIVING IN URBAN AREAS IN SAMPLE COUNTIES**

| Degree of Urbanization | Percent Urban | Percent of Counties | Percent of People Living in These Counties |
|---|---|---|---|
| Predominately urban | 75-100% | 10.7% | 56.3% |
| Mainly urban | 50-74% | 18.7% | 18.7% |
| Mainly rural | 25-49% | 30.3% | 14.9% |
| Predominately rural | 1-24% | 11.0% | 5.7% |
| Completely rural | 0% | 29.3% | 4.4% |
| | | 100.0% | 100.0% |

SOURCE: The per cent of urban population in a sample of 310 counties was computed from population data in U.S. Bureau of Census, *1970 Census of Population Volume 1, Characteristics of the Population* (Washington: U.S. Government Printing Office, 1973). The sample was randomly selected within population groups so it was not over weighted with either populous or sparsely populated counties.

into urban areas while 26½% resides in the remaining 98½% of the land which is considered rural.

Another way of examining whether counties as a whole may be considered urban or rural is to determine what percent of the nation's counties have more than half their population living in urban areas. Table 1-3 divides a representative sample of counties into five groups depending upon the percent of county population living in urban areas in 1970. The table shows that 29.4% of all counties are 50% or more urban. Of greater significance is the fact that 75% of the people in the nation live in counties that are at least half urban. Only about 10% of the people in the nation live in the completely or predominantly rural county that many people consider the typical county.

**Economic Base.** The economic base and degree of urbanization of counties affect the types of services their citizens expect from government. In populous, predominantly urban counties, concentrations of manufacturing plants and large numbers of motor vehicles cause high levels of air pollution; citizens in these counties often expect their county government to have an air pollution control program. The existence of extensive areas of slum housing and a large number of low income residents in the older areas of these counties will generally require more extensive county social services, employment, maternal and child health, and rodent control programs.

Some "mainly urban counties" are within commuting distance of metropolitan cities, and their residents are concerned about the adequacy of the county highway systems. In other urban counties, there are large areas of unincorporated land being subdivided for housing or being developed as shopping and office centers. County governments are often called upon to provide education, water supply, sewage treatment, refuse disposal, street maintenance, zoning, subdivision controls, parks, and recreation programs for these areas.

The economy of many predominantly rural counties is farming and ranching. Farm families in these counties rely on agricultural extension agents and other county officials to help control insect pests, supply information on the best types of fertilizers to use, prevent the spread of noxious weeds, and provide a county fair. The economy of many "entirely rural counties" is based on ranching lumbering, and tourism, and their residents are concerned about the adequacy of rural roads and rural law enforcement.

## A PROFILE OF COUNTIES

There is no "typical" county just as there is no typical American, English, German or Japanese person. If counties were ranged on a scale from highest to lowest in population, area, and percent of urban population, the county at the middle of the scale would have a population of about 20,000, of which almost 34% would be urban residents. However, the average person lives in a county that is more than 75% urban. This type of comparison does not reveal the significant differences between groups of counties which are of great importance to a study of county government. To develop a profile of typical counties, it is first necessary to group counties into meaningful classifications.

**Department of Agriculture County Classification.** The Economic Research Service of the U.S. Department of Agriculture has developed a classification of counties used to accumulate key demographic, economic, and social statistics about counties.[10] The classification makes a basic division of counties into two groups: those

Table 1-4

CLASSIFICATION OF COUNTIES AS OF DECEMBER, 1975

1. Metropolitan counties (627)

   a. Counties in large metropolitan areas having at least one million people in 1970

| | | | |
|---|---|---|---|
|      1. Core counties (counties containing the central city in the metropolitan area) | 49 | | |
|      2. Fringe counties (those on the fringe of the metropolitan area) | 132 | 181 | |

   b. Counties in a medium metropolitan area having a 1970 population of 250,000 to 999,999. These can be both core counties and fringe counties. — 260

   c. Counties in a small metropolitan area having a 1970 population of less than 250,000. — 186 — 627

2. Non-metropolitan counties (2,470)

   a. Urbanized counties having 20,000 or more urban residents in 1970

| | | |
|---|---|---|
|      1. Counties adjacent to metropolitan areas | 189 | |
|      2. Counties not adjacent to metropolitan areas | 132 | 321 |

   b. Less urbanized counties having 2,500 to 19,999 urban residents in 1970

| | | |
|---|---|---|
|      1. Counties adjacent to metropolitan areas | 576 | |
|      2. Counties not adjacent to metropolitan areas | 707 | 1,283 |

   c. Thinly populated counties having no urban residents in 1970

| | | | |
|---|---|---|---|
|      1. Counties adjacent to metropolitan areas | 247 | | |
|      2. Counties not adjacent to metropolitan areas | 619 | 866 | 2,470 |

Total number of counties       3,097

SOURCE: Data supplied by David L. Brown, Economic Development Division, Economic Research Service, U.S. Department of Agriculture in a letter dated December 24, 1975. The data came from a computer printout of counties.

The 3,097 county areas in this table differ slightly in number from the 3,104 county-type governments listed in the *1976 County Year Book.* The main differences between the two sets of figures lie in the way independent cities in Virginia, boroughs in Alaska, and counties in Connecticut and Rhode Island are listed.

within standard metropolitan statistical areas (SMSA's) and those outside of these areas. To understand the classification, it is important to know that a metropolitan area (in most of the nation) is basically a county or group of contiguous counties containing at least one city (or twin cities) of 50,000 or more people. The metropolitan area contains the county in which the city (or twin cities) or 50,000 or more is located plus adjacent counties "which are metropolitan in character and are economically and socially integrated with the central city."[11] In New England, cities and towns are used to define the boundaries of metropolitan areas rather than counties.

The Department of Agriculture classification also distinguishes between counties having 20,000 or more urban residents and those with fewer or no urban residents. Urban residents are those who live in cities of 2,500 or more people or in other "urban areas." Table 1-4 shows the Department of Agriculture classification.

Table 1-4 reveals some important information about American counties. Contrary to the popular image of the county as rural and non-metropolitan, 20% of all counties or county-type areas (627) are located within metropolitan areas. An additional 33% (1,012) are located outside but adjacent to a metropolitan area.

As can be seen from Table 1-5, the largest number of metropolitan counties are in densely populated states in the East and Midwest, and the most thinly populated counties tend to be in Plains and Rocky Mountain states.

**Characteristics of Typical Groups of Counties.** It is difficult to describe the characteristics of counties from statistics. To better portray the location and characteristics of individual counties, six groups of counties have been compiled. These classifications are similar to the Department of Agriculture classifications except that a new class (single county metropolitan areas) has been established, and fringe counties include those in all sizes of metropolitan areas. A synopsis of each class follows.

*Metropolitan core counties.* Core counties contain most of the nation's largest cities, and all have a city (or twin cities) of 50,000 or more people. Many people commute into the central city of the core county from surrounding counties and from smaller cities within the core county. The core county is the center of a multi-county regional wholesale, retail, and business area. The core county is likely to have an extensive industrial area, a large minority population, and a higher-than-average percentage of both low-income and wealthy persons. As Table 1-6 shows, the larger core counties have a high population density.

Although, most core counties gained population from 1960 to 1970, many of the same counties lost population after 1970. The recent decline in population of the core county and the even greater decline in the population of the central cities in these counties will be discussed in further detail in the final chapter.

*Metropolitan fringe counties.* Fringe counties completely or partially surround the core county of a multi-county metropolitan area. The inner fringe of counties around our largest metropolitan areas may contain densely populated, predominantly urban counties like Westchester, Nassau, and Suffolk Counties in New York; Delaware and Montgomery Counties in Pennsylvania; and Prince George's and Montgomery Counties in Maryland. These counties have large industrial and/or commercial centers, and many of their residents work within the county while many other commute to New York, Philadelphia, or Washington, D.C.

The outer fringe counties around a large metropolitan area (like Putnam County, New York) are not as densely populated and contain small cities, farm areas, and semi-rural residential areas. The fringe counties around smaller metropolitan areas, such as Indianapolis and Nashville, are also generally less densely populated and may be less than 50% urban. In general, fringe counties have a high growth rate and a high median per capita income. Almost all fringe area counties gained in population between

Table 1-5

NUMBER OF COUNTIES BY DEPARTMENT OF AGRICULTURE CLASSIFICATION, IN DECEMBER, 1975 IN SELECTED STATES

| State | 1970 Population Density | Metropolitan Counties | | | Non-Metropolitan Counties | | | Total |
| | | Large Metro | Medium Metro | Small Metro | Urbanized | Less Urbanized | Thinly Pop. | |
| --- | --- | --- | --- | --- | --- | --- | --- | --- |
| New Jersey | 953.1 | 9 | 6 | 2 | 3 | 1 | 0 | 21 |
| Massachusetts | 727.0 | 4 | 5 | 1 | 2 | 0 | 2 | 14 |
| Maryland | 396.6 | 9 | 1 | 0 | 3 | 7 | 4 | 24 |
| New York | 381.3 | 12 | 17 | 2 | 14 | 16 | 1 | 62 |
| Pennsylvania | 262.3 | 9 | 16 | 3 | 15 | 18 | 6 | 67 |
| Ohio | 260.0 | 12 | 16 | 11 | 17 | 28 | 4 | 88 |
| Illinois | 199.4 | 10 | 7 | 5 | 13 | 54 | 13 | 102 |
| Michigan | 156.2 | 6 | 11 | 8 | 7 | 32 | 19 | 83 |
| Indiana | 143.9 | 9 | 14 | 7 | 9 | 43 | 10 | 92 |
| California | 127.6 | 11 | 9 | 5 | 11 | 15 | 7 | 58 |
| Florida | 125.5 | 4 | 10 | 10 | 9 | 20 | 14 | 67 |
| North Carolina | 104.1 | 0 | 9 | 10 | 14 | 38 | 29 | 100 |
| Tennessee | 94.9 | 0 | 17 | 3 | 8 | 41 | 26 | 95 |
| Alabama | 67.9 | 0 | 9 | 9 | 7 | 31 | 11 | 67 |
| Arkansas | 37.0 | 0 | 3 | 7 | 5 | 39 | 21 | 75 |
| Kansas | 27.5 | 2 | 2 | 3 | 10 | 44 | 44 | 105 |
| Utah | 12.9 | 0 | 3 | 2 | 1 | 9 | 14 | 29 |
| North Dakota | 8.9 | 0 | 0 | 1 | 6 | 8 | 38 | 53 |
| Montana | 4.8 | 0 | 0 | 2 | 3 | 19 | 32 | 56 |
| Wyoming | 3.4 | 0 | 0 | 0 | 3 | 13 | 7 | 23 |

SOURCE: U.S. Bureau of the Census, *Statistical Abstract of the United States, 1975,* (Washington: U.S. Government Printing Office, 1975), p. 15, and data supplied by the Economic Research Service of the U.S. Department of Agriculture. Large metropolitan areas are those with one million or more people in 1970, medium metropolitan areas had 250,000 to 999,999 people, and small metropolitan areas had less than 250,000 people.

1960 and 1970, as did the six counties shown in Table 1-6.

*Single county metropolitan areas.* Single county metropolitan areas do not usually receive as large an influx of commuters from surrounding counties as do core counties. A few one-county metropolitan areas (such as Dade County, Florida) are as densely populated and highly urbanized as core counties, but in general this type of county has less than 500,000 people and less than 500 people per square mile.

The county seats of most of these counties are located in the center of the counties and serve as shopping and trade centers for a multi-county area. The outlying part of some single county metropolitan areas (like Spokane County, Washington) contains farms, forests, and unincorporated rural subdivisions and homes. Most single county metropolitan areas gained population between 1960 and 1970 as did all but one county in this group listed in Table 1-6.

*Urbanized non-metropolitan counties.* These counties have an urban population of 20,000 or more residents and some, like Orange County (New York), may have as many as 100,000 urban residents in a dozen or more small cities. Generally, the county seat of the urbanized county has 20,000 to 40,000 people and is developing into a trade center for surrounding counties. For example, Bowling Green (36,253) in Warren County (Kentucky) is a growing commercial, industrial, and educational center for an eight county region.

Often the urbanized county, such as Weld County (Colorado), has an extensive farm area as well as a growing commercial center. Sometimes, as is the case with Nez Perce County (Idaho), an urbanized county has a large industrial plant and a percent of urban population. Urbanized counties tend to have higher growth rates and higher median incomes than other non-metropolitan counties. Most of these counties gained population between 1960 and 1970.

*Less urbanized counties.* A less urbanized county is one with an urban population of 2,500 to 19,999 people. There is generally one city in this county with a population large enough to support a shopping area which meets the weekly needs of its residents. Several times a year, a resident of a less urbanized county will need to travel to a larger city in a nearby county for specialized purchases or medical care.

Although less urbanized counties have no city of 20,000 or more people, many are not predominantly rural. While Baker County (Oregon) (14,919) is a cattle ranching, wheat farming, and lumbering county, 63% of its people live in one urban city—the county seat. Asotin County (Washington) is 73% urban with many of its residents working in a pulp and paper mill in a nearby county. There are a number of less urbanized counties with a predominantly rural, farm based economy such as Henry County (Iowa). Some less urbanized counties, such as Henry County (Iowa) and (Bullock County (Alabama), lost population between 1960 and 1970.

*Thinly populated counties.* A thinly populated county does not have any urban residents since it has no city or other urban area with 2,500 or more people. Thinly

Table 1-6

EXAMPLES OF POPULATION, POPULATION DENSITY, POPULATION CHANGE,
AND PERCENT OF URBAN POPULATION IN TYPICAL COUNTIES BY GROUP

| County, State and County Seat* | 1970 Population | People Per Square Mile | Percent of Urban Population | Percent of Population Increase 1960-1970 |
|---|---|---|---|---|
| Metropolitan Core Counties | | | | |
| Cook, Illinois (Chicago) | 5,492,369 | 5,473 | 99.7% | 7.1 |
| Wayne, Michigan (Detroit) | 2,666,751 | 4,408 | 98.2% | +.0** |
| Milwaukee, Wisconsin (Milwaukee) | 1,054,063 | 4,447 | 100.0% | 1.7 |
| Marion, Indiana (Indianapolis) | 792,299 | 2,021 | 99.8% | 13.6 |
| Davidson, Tennessee (Nashville) | 448,003 | 882 | 97.4% | 12.0 |
| Metropolitan Fringe Counties* | | | | |
| Westchester, New York (New York inner fringe)* | 894,104 | 2,018 | 93.9% | 10.5 |
| Prince George's, Maryland (Washington area)* | 660,657 | 1,362 | 92.2% | 84.8 |
| Montgomery, Pennsylvania (Philadelphia area)* | 623,799 | 1,257 | 81.6% | 20.7 |
| Waukesha, Wisconsin (Milwaukee area)* | 231,365 | 418 | 80.2% | 46.2 |
| Putnam, New York (New York outer fringe)* | 56,696 | 245 | 37.8% | 78.7 |
| Hendricks, Indiana (Indianapolis area)* | 53,974 | 129 | 32.4% | 32.0 |
| Single County Metropolitan Areas | | | | |
| Dade, Florida (Miami) | 1,267,792 | 621 | 98.3% | 35.6 |
| Spokane, Washington (Spokane) | 287,487 | 126 | 85.7% | 3.3 |
| Fresno, California (Fresno) | 413,053 | 69 | 75.0% | 12.9 |
| McLennan, Texas (Waco) | 147,553 | 147 | 83.5% | -1.7 |
| Boone, Missouri (Columbia) | 80,911 | 118 | 77.7% | 46.6 |
| Urbanized Non-Metropolitan Counties | | | | |
| Orange, New York (Newburg) | 221,657 | 266 | 51.1% | 20.6 |
| Weld, Colorado (Greeley) | 89,197 | 22 | 46.4% | 23.4 |
| Warren, Kentucky (Bowling Green) | 57,432 | 105 | 63.1% | 26.2 |
| Saline, Kansas (Salina) | 46,592 | 65 | 80.9% | -14.8 |
| Nez Perce, Idaho (Lewiston) | 30,376 | 36 | 85.8% | 12.2 |
| Less Urbanized, Non-Metropolitan Counties | | | | |
| Laurens, Georgia (Dublin) | 32,738 | 40 | 46.3% | 1.3 |
| Knox, Maine (Rockland) | 29,013 | 79 | 41.4% | 1.5 |
| Henry, Iowa (Mount Pleasant) | 18,114 | 41 | 38.7% | -.4 |
| Baker, Oregon (Baker) | 14,919 | 5 | 62.7% | -13.7 |
| Asotin, Washington (Asotin) | 13,799 | 21 | 73.3% | 6.9 |
| Bullock, Alabama (Union Springs) | 11,824 | 19 | 36.6% | -12.2 |
| Thinly Populated, Non-Metropolitan Counties | | | | |
| Gates, North Carolina (Gatesville) | 8,524 | 25 | 0.0% | -7.9 |
| Bland, Virginia (Bland) | 5,423 | 15 | 0.0% | -9.3 |
| Sheridan, North Dakota (McClusky) | 3,232 | 3 | 0.0% | -25.7 |
| Harding, New Mexico (Mosquero) | 1,348 | 1 | 0.0% | -28.1 |
| Petroleum, Montana (Winnett) | 675 | *** | 0.0% | -24.5 |

\*    Designation of Metropolitan Area
\*\*   Denotes an increase of less than .005%.
\*\*\* Denotes less than 1/2 persons per square mile.
SOURCE: U.S. Bureau of the Census, *Census of Population, Vol. I, Characteristics of the Population.* (Washington: U.S. Government Printing Office, 1973). The information is taken from Tables 9 and 10 of the report of each state.

populated counties have low population densities and usually have economies based on farming, ranching, lumbering, or tourism. Petroleum County (Montana), for example, has a population density of less than half a person per square mile and is a rolling, treeless cattle ranching area with some irrigated farming along river bottoms. Its county seat, Winnett (271), has two stores, but most residents must drive forty miles or more to cities in nearby counties to shop in a supermarket, furniture, or auto supply store. Some thinly populated counties, like Bland County (Virginia), have a number of small cities, a few small industrial plants, and a population of more than five thousand. Thinly populated counties tend to have the lowest per capita income.

With some exceptions, the thinly populated county best fits the stereotype of the rural county. Many thinly populated counties lost population between 1960 and 1970, as did all five counties in this group listed in Table 1-6.

## COUNTIES AS SERVICE AREAS

Counties are not merely geographic areas on a map; they are service areas within which people utilize a wide variety of governmental, retail, banking, utility, medical, and other types of services. The concept of a service area is potentially useful for a study of county government. If the county is a natural service area for retail stores, newspapers, and other business firms, it can be argued that it is likely to be a natural area for many of the governmental services per-

formed by counties. From the consumer's standpoint, there are three types of service areas:

(1) *A neighborhood service area close enough for a consumer to use daily, if necessary, in purchasing groceries, gasoline, and similar products.*

(2) *A general service area close enough for one or more trips a week to a supermarket, bank, clothing store, hardware or sporting goods store, and similar establishments. A general service area should have a newspaper, radio station, hospital, dentist, and other services needed for daily living.*

(3) *A regional service area close enough for several trips a year for specialized medical services such as those requiring a doctor who can perform open heart surgery or for shopping for expensive or hard-to-find items.*

A preliminary study of services in a sample of forty counties indicates that the county is a natural service area for retail trade, newspapers, banks, and other businesses.[12] In thirty-seven of the forty counties, the county had a general service trade area that satisfactorily served the weekly needs of its citizens. Nine counties had a regional service area as well as a general service area. In all but six of the counties (85% of the sample), the county courthouse was located in the largest city in the county, and in the remaining counties the county seat was centrally located.

One example of a county which is a natural trade area is Latah County, Idaho (1970 population - 24,891). Its county seat, Moscow (14,146), is located at the junctions of the major north-south and east-west routes in the county. While the smaller communities in the county have grocery stores, gas stations, and similar establishments, the only department store, the largest clothing stores, the only jewelry stores, and nearly all the physicians, attorneys, accountants, and insurance agencies are in the county seat. The only hospital is in the county seat as are the only daily newspaper and radio stations. In other words, the county may be a centralized self-contained unit.

There are some counties, however, which are not natural trade areas. The three counties in the sample which contained only a neighborhood shopping area were not natural retail centers since their residents frequently had to shop in neighboring counties. Moreover, some counties, such as Orange County, New York (221,657), have two or more cities of sufficiently equal population, each with a general service area of its own. However, these counties, like Orange, may have a centrally located county seat on good highways which serves well as a center for governmental services.

**Counties as Governmental Service Areas.** With the county a natural geographic area for many types of retail, medical, and other services, it is not surprising that the county is a center for governmental services as well. In the county seats of many metropolitan counties are the offices of the Internal Revenue Service, Social Security Administration, Justice Department, Federal Aviation Agency, and other federal agencies. In rural counties, the U.S. Soil Conservation Service, Agricultural Marketing Service, Agricultural Stabilization and Conservation Service, and Farmers Home Administration will often have offices in or near the county courthouse. State agencies providing public assistance, health services, employment, vocational rehabilitation, and other services will frequently be organized on a county basis or be located in or near the county courthouse.

Since colonial times, the county has been used as a central administrative unit to provide many types of local government services. The recording of deeds, mortgages, marriage licenses, and other legal documents is generally provided for the entire county at the county courthouse. The county is often a good geographic area for solid waste disposal, assessment and collection of property taxes, and many types of health, welfare, and manpower services. The city and (in some parts of the nation) the town or township are also good geographic areas for other types of services. School districts and special districts provide specific services in areas generally larger than a city and smaller than a county. Each unit of local government has a different area within which it is effective in providing services.

**The Systems Approach to County Services.** This book also uses a systems approach to describe the integration of services within county government and within a county area to carry out county responsibilities. A county service delivery system can be defined as a collection of people, procedures, physical facilities, organizational and financial arrangements, service needs and expectations within the area of a county.[13]

One illustration of a system serving a county area is the county hospital. The hospital has physicians, nurses, dietitians, laboratory technicians, and many other types of personnel working together to provide health care. Those who operate the hospital system are dependent on having a hospital building, operating rooms, and many types of equipment. A hospital must have a manager, an organizational system, and sources of funds. Hospitals have established procedures which begin when the patient approaches the admitting desk or emergency room and may end only after the patient is wheeled out to a waiting car after being discharged. The county hospital is a relatively self-contained system although it may be linked to a county ambulance system, receive funds by action of the county governing board, and may work with county health, social services, and law enforcement officials on certain cases. Clearly there may be an interlocking relationship among apparently independent county systems.

A second illustration of a county system is the coalition of county and other agencies that may work with an alcoholic at the county level. This may include: the law enforcement officer who refers the alcoholic to a county detoxification center, the staff of the detoxification center, the social worker who places the children of the alcoholic temporarily in a foster home, the county mental health center which provides group therapy, and members of Alcoholics Anonymous who provide supportive services. In time, the state vocational rehabilitation service, the county community college, and the county manpower office (or state employment service) may all help the alcoholic become a contributing member of society. The treatment of alcoholism as a disease with an eventual cure requires health, mental health, social services, educational training, manpower, and other programs, each of which has a role in helping alcoholics resolve their problems. The entire system is an alternative to keeping alcoholics in jail, provides a framework for their rehabilitation, and frees the criminal justice system from an excessive overload.

The systems approach to county services requires an examination of the relationships of county offices and departments in providing services. It also includes a study of the relationship of federal, state, county, and other local government agencies in providing services within a county area.

**Differing Roles in Providing Services.** In providing services, county governments frequently find themselves in one or more of the following twelve roles.

*Sole provider for the entire county.* For example, the county may be the only unit of government assessing property, disposing of solid waste, or operating an airport within the county.

*Sole provider for part of the county.* As an example, the county may provide police, planning, recreation, or other services for the unincorporated area of the county or some other portion of the county.

*Provider of specialized services.* The county, for example, may provide specialized facilities and services to city police departments such as a communications service, jail, or crime laboratory.

*Administrative partner.* In this role, the county participates with the city or some other unit in a jointly administered agency such as a county-city planning department.

*Intergovernmental partner.* In a given criminal justice case, the city police, county sheriff's office, state patrol, and even federal investigators may have roles in the investigation of a particular crime and the apprehension of a suspect. After the suspect's arrest, he is given a preliminary hearing before a county judge and tried before a state trial court with the county prosecuting attorney representing the state's case. If the person is found guilty, a pre-sentence investigation is conducted by a county probation officer, he is sentenced by a state judge, and he is placed in a county, state or federal prison. In the criminal justice system, county agencies are part of a complete intergovernmental partnership.

*Intergovernmental cooperator.* The county government, in this role, participates in mutual aid agreements, exchanges of information, cooperative purchasing, and other forms of intergovernmental cooperation.

*Subcontractor.* In this role, a county agency receives a contract to provide services under the supervision of another unit of government. County manpower agencies may act as sub-grantees for a state employment department in administering the comprehensive employment and training program.

*Fiscal agent.* In this role, the county serves to collect funds for other units of government or disburse funds to other units. The property tax collection function of county government is an example of this role.

*Purchaser of services.* In this case, county governments purchase supplies or services from other units of government.

*Vender of services.* The county may sell police, fire, planning or other services to cities or towns within the county.

*Creator of dependent districts and service areas.* In this role, the county government establishes special districts and service areas in particular areas of the county.

*Participant in regional governmental agencies.* The county government, in this role, contributes to the governing and financing of councils of governments and regional service departments in a multi-county region.

The roles of county government in providing services cannot, of course, be neatly categorized into a dozen types, for they differ by state and, sometimes by county. In the chapters on county services in this book, the role of county government in providing more than eighty services are described in detail.

## COUNTY DIVERSITY

A significant characteristic of American counties is their diversity.

## 16 • *Modern County Government*

Counties differ significantly in area, population, population density, geography, and economic base. It is important to remember that there are densely populated counties that form the core of metropolitan areas, counties on the fringe of these areas, urbanized counties with growing cities of 20,000 to 50,000 people, as well as counties with a predominantly agricultural economic base.

Counties vary in the services that they offer and these differences are related, not only to urbanization, but also to the section of the nation in which the counties are located. To understand regional differences in county government and county services, one must study the history of the American county and its predecessor, the English shire.

REFERENCES

1.  Avery v. Midland County, 406 S.W. 2d 422, 428 (1966).

2.  U.S. Bureau of the Census, *Census of Governments, 1972, Vol. I, Governmental Organization* (Washington: U.S. Government Printing Office, 1973), p. 14. In other figures, the Census Bureau shows 3,118 county areas because it has excluded 23 census divisions in Alaska and the part of Yellowstone Park in Montana, and has combined five counties in New York City into one county. A comprehensive census of local governments is taken once every five years and the latest census was taken in 1972.

3.  National Association of Counties and International City Mangement Association, *The County Year Book, 1976* (Washington: National Association of Counties and International City Management Association, 1976), Table 1-2. The Bureau of Census classifies city-county consolidations and independent cities as county-type areas but not as county-type governments, so Bureau of Census figures for county-type governments differ from those of *The County Year Book.*

4.  There were 3,053 counties with county governments during the 1930-33 period, 3,050 in 1942, 3,049 in 1952, 3,043 in 1962, 3,049 in 1967, and 3,042 in 1976. The 1930-1967 figures are from U.S. Bureau of the Census, *Historical Statistics of the United States, Colonial Times to 1970* (Washington: U.S. Government Printing Office, 1975), p. 1086. The 1976 figures are from National Association of Counties and International City Management Association, *The County Year Book, 1976,* Table 1-2.

5.  Clyde F. Snider, *Local Government in Rural America* (New York: Appleton-Century-Crofts, 1957), pp. 533,534 has an excellent description of early consolidations and the difficulties of county consolidation.

6.  Idaho, *Constitution,* Article 18, Section 4A.

7.  Quoted in National Association of Counties, *From America's Counties Today, 1973* (Washington: National Association of Counties, 1973), p. 4.

8.  U.S. Bureau of the Census, *1970 Census Users' Guide, Part 1* (Washington: U.S. Bureau of the Census, 1970), p. 82.

9.  U.S. Bureau of the Census, *Statistical Abstract of the United States, 1975* (Washington: U.S. Government Printing Office, 1975), p. 17.

10. A full explanation of the Department of Agriculture classification may be found in Fred K. Hines, David L. Brown and John M. Zimmer, *Social and Economic Characteristics of the Population in Metro and Nonmetro Counties, 1970* (Washington: Economic Research Service, U.S. Department of Agriculture, 1975), pp. 3,4.

11. U.S. Bureau of the Census, *1970 Census User's Guide*, p. 83.

12. The writer used personal visits to 35 of the counties and information provided by Chambers of Commerce and other sources for the remaining five counties.

13. The term "service delivery system" is widely used in criminal justice administration. Alfred Blumstein, "Systems Analysis and the Criminal Justice System," *The Annals of the American Academy of Political and Social Science* (November, 1967), p. 93 has defined a particular system as "a collection of people, devices, and procedures intended to perform some function." The concept of "service delivery system" is related to the conceptual framework developed by Sharkansky, Dye, Hefferbert and others to study political and administrative processes. Ira Sharkansky, *Public Administration* (Chicago: Markham Publishing Company, 1970), p. 9 describes a system as, not only the administrative unit, but also the environment within which the administrative unit operates, the inputs and outputs of the unit, the process of converting inputs to outputs, and the feedback mechanism.

Chapter 2

# The History of County Government—Traditional and Modern

"A municipal corporation proper is created mainly for the interest, advantage, and convenience of the locality and its people; a county organization is created almost exclusively with a view to the policy of the state at large, for purposes of political organization and civil administration, in matters of finance, of education, of provision for the poor, of military organization, of the means of travel and transport, and expecially for the general administration of justice. With scarcely an exception, all the powers and functions of the county organization have a direct and exclusive reference to the general policy of the state and are, in fact, but a branch of the general administration of that policy."[1]

The traditional view of the power and role of county government has many components. One is the traditional legal view of the county in the above quotation from an Ohio Supreme Court opinion in 1857. Written at a time when counties had far fewer functions than they have today, the opinion pictures county government as an arm of the state with functions prescribed by state government. Related to this traditional view of county legal powers is the concept of traditional county services. These are services which counties have provided for many years as an arm of the state.

The term "traditional" has also been applied to the commission form of county government.[2] This form (which will be described at length in Chapter 3) consists of a governing body of three to nine members in most states and a number of independently elected county officials. The governing body (usually called a board of commissioners or board of supervisors) has both executive and legislative powers. The independently elected officials, such as the clerk, auditor, treasurer, prosecuting attorney, sheriff, assessor, and coroner, also have significant areas of executive responsibility. H.S. Gilbertson, writing in 1917, called counties "a creature of tradition" and stated that: "Counties, once established, acquired a tendency to 'stick' tenaciously to their original form."[3]

The extent to which counties are, or are not, traditional can be explored only with reference to the history of county government. Those characteristics of county government which have existed for half a century or more may be considered traditional, while newer features of county government may be considered less traditional or "modern." In the concluding sections of this chapter, the concept of county modernization will be explored.

## ENGLISH ORIGINS

The origins of the American county can be traced back to the shires of Anglo-Saxon local government a thousand years ago.[4] The shire of that time performed judicial, police, public works, and military functions. The shire-moot, which met twice a year, was the legislative and judicial body of the shire. The earl, a large landowner in the district, presided over the shire-moot and was commander of the king's military forces in the shire. A shire-reeve, the predecessor of the present sheriff, was an assistant to the earl and later gained police, financial, and judicial power. The shire provided Anglo-Saxon Britain with a government which met the needs of the times for limited governmental services.

The shire came to be called the "county," and significant changes occurred in the next few centuries. William the Conquerer and his successors brought greater centralized control over local government. The shire-moot evolved into a county court of large landowners which had little real authority, while the sheriff gained increasing influence as the king's military representative, chief of county police, and steward of the royal estates.

At the time the first British colonists landed in Virginia, English counties were still largely an arm of national government with an element of local autonomy. The most important administrative functions of counties at the time were performed by justices of the peace who were appointed by the king and supervised by the royal Privy Council. The sheriff, an appointee of the king, had lost some of his former power but still retained a position of importance in the court system.

The parish (forerunner of the American town) was a unit of church and civil government in England at the time. It encompassed a small rural area in the county and provided mainly for church affairs and the administration of elementary education, highways, and poor relief. The borough (predecessor of the American city) was generally ruled by a small self-perpetuating oligarchy and provided police and judicial functions.

In the six centuries before the English colonists established large permanent settlements in America the shire (or county) had been, at different times in England, both a unit of local government and the local arm of national government. Thus there is support rooted in English history for both the traditional view of the county as an arm of the state and the view of the county as a self governing unit established for the benefit of its citizens.

## THE COLONIAL COUNTY

The English colonists were familiar with the organization of shires, boroughs, and parishes and adapted these to meet the needs of the eastern seaboard of the new continent.[5] The colonists, settling in the Virginia tidewater region, found an area well suited to small agricultural settlements and dispersed plantations and farms. Land grants were generally made to individuals rather than groups and, after the early years, the development of closely knit agricultural communities was not necessary to protect the colonists from Indian attack. Although many of the first units of local government in Virginia were similar to English parishes at the time, the plantations, farms, and small agricultural communities in Virginia were too widely dispersed to be effectively governed by the parish form of government. Recognizing the need for a form of local government with a much larger area than a parish, the settled part of Virginia was divided into eight shires or counties in 1634. Additional counties were organized as the population spread inland.

Virginia counties served as election districts for the colonial House of Burgesses with the sheriff as election officer. There were also military districts with the power to call all males over eighteen to active duty vested in a lieutenant appointed by the colonial government. Counties were also judicial districts as well as important units of civil administration reponsible for the construction and repair of highways and bridges, keeping rivers navigable, controlling the erection of water mills, and licensing private ferry keepers. The county court, composed mainly of large landowners commissioned by the colonial governor, was the governing body of the county. The sheriff was executive officer of the county court, collected county taxes, and acted as county treasurer. The sheriff, county coroner, surveyor, lieutenant, and justice of the peace were appointed by the colonial governor on the recommendations of the county court. The Virginia system of local government, with strong county government based upon an agrarian society, influenced the development of county government in America, particularly in the South.

The colonists settling in Massachusetts found a colder climate, rockier soil, and circumstances unlike those found in the South. They settled in compact communities that could be more easily protected against the Indians rather than in the dispersed plantations and agricultural settlements common in colonial Virginia. Massachusetts settlers found that the smaller and more compact English parish government was best suited to the needs of their shipping, fishing, and farming communities. They formed towns of about twenty to forty square miles which included a village and the surrounding rural area to perform a number of functions which in Virginia, were county responsibilities.

The first counties in Massachusetts were formed in 1643 and were governed by a county court composed of justices appointed by the governor and by a treasurer and sheriff also appointed by the governor. The Massachusetts county had highway maintenance, licensing, and judicial functions. With strong towns and weaker counties, the Massachusetts system of local government spread throughout New England; thus, the county has never gained the prominence there that it has in other areas of the nation. In fact, counties do not exist as organized units of government in Rhode Island and Connecticut.

New York, New Jersey, and Pennsylvania developed forms of colonial local government that differed from Massachusetts and Virginia. In New York, one supervisor was elected from each town to levy and assess local taxes, and this supervisor automatically became a member of the county board of supervisors. The board assumed control of highways and other county administrative functions. Similarly, assessors were elected in New Jersey from each township to help assess property. Later, they evolved into the county board of freeholders.

In Pennsylvania, counties developed as administrative units before towns. In 1724, the county governing body became a board composed of three county commissioners, each elected at-large from the county. Unlike those in New York and New Jersey, Pennsylvania townships were not represented in the county governing body and were less important than those in New York and New England.

The structure of colonial local government has had a significant effect on county and town government to this day. The Virginia system of a strong county government with no towns spread to the remainder of the South. Today, southern counties perform many more functions than counties in New England, which were influenced by the Massachusetts form of local government. The New York supervisor form of county government, in which the county governing body is composed of supervisors elected by towns or townships, spread to Michigan and parts of Illinois and Wisconsin. The county commissioner form of county government, found today in most midwestern and western states, is a direct descendent of the form of county government established in colonial Pennsylvania. The basic relationships between county and township governments, established in colonial times in New England, the Mid-Atlantic States, and Virginia, continue to affect county functions in many parts of the nation today.

## FROM THE REVOLUTION TO THE CIVIL WAR

County governments were not greatly affected by either the American Revolution or the sweeping changes made by the United States Constitution. The American Revolution brought a gradual rather than abrupt change in the manner of choosing county officials. In Virginia, for example, county officers were commissioned by the Governor after nomination by county court justices as they were in colonial days.[6] In New York, county officers formerly appointed by the royal Governor were now appointed by a council consisting of the Governor and four members of the state senate. However, more county offices gradually became elective as did the office of sheriff in New Jersey and Maryland.[7]

The United States Constitution, drafted in 1787, made no mention of county government or any other unit of local government. It established a federal system of government with two centers of power—the national government and state governments. Control over local government was reserved to the states and the people by the Tenth Amendment. Thus, the Constitution had much less impact on American county government than changes which occurred in state constitutions.

Early state constitutions maintained the status of counties as primarily an arm of state government. The structure of county government tended to be established in state constitutions, while these documents remained largely silent on municipal government. During the 1800s, the legal distinction between counties and municipalities was made more explicit. Chief Justice Taney of the U.S. Supreme Court stated in 1845 that: "The several counties are nothing more than certain portions of the territory into which the state is divided for a more convenient exercise of the powers of government."[8] The Hamilton County decision, quoted at the beginning of this chapter, made a widely used distinction between a municipal corporation (created for the convenience of the locality) and a quasi-municipal corporation (such as the county) created with a view to the policy of the state at large. This legal view of the county as merely an arm of the state had a stultifying

effect on the powers of county government throughout the 1800s, and has hindered counties in providing municipal services in the 1900s.

During the early 1800s, the trend toward elective county officers accelerated. New York abolished its council of appointment and made a number of county positions elective in 1821.[9] The Governor of Pennsylvania was stripped of his remaining discretion in the appointment of county sheriffs in 1838. When new states were established in the South and Midwest, county officials were generally elected rather than appointed by the state governor or legislature.

The number of independently elective offices was increased as well. Indiana, for example, had only two elective offices (other than the county commissioners) in 1816; by 1851 the Indiana Constitution required the election of an auditor, recorder, treasurer, surveyor, and clerk of the district court as well as the sheriff, coroner, and county commissioners.[10] The period of the greatest increase in the number of independently elected officials coincided with an extension of suffrage, and both movements may have been associated in the minds of many with the extension of democracy. The increase in independently elective county offices undoubtedly appealed to the Jacksonian frontiersman with his suspicion of aristocratic cliques and expertise.[11] Through a large number of elective county officers and frequent rotation of these officers, Jacksonians attempted to insure that a small clique would not hold power in the county and that county jobs would be passed around so that small farmers and tradesmen would have a chance to hold them.

By the Civil War, county government had established its present traditional structure with nearly all of the states having an elected county board. Counties had many independently elected officials whose powers reduced those of the county board. State constitutions became increasingly detailed covering such matters as the qualifications, powers, and selection of county officers.

During the late 1700s and early 1800s, the most common county functions were assessment and collection of property taxes, law enforcement in rural areas, maintenance of rural roads, and administration of justice. In New Jersey, the county board of freeholders or the sheriff was given the responsibility of operating jails and workhouses.[12] An 1847 New Jersey act also made counties responsible for part of the state's cost for care of the insane, while two 1798 laws gave New Jersey counties control of bridges.[13] During the early 1800s, county government was not involved in planning, although planning street systems had been a municipal function as early as 1682 in Philadelphia.[14]

## THE TRADITIONAL COUNTY: THE CIVIL WAR TO WORLD WAR I

The traditional structure of county government and many of its traditional functions had largely been established by the time of the Civil War. The county had the plural executive form of government with a board of county commissioners or supervisors, and a number of independently elected officers such as the sheriff, coroner, clerk, assessor, treasurer, and surveyor. The primary functions of county government involved judicial, road, law enforcement, and other responsibilities in which the county acted mainly as an arm of the state. The Civil War brought no significant change in county government except the unsuccessful attempt to transplant the township system into the South. As new states were established west of the Mississippi, counties were made the main unit of rural government. With a few exceptions, townships were not established west of the Dakotas and Kansas where the sparse settlement made the township unsuitable for local needs.

**Urban Growth and Problems.** The tremendous growth of urban centers from the Civil War to World War I placed great stress on both city and county government. In 1860, there were 6.2 million people living in urban centers; in 1880, there were 14.1 million; in 1900, 30.1 million; and in 1920, 54.2 million. Cities were faced with increased demands for services at a time when they were weakened by extensive use of the spoils system. The absence of comprehensive social welfare programs left the immigrants who moved into slum neighborhoods of the larger cities vulnerable to major illnesses, unemployment, and death.

**Political Bossism.** In urban centers, political machines developed which provided patronage positions for the unemployed, food for the needy, and medicines for the sick. The political boss and his ward leaders expected and received political support from those they helped and, once entrenched in city government, enriched themselves through such fraudulant practices as kickbacks on purchases and land sales to the city at exhorbitant prices. County governments faced the same pressures and problems and succumbed to the same political machines. The political boss of a large urban area ruled both the city and the county and frequently used county political office as a springboard to greater power.[15]

To Lord Bryce, an English observer of the American political scene in the late 1800s, the political bosses were "the ugliest feature in the current politics of the country."[16] He described in detail the machinations of the Philadelphia Gas Ring which enriched its members through charging high prices for gas, receiving commissions on public works, and requiring kickbacks from public employees.[17] H.S. Gilbertson, writing in 1917, documented the inefficiency and corruption of county government of his day and described the evils of the fee system in which the sheriff of New York County pocketed fees of $60,000 a year as well as a $12,000 annual salary.[18] He depicted the workings of the spoils system, the salary kickbacks, the abuses of fee-paid overseers of the poor, the unsanitary county penal institutions, and the poorly planned county public works projects.

The problems of county government stemmed mainly, Gilbertson thought, from a long "bed quilt" ballot of county officers that "deceived, misled and disfranchised the 'average citizen'."[19] As the population of urban counties grew, few people knew elective county officials personally, and few could evaluate their qualifications. Boss rule, he believed, was the inevitable outcome of the splintering of political responsibility in county government.[20] In a government without a single legal head, he stated, the political boss provided needed stability and made "an altogether unworkable system... tolerably workable."[21] The boss controlled the party machine, and the people, unable to know the qualifications of the large numbers of elective county officials, tended to vote the straight party ticket. The voters' only real choice was between the machines of both political parties. The real allegiance of the independently elected county officials was to the party boss, not to the people.

**Early Failure of Urbanized County Government.** Metropolitan counties in the late 1800s and early 1900s were facing particularly difficult problems adjusting to the needs for new and expanded services. Popular distrust of county officials, in some instances, undermined the capability of counties to provide new services.[22] H.S. Gilbertson, for example, criticized counties for the overcrowded conditions in county prisons of the time, the indiscriminate association of first offenders with hardened criminals, the miserable conditions of alms houses, and the lack of proper care of the insane.[23] Gilbertson pointed out that competent professional administration was needed in county functions, and that the many independently elected officials of the time did not provide the leadership required. While he gave some examples of inefficiency, corruption, and poor administration in rural counties, he stated that "without a doubt, the urban, and particularly the metropolitan county, is the county at its worst."[24]

The failure of county governments to meet the needs of urban residents in the first decade of the twentieth century stemmed from several factors. The plural executive form of county government, with many independently elected officials, did not provide strong executive leadership. Because of boss rule, corruption, and lack of leadership, popular opinion of county governments was low, and state legislatures were not about to entrust county governments with major new responsibilities. The legal viewpoint that counties were quasi-municipal corporations and an arm of the state resulted in excessively specific state constitutional provisions and laws which stifled county initiative.

**Government Reform.** As the chief critic of county government before World War II, Gilbertson pointed the way to county reform. Although the subtitle of his book, which labels county government as "the dark continent of American politics," has been widely used by subsequent writers to attack county government, Gilbertson sought to reform the county, not abolish it. He favored home rule and thought counties should be able to adopt one of several optional plans for county government.[25] He favored reducing the number of elected county officials, and one can find favorable comment in his book for the county executive and manager plans. He saw ad-

vantages, in some urban counties, of consolidating city and county government. He advocated a comprehensive merit system for county employees, a modern executive budget, a professional accounting system, purchasing standards, bid procedures, and citizen organizations that would take a greater interest in county government.

His final chapter was a picture of the county of the future in which "the county politician of the conventional type has been extinguished."[26] Gilbertson's book marks a critical point in the history of the county. The traditional county government of the 1800s was failing (particularly in metropolitan areas) to meet the service needs of the times and would need to change or face slow extinction.

## THE COUNTY IN TRANSITION 1917 to 1950

The thirty-three years between Gilbertson's book and 1950 saw sporadic progress in county government. The most significant change was the growth in county functions. In 1913, the most important county functions were general governmental services such as judicial administration, assessment and collection of property taxes, election administration, and the recording of legal papers.[27] Other major county programs at the time were the maintenance of county roads, the operation of schools and county school superintendents' offices, and the provision of police protection through the sheriff's office. In most functions, the county served primarily as an administrative arm of the state.

**Shifting Responsibilities.** Between World War I and the early 1950s, responsibility for some of the traditional county services shifted to state and national government. In a mid-century review of county government, written in 1952, Clyde Snider stated that in Delaware, North Carolina, West Virginia, and in most counties in Virginia, county roads had been transferred to the jurisdiction of the state.[28] The inability of local government to finance relief costs during the 1930s resulted in the shifting of much of the financing of public assistance to the national level and the shifting of welfare administration. from the county to the state in some areas of the nation. Some specialized health institutions, such as tuberculosis and mental hospitals, were also shifted from the county to the state level.

There was a compensating trend toward the transfer of some responsibilities from township and special district governments to counties, such as highway administration, as it was recognized that these units were geographically too small to provide efficient service. Snider reported in 1952 that township roads had been transferred to county administration in states such as Indiana and Michigan, and that in other states such as Kansas and Texas individual counties assumed control over township or special district roads.[29] Property assessment and minor judicial functions were also being transferred from township to county government.

**New County Services.** Of greater significance, was the emergence of newer services in which the county acted, not as an administrative arm of the state, but as an autonomous unit of local government. The establishment of county parks was one of these newer services. Although the first county park was established in the 1890s in Essex County (New Jersey), county park and recreation expenditures nationwide amounted to only $419,000 by 1913.[30] By 1928, they had grown to $7.6 million and $67 million by 1957. Many counties established park systems when citizen pressure for new parks grew, and the most suitable undeveloped land for larger parks was found to be beyond city limits.

Among the newer county functions listed by Clyde Snider in 1952 were: health protection, hospitals, conservation of natural resources, fire protection, veterans' services, libraries, planning and zoning, airports, housing, and utility services.[31] The first full-time county health department was established in Yakima County, Washington in 1911, and by 1926 there were 307 full-time health departments.[32] Expenditures for county libraries increased from less than half a million dollars in 1913 to $4 million in 1932 and to $31 million in 1957. As airports grew in size after World War I and became more expensive to operate, some were transferred from city to county ownership because city residents had grown tired of subsidizing a service used by all residents of the county. County services grew swiftly after World War II when general prosperity and easy money for housing led to rapidly expanding populations in the unincorporated areas and small suburban communities surrounding our large cities. As the strongest unit of government in the area, counties were called on increasingly to meet many of the service needs of the expanding residential area.

**Urbanization.** The automobile was a major influence in bringing county government into the planning process and into many types of urban services. Automobile registrations increased from 458,000 in 1910, to 8,132,000 in 1920, and 22,973,000 in 1930.[33] Automobiles made it possible for millions of upper and middle income residents to escape city congestion and commute to cities from suburban communities and rural areas around the fringes of cities. Urban problems, such as traffic congestion, inadequate water supply and sewage disposal, and mushrooming residential areas, became county-wide. The first county planning commissions were created in the 1920s, and counties were soon providing urban services to unincorporated areas around the fringes of cities.

As counties began to provide more services formerly performed only by municipalities, a gradual change in the status of counties occurred. In practice, the status of county governments in many urban areas of the nation changed from that of a quasi-municipal corporation to one more nearly resembling a municipal corporation.

With increasing urbanization in the 1930s and 1940s, other changes came gradually. Larger county governments developed professional accounting systems, purchasing standards, and bid procedures recommended by Gilbertson. Other counties dropped hiring procedures based on patronage and established civil service merit systems.

The home rule charters which Gilbertson recommended in 1917 have developed more slowly. In 1917, California and Maryland were the only two states having constitutional provisions which permitted home rule charters for all counties, and only four of the eighty-two counties in those two states had charters.[34] In 1933, constitutional amendments in Texas and Ohio provided a degree of home rule for counties in these two states. Missouri adopted a constitutional amendment in 1945 providing that any county having more than 85,000 inhabitants could adopt a charter, while Washington State granted authority to counties to adopt charters in 1948. However, it was not until 1968 that a county in either Missouri or Washington adopted a charter. By the beginning of 1950, this authority had been granted counties in only six states, and only about a dozen counties actually had charters.

Changes in organizational structure also came slowly in the period from World War I to 1950. In 1917, the traditional commission form of government that Gilbertson criticized was found in all, or nearly all, counties. In 1927, Iredell County (North Carolina) became the first county in the nation to adopt a council-administrator form of county government.[35] In the late 1930's, Westchester and Nassau Counties in New York secured special legislative charters enabling them to adopt an elected executive form of government. By 1950, sixteen counties had appointive managers recognized by the International City Manager's Association, and several counties had county executives.[36]

Changes in relationships between counties and other units of local government were also developing slowly. City-county consolidation combined city and county governments in Boston, Philadelphia, New Orleans, and New York in the 1800s, but there were no further consolidations for many years.[37] In 1949, the City of Baton Rouge merged with East Baton Rouge Parish causing a renewal of interest in city-county consolidation.[38]

According to Clyde Snider, one of the most encouraging developments in local government during the 1930s and 1940s was functional consolidation by which counties and other local units cooperated in performing certain governmental functions.[39] Snider, however, concluded his mid-century review of county government by stating: "In overall appraisal, the first half of the twentieth century must be considered as a period of progress, albeit slow and halting progress, in the field of county government. Functionally, the county is of greater importance today than a generation ago, and expansion of the services provided by its government appears likely to continue."[40]

## COUNTY MODERNIZATION SINCE 1950

The term "county modernization" will be used in this book to describe the trend in county government away from the traditional mold. Characteristics of the traditional mold include: the performance of mainly state-mandated functions; the concept of the county as an arm of the state; the traditional commission form of county government; and the lack of extensive cooperation with other units of local government.

County modernization is also related to the index of county political vitality developed by John Bollens. The five components of this index are: "(1) resource utilization; (2) volume of intergovernmental linkages; (3) changes in organization and processes; (4) adequacy of public accountability; and (5) extent of voting and competition in elections."[41] Bollens comments that these "components tell us a great deal about the capability of counties to decide upon and carry out policies and to respond quickly, responsibly, and efficiently to problems and demands."[42]

While data is not readily available on all elements of county modernization, there is sufficient information to identify certain trends: (1) changes in county services; (2) the home rule movement which is altering the relationship of state and county government; (3) the adoption of newer forms of county organization; (4) the growth of cooperative intergovernmental linkages; (5) the growth in county revenues; and (6) the increase in political accountability brought by reapportionment.

**Changes in County Services.** The traditional services (such as assessment and collection of property taxes, election administration, and police protection) continue to be provided. However, since 1950 many new county services have been added such as: job training, work experience programs, public service employment, drug control programs, food stamps, bikeways, coastal zoning, energy conservation, leased public housing, cable television, and consumer protection. Counties assumed these new functions for many reasons. In the case of consumer protection, counties were reacting to the rising demand of their citizens in the 1970s for some unit of government to investigate legitimate consumer complaints about poor service or shoddy merchandise.[43] In the case of energy conservation, counties were reacting to the oil crisis of 1973 by conserving their own fuel and encouraging conservation by citizens and businesses within their boundaries.[44] The entry of county government into job training, work experience, and pub-

lic service employment fields was accelerated by the passage of the Comprehensive Employment and Training Act of 1973, which provided funds to counties to operate county manpower programs or join with other units of government in providing manpower services.[45]

While counties were adding new functions, significant transfers of functions from cities, towns, townships, and special districts to county governments were also occurring. Table 1, developed from a 1971 study, published by the Advisory Commission on Intergovernmental Rela-

Table 2-1

**TRANSFER OF SELECTED FUNCTIONS OF SUBCOUNTY GOVERNMENTS TO COUNTIES AND FROM COUNTIES TO SUBCOUNTY GOVERNMENTS BETWEEN 1960 AND 1970**

| | Transfer from Subcounty to County | | Transfer from County to Subcounty | |
|---|---|---|---|---|
| No. of Counties Reporting (A)-78 Total No. Counties—1,026 | | | | |
| Function | No. | Percent of Counties | No. | Percent of Counties |
| Police Protection | 31 | 40 | 2 | 3 |
| Correction Jails and Detention Homes | 21 | 27 | 1 | 1 |
| Fire Protection | 10 | 13 | 6 | 7 |
| Public Welfare | 18 | 23 | 0 | 0 |
| Education | 9 | 12 | 4 | 5 |
| Libraries | 29 | 37 | 4 | 5 |
| Roads and Highways | 18 | 23 | 7 | 9 |
| Sewers and Sewage Disposal | 17 | 22 | 4 | 5 |
| Refuse and Garbage Collection | 18 | 23 | 2 | 3 |
| Parks and Recreation | 10 | 13 | 3 | 4 |
| Hospitals | 8 | 10 | 1 | 1 |
| Other Health Services | 34 | 46 | 0 | 0 |
| Natural Resources Services | 0 | 0 | 0 | 0 |
| Housing and Renewal | 6 | 7 | 0 | 0 |
| Water Supply | 8 | 10 | 1 | 1 |
| Transportation | 3 | 4 | 1 | 1 |
| Power Supply | 0 | 0 | 0 | 0 |
| Planning | 35 | 45 | 5 | 6 |
| Total | 275 | | 41 | |

SOURCE: Advisory Commission on Intergovernmental Relations, *Profile of County Government* (Washington: Advisory Commission on Intergovernmental Relations, 1972), p. 26. The term "subcounty" refers to cities, towns, townships, and special districts.

tions, lists the following types of transfers in Table 2-1.[46]

To what extent has the percentage of counties performing the newer county services increased since 1950? Unfortunately, there were no surveys of county functions in 1950 which could be compared to the statistical information available in 1975.

An indication of the trend is given by Table 2-2 which compares the percent of metropolitan counties providing certain services in 1971 and in 1975. In each category, the percent of counties performing the service increased.

**Acceleration in Adoption of County Charters.** Since 1950, county home rule provisions have been passed in more than a dozen states including Alaska, Florida, Georgia, Illinois, Kentucky, Montana, Pennsylvania, South Dakota, and Utah.[47] In addition, some counties in other states (such as Louisiana, New York, New Mexico, and Tennessee) have received charters or have adopted optional forms of government.

Kansas and Minnesota have constitutional provisions authorizing county home rule, although the state legislatures have not enacted the necessary authorizing legislation. Even more significant is the fact that the number of county charters increased from about a dozen in 1950 to seventy-one in 1973 with most of the new charters adopted after 1960.[48]

Table 2-2

SELECTED FUNCTIONS PERFORMED BY
METROPOLITAN COUNTY GOVERNMENTS, 1971 AND 1975

| Function | 1971 | | 1975 | | Percent Increase |
|---|---|---|---|---|---|
| | No. | Percent of Total | No. | Percent of Total | |
| Total metropolitan counties responding to questionnaire | 150 | 100 | 291 | 100 | ... |
| Fire protection | 47 | 31 | 139 | 48 | 17 |
| Mental health | 104 | 69 | 240 | 82 | 13 |
| Animal control | 75 | 51 | 204 | 70 | 19 |
| Hospitals | 61 | 41 | 137 | 47 | 6 |
| Mass transit | 7 | 5 | 81 | 28 | 23 |
| Airports | 36 | 24 | 121 | 42 | 18 |
| Water supply | 31 | 21 | 90 | 31 | 10 |
| Solid waste collection | 31 | 21 | 124 | 43 | 22 |
| Solid waste disposal | 55 | 37 | 190 | 65 | 28 |
| Water pollution control | 45 | 30 | 131 | 45 | 15 |
| Air pollution control | 55 | 37 | 115 | 40 | 3 |
| Subdivision control | 77 | 51 | 226 | 78 | 27 |
| Industrial development | 32 | 21 | 143 | 49 | 28 |
| Museums | 25 | 17 | 75 | 26 | 9 |
| Libraries | 86 | 57 | 216 | 74 | 17 |

(...) Leaders indicate percent increase not relevant.

SOURCE: Carolyn B. Lawrence and John M. DeGrove, "County Government Services" in National Association of Counties and International City Management Association, *The County Year Book, 1976* (Washington: National Association of Counties and International City Management Association, 1976), p. 98.

In 1973, thirty-five million Americans lived in charter counties.[49]

**Accelerating Change in Organizational Structure.** Approximately two dozen counties operated under non-traditional county government in 1950. Since 1950, the council-elected executive form of county government has spread from eight to 142 counties and city-counties.[50] In 1977, more than forty-three million people were governed under the council-elected executive form.[51] Council-administrator forms, including the county manager plan and the council-administrative officer plan, were more widely adopted after 1950.[52] California, North Carolina, and Virginia have led the way with more than forty counties in each state having this form of government in 1976.[53] It was estimated that more than sixty million persons in about five hundred counties were served under one of the council-administrator forms of county government in 1975.[54]

**Growth of Local Intergovernmental Linkages.** Comprehensive statistical comparisons of intergovernmental linkages in 1950 and a quarter century later are lacking. However, certain types of structural, program, and cooperative linkages are known to have increased greatly. For example, in 1950 there had been only one city-county consolidation in fifty years. In the quarter century which has followed, there have been a dozen city-county mergers.[55] Since 1950, the number of counties contracting with cities to provide services has increased greatly, with Los Angeles County providing services to seventy-eight cities.

John Bollens believes that the growing use of the county as a provider of contractual services to cities has been stimulated by the wider range of services of counties and increased confidence in the competence of county government.[56] City-county and multi-county administration of airports, health departments, mental health clinics, and other services are also increasing. Perhaps, the most significant increase in intergovernmental linkages has resulted from the establishment of more than six hundred councils of governments and other regional agencies which have brought county officials into closer contact with officials of other units of local government.

**Growth in County Revenues.** While county revenues grew from $896 million in 1913 to $4.0 billion in 1952, the increase in county revenues was greater still in the next twenty years reaching $32.4 billion in the fiscal year 1974-75.[57] The percent of county revenues coming from the property tax declined from 46% to 31% in the 1952-75 period, as counties became less dependent on a single source of revenue.[58] Non-property taxes, such as the income tax, sales tax, and selective sales taxes on cigarettes, gasoline, and other products, are becoming increasingly productive and giving counties a broader tax base. County revenue from state and federal sources has increased almost tenfold since 1952.

**Political Accountability and Reapportionment.** An important measure of political accountability, according to John Bollens, is "the degree of equitability employed in apportioning seats on the county governing body when all or most of its members are elected from districts or are elected at large but must reside within specified local areas."[59] If county electoral districts contain substantially unequal populations, Bollens contends that some persons have less voting power and ability to hold elected officials responsible than other persons. Equitable apportionment, Bollens feels, produces more responsive and responsible government.

In 1950, county governing boards were able to reapportion their own districts with few requirements established by state constitutions, state laws, or court decisions.[60] The township supervisory type of county board in New York, Michigan, New Jersey, and Wisconsin had one supervisor representing each township regardless of population and additional board members representing cities. There were great disparities in some of these counties between the populations of townships.

In 1962, the U.S. Supreme Court entered the reapportionment thicket and made clear, in Baker v. Carr, that reapportionment suits were within the jurisdiction of federal courts and could be settled by judicial action. In 1964, U.S. Supreme Court, in Reynolds v. Sims and in other cases, applied the "one man, one vote" principle to the reapportionment of both houses of the state legislature and congressional redistricting. In 1968, the U.S. Supreme Court applied the "one man, one vote" principle to counties. The case involved Midland County (Texas), in which more than 95% of the people of the county lived in one of four commissioner districts and the

county judge was elected at large. The Texas Supreme Court upheld this apportionment system stating that "the voice of the rural areas will be lost for all practical purposes if the commissioner precincts of counties are apportioned solely on a population basis except, perhaps, in those few sparsely settled counties without a concentration of urban centers."[61] The U.S. Supreme Court overturned the Texas Supreme Court decision and applied the "one man, one vote" principle to counties.[62]

In dozens of cases since the 1960s, federal and state courts have related the "one man, one vote" principle to county government. The most sweeping change has come in township supervisory boards. In New York State, at least twenty-five counties were involved in reapportionment litigation in the 1960s.[63] In Goldstein v. Rockefeller, the requirement that each township supervisor have one vote on the county board was declared invalid.[64] As a result of court cases in New York, New Jersey, Michigan, and Wisconsin, the township supervisory board has been largely replaced with a county legislative body with legislators elected by districts rather than townships. Substantial change has also occurred in states such as Texas, California, Kansas, and South Dakota where county commissioners are elected by district.

In South Dakota and Minnesota, for example, the state courts have invalidated state laws which have interfered with relatively equal apportionment of commissioner districts.[65] Some county boards with at-large elections and residence requirements by district also had to be reapportioned. In Maryland, the Montgomery County Council apportionment system was declared unconstitutional because the five council districts varied in population.[66] The only types of county boards which have not been affected by apportionment cases are those in which all county commissioners are elected at large and live anywhere in the county. Reapportionment has undoubtedly brought some increase in county government accountability since 1950. In other, harder to measure ways, new county services and newer forms of county government may also have increased political accountability. As counties have provided more services, county officials may have become more subject to scrutiny by the press. As more counties have adopted the county executive forms of government, the people of the county may have had an easier time holding one county official responsible for much of the executive branch of county government.

## MODERNIZATION AND ORGANIZATIONAL CHANGE

Modernization is the trend away from the traditional mold of county government, which has been criticized by writers from the time of Henry S. Gilbertson to the present. In the past half century, county modernization has been marked by increases in newer types of services not required by state law and the adoption of newer forms of county organization. The home rule movement, the growth of cooperative relationships between the county and other units of local government, the increase in county revenues, and reapportionment have also had part in county modernization. Future studies of county government should try to measure trends in county government with an index of modernization developed in a way similar to John Bollens' index of political vitality. In the final chapter, the author takes a step in this direction by developing a partial index of modernization and applying it to determine the degree of modernization in certain types of counties.

One of the factors in county modernization has been a change in the form of county government particularly in the most populous counties. The next chapter examines the organization of county government.

### REFERENCES

1. Commissioners of Hamilton County v. Mighels, 7 Ohio St. 110, 118-119 (1857).

2. Herbert Sydney Duncombe, *County Government in America* (Washington: National Association of Counties Research Foundation, 1966), p. 9.

3. H.S. Gilbertson, *The County, The "Dark Continent" of American Politics* (New York: The National Short Ballot Organization, 1917), p. 23.

4. For further information on the development of the English shire see John A. Fairlie, *Local Government in Counties, Towns and Villages* (New York: The Century Company, 1914), pp. 5,6, Herman G. James, *Local Government in the United States* (New York: D. Appleton and Company, 1921), pp. 4-6, and Herbert Sydney Duncombe, *County Government in America*, pp. 18, 19.

5. See Henry S. Gilbertson, pp. 16-18, Herman G. James, pp. 72-90, and James A. Fairlie, pp. 20-30 for further information on the colonial county.

6. John A. Fairlie, p. 33.

7. Francis Newton Thorpe, *The Federal and State Constitutions, Colonial Charters, and Other Organic Laws of the States, Territories, and Colonies* (Washington: U.S. Government Printing Office, 1909), Vol. 5, p. 2597.

8. State of Maryland v. Baltimore and Ohio R.R., 44 U.S. 534,550 (1845).

9. The change in state constitutions can be traced in Francis Newton Thorpe, p. 2633.

10. Ibid., pp. 1063, 1085.

11. H.S. Gilbertson, pp. 29, 30, blames Jacksonians for weakening the power of the county governing board.

12. The writer is indebted to Harris I. Effross, *County Governing Bodies in New Jersey* (New Brunswick: Rutgers University Press, 1975), pp. 8-11 for his description of the functions of New Jersey counties of this period. The book contains an excellent history of New Jersey county government.

13. Ibid., p. 9.

14. For a history of American planning in the 16th and 17th centuries, see James G. Coke, "Antecedents of Local Planning," *Principles and Practice of Urban Planning*, William I. Goodman and Eric C. Freund, ed.(Washington: International City Management Association, 1968), pp. 8-12.

15. William M. Tweed was Alderman of the City of New York, Congressman, Commissioner of the New York Board of Education, and finally a member of the Board of Supervisors of the County of New York. As a county supervisor, he once purchased 300 benches at $1,500 and resold them for use of county armories at a price of $169,800. For further information on how Boss Tweed used his county and city offices for personal gain, see Seymour J. Mandlebaum, *Boss Tweed's New York* (New York: John Wiley and Sons, Inc., 1965) and Dennis T. Lynch, *"Boss" Tweed* (New York: Boni and Liveright, 1927).

16. James Bryce, *The American Commonwealth*(New York: Macmillan and Co., 1891), Volume II, p. 470. Bryce stated that this corruption was one of the faults of American democracy, but it could be prevented. He commented that "The city masses may improve if immigration declines, offices may cease to be the reward of party victory," and "the better citizens may throw themselves more actively into political work." Ibid., pp. 470, 471.

17. Ibid., pp. 367-384.

18. H.S. Gilbertson, p. 51.

19. Ibid., p. 34. Gilbertson was quoting a Chicago newspaperman whom he did not identify by name.

20. Gilbertson stated: "In their theory of pure democracy via the ballot, they spread out their interest in county officers so thin that no single officer got sufficient attention to make him realize their influence." Ibid., p. 44.

21. Ibid., pp. 49, 50. Gilbertson reasoned that to survive as a functioning unit of government with a splintered executive, counties adopted a boss system.

22. For example, mistrust of county officials in Hudson County (New Jersey) in 1877 led to the defeat of funds for a badly needed road in the county. The mistrust stemmed from a questionable action of the County Board of Freeholders in building a new courthouse. Harris Effross, p. 17.

23. H.S. Gilbertson, pp. 86-91. Gilbertson was concerned because sheriffs were under contract with boards of supervisors to provide food for prisoners and made a profit at the expense of the prisoners' diets.

24. Ibid., p. 65.

25. Ibid., Chapter 15.

26. Ibid., p. 193.

27. More than a quarter of all county government expenditures were for general government. Information on county government expenditures in 1913 is provided by U.S. Bureau of the Census, *Wealth, Debt and Taxation, Volume II, 1913* (Washington: U.S. Government Printing Office, 1915), p. 210.

28. Clyde F. Snider, "American County Government: A Mid-Century Review," *American Political Science Review*, 46: 74, March, 1952.

29. Ibid.

30. For an excellent description of newer county functions in the 1900-1930 period, see Charles M. Kneier, "Development of Newer County Functions," *American Political Science Review*, 24: 134-140, February, 1930.

31. Clyde F. Snider, p. 74.

32. Charles M. Kneier, p. 139.

33. James G. Coke, p. 23.

34. National Association of Counties, *From America's Counties Today* (Washington: National Association of Counties, 1973), pp. 52-70 is the source of the information in this section on charter counties. The four counties having charters in 1917 were all in California. The City and County of Denver also had a charter adopted in 1904.

35. Florence Zeller, "Forms of County Government" in National Association of Counties and International City Management Association, *The County Year Book, 1975* (Washington: National Association of Counties and International City Management Association, 1975), p. 28.

36. Clyde F. Snider, p. 71.

37. For a listing of city-county consolidations see National Association of Counties, *From America's Counties Today*, p. 60.

38. William Havard and Floyd Corty, *Rural-Urban Consolidation: The Merger of the Governments in the Baton Rouge Area* (Baton Rouge: Louisiana State University Press, 1964) contains an excellent description of this merger.

39. Clyde F. Snider, p. 77.

40. Ibid., p. 78.

41. John C. Bollens, *American County Government* (Beverly Hills, California: Sage Publications, Inc., 1969), p. 41.

42. Ibid.

43. Consumer protection is described in more detail in Chapter 6.

44. Energy conservation is described in further detail in Chapter 8.

45. County governments may be prime sponsors of manpower programs, may join with other units of governments in consortia, or may be sub-grantees. For further information see Chapter 7.

46. Advisory Commission on Intergovernmental Relations, *Profile of County Government* (Washington: U.S. Government Printing Office, 1972) provides a valuable source of information on county services.

47. National Association of Counties, *From America's Counties Today,* pp. 53-58.

48. Ibid., pp. 68, 69.

49. National Association of Counties, "List of Charter Counties," January, 1976. (Mimeographed.)

50. The council-elected executive form of county government is similar in many respects to the predominant form of state government. The voters elect a county executive powers similar to a governor and a county legislature often called a county council. As in state government, there are some other elected executives. The National Association of Counties, *NACo Fact Sheet - Elected Executives* (Washington: National Association of Counties, 1977) lists 142 counties and city-counties with an elected county executive.

51. Ibid.

52. These forms of county government have an appointed administrative officer with important powers. For further information on these forms of county government see Chapter 3.

53. For further information see Table 3-3 in Chapter 3.

54. Florence Zeller, p. 28.

55. National Association of Counties, *From America's Counties Today,* p. 60.

56. John C. Bollens, p. 47.

57. U.S. Bureau of the Census, *Wealth, Debt and Taxation, 1913, Vol. II,* p. 81 and U.S. Bureau of the Census, *1957 Census of Governments, Vol. III, No. 4, Finances of County Governments* (Washington: U.S. Government Printing Office, 1959), p. 6.

58. Computed from data in the U.S. Bureau of the Census, *1957 Census of Governments,* p. 6 and U.S. Bureau of the Census, *1972 Census of Governments, Vol. IV, No. 3, Government Finances* (Washington: U.S. Government Printing Office, 1974), p. 9.

59. John C. Bollens, pp. 57, 58.

60. An exception was a Nebraska Supreme Court decision in 1916 which declared uncohstitutional a Nebraska state law redistricting the Board of Commissioners of Douglas County because it gave disproportionate weight to the rural areas surrounding Omaha. State ex rel Harte v. Moorehead, 156 N.W. 1067, 1070-71, (1916).

61. Avery v. Midland County, 406 S.W., 2nd, 422 (1966).

62. Avery v. Midland County, 390 U.S. 474, 485 (1968). The court reaffirmed the requirement that local government units with general government powers for an entire geographic area should not be apportioned among single member districts of substantially unequal population.

63. For a comprehensive state-by-state review of county apportionment cases up to 1968, see Herbert Sydney Duncombe and Clifford I. Dobler, "Local Legislative Apportionment" in National Association of Counties, *Guide to County Organization and Management* (Washington: National Association of Counties, 1968), pp. 123-133.

64. Goldstein v. Rockefeller, 257 N.Y.S. 2d 994, 995 (1965).

65. Herbert Sydney Duncombe and Clifford I. Dobler, p. 125.

66. Montgomery County Council v. Garrott, 222 A. 2nd 164 (1966).

# Chapter 3

# County Government Organization

"County governmental organization is characterized by diversity, not only from state to state but even within states . . . As has been aptly observed, if any 'principle' could be distinguished in American county government, it is the principle of confusion."[1]

"On the average, counties have not been viewed by political scientists as particularly flexible and modern instruments of grassroots democracy. The two most common criticisms are that county governments have archaic organizational structures and that these units have only limited, if any, capacity to perform nonroutine and nonrural functions, being ill-equipped in most instances to handle the most pressing demands of a rapidly growing urban society."[2]

"During most of the 330-year history of counties in the United States the traditional plural executive, or commission, plan has been maintained for administering the county government. Over the past 15 years, however, widespread reform of county government structure has occurred."[3]

County government organization is undoubtedly the most criticized feature of county government. The first two quotations, cited above, are from excellent state and local government textbooks and give the impression that county government organization is confusing and archaic. The third quotation is from *The County Year Book of 1975* and em- phasizes the reform that has occurred in county government in the 1960s and early 1970s.

Before describing the forms of county government today, it is important to describe the nature of the criticism of county organization. In 1917, H.S. Gilbertson focused his attack on the many elective officials which he felt misled the average voter and splintered executive responsibility within the county.[4] Lane Lancaster has contended that the county is too small in population and too weak financially to support an efficient administrative organization.[5] More recently, Maddox and Fuquay stated that:

> *"One outstanding weakness of county government in general is the absence of a chief executive. There are far too many independent 'executives' and department heads whose activities are subject to no effective supervision and coordination."*[6]

The criticisms of county government organization are primarily criticisms of the traditional commission (or plural executive) form of county government. Gilbertson, Maddox and Fuquay, and others favored alternative forms of county government featuring an elective or appointive county executive.

Were past criticisms of county organization valid or did the critics of county government misunderstand the strengths of the collegial decision-making process which occurred in county boards of commissioners? If these criticisms were accurate at the time Gilbertson wrote in 1917, are they still valid or have they become outdated as county government organization has changed in the past two decades? Have counties, in fact, actually changed or are their new organizational structures a facade covering inherent weaknesses? The

Table 3-1

BASIC FORMS OF COUNTY GOVERNMENT

| Form of County Government | % of Counties | % of People with This Form of County Government |
|---|---|---|
| 1. Commission form (In this form, a governing board has both administrative and legislative functions, and a number of independent officials such as the county auditor and treasurer are elected. This is sometimes called a plural executive form of county government.) | 77 | 49 |
| 2. Council-administrator form (In this form, the council has mainly legislative and policy-making functions, and the council appoints a manager or some other administrator to be responsible for important staff and/or administrative functions. | 18 | 31 |
| 3. Council-elected executive form (In this form, the citizens of the county elect a council as the legislative body and an elected executive to be the chief executive official.) | 5 | 20 |
| | 100 | 100 |

SOURCE: Information provided by the staff of the National Association of Counties, in April, 1977.

strengths and weaknesses of the current forms of county government organization will be examined in this chapter.

## ALTERNATIVE FORMS OF COUNTY GOVERNMENT

The form of local government determines the major organizational features such as the relationship between the voters, the legislative body, and the major elective and appointive officials. For example, one major form of city government is the mayor-council form in which voters elect separately a mayor (as chief executive) and council (as legislative body).

There are three basic forms of county government and several important variations of each. As the Table 3-1 shows, the commission form of county government accounts for about 77% of all counties but governs only about 49% of the people of the United States having county-type government. More populous counties tend to use the council-administrator or council-elected executive forms.

**Commission Form.** Florence Zeller estimates that more than 2,500 counties, of a total of 3,101 county-type governments, operate under the traditional commission form of government.[7] In Idaho, Iowa, Massachusetts, Oklahoma, Texas, Vermont, West Virginia, and Wyoming, it is the only form of county government permitted. Frequently called a board of county commissioners or a board of supervisors, the governing body has legislative functions such as enacting ordinances, adopting a budget, and setting county tax rates. The county board also has numerous executive and administrative functions such as appointing certain county employees, reviewing applications for licenses, and supervising county road work. A characteristic of the commission form of organization is that the county commissioners share administrative responsibility with a number of independently elected "row" officers who frequently include: a county clerk, auditor and recorder, assessor, treasurer, prosecuting attorney, sheriff, and coroner. Chart 3-1 illustrates this traditional arrangement.

Chart 3-1

TRADITIONAL COMMISSION FORM OF ORGANIZATION
IN LATAH COUNTY, IDAHO

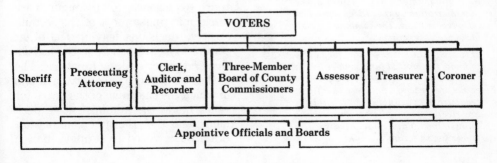

*The pros and cons.* A 1975 study of county organization summarizes the frequently cited advantages and disadvantages of the commission form of government as follows:

*Advantages of Commission Form*

*Longevity: the commission form of government is the traditional structure in county governments.*

*The commission plan brings government administration close to the people through the independent election of government department heads: therefore, it is the most democratic form of government.*

*A broadened system of checks and balances is provided by the individual election of officials: there is less chance of a totally corrupt government.*

*It promotes a unified administration and policy-making government because, with legislative and executive functions combined in one branch, conflicts are avoided.*

*Disadvantages of Commission Form*

*The commission plan is antiquated: a form of government that predates the American Revolution cannot answer the complex needs of the twentieth century.*

*Lack of a chief executive officer is one of the most glaring deficiencies of most local governments, and results in a lack of efficiency in delivering governmental services to citizens.*

*Technology and increased citizen dependence on government service and government regulation make administration by the citizen legislator no longer feasible. The commission plan lacks professionalism.*

*It is often nearly impossible for voters to know the myriad functional officials they are electing. Quite frequently clerks, recorders, engineers, auditors, treasurers, coroners, and sheriffs are elected term after term without opposition. This concentrates the power for selection of county officials in political parties and special interest groups.*

*The commission plan lacks accountability because responsibility for legislative and executive functions is so diffused.*

The first three advantages cited are largely the traditional, Jacksonian arguments which are extremely difficult to prove or disprove. The fourth advantage (that the commission form results in unified administration and policy-making) is particularly debatable. Unified administration and policy-making can occur if there is strong party leadership in the county and the commissioners and other elected county officials are of the same party and follow agreements worked out with party leaders. Unified administration can also occur if commissioners and other elected officials are in basic agreement on county programs. However, in the absence of these conditions, there may be major divisions of opinion among the commissioners or sharp differences between the commissioners and one or more of the independently elected officials. The resulting conflicts can be severe.

*Variations in practice.* There are important differences in how the commission form of government operates. In some counties, the chairman of the county board of commissioners, as a result of seniority, greater ability, more experience, (or a longer work week) may make most of the administrative decisions leaving the other commissioners to share in the legislative and policy-making functions. The author observed one county in Idaho in which the chairman of the board for years made the administrative decisions, and the other two commissioners always voted to support him. A second example of the strong board chairman was observed in Baker County (Oregon) which has a full-time elected County Judge with no judicial duties but considerable executive responsibilities for supervision of most county departments. Baker County also has two part-time Commissioners who meet with the County Judge about five or six days a month primarily on legislative and policy matters.

A second variation in the commission plan occurs when the county clerk is an experienced, full-time county official with many fiscal and administrative duties, and the county commissioners are part-time officials with time consuming non-governmental responsibilities. An able, experienced county clerk (with the approval of the commissioners) can make many of the day-to-day administrative decisions that the board of county commissioners would otherwise have to make.

A third version is found when there is an appointed county clerk or administrative assistant who aids the county commissioners in preparing the budget, developing agendas for board meetings, following-up on board decisions, and advising the commissioners on emergencies that require their attention. In Franklin County (Ohio), this administrative assistant is called a "county administrator" and functions almost as a county administrator in a council-administrator form of government.

Still another variety can be observed in some Texas, Tennessee, and Alabama counties where a county judge is elected at large and is the presiding officer of the county board. The judge (who has judicial functions) also has important financial and administrative powers. In many cases, the county judge has most of the strengths of a county executive.

The strongest criticism of the commission form is that it lacks a chief executive officer to unify administration and be accountable to the people. This is a valid argument in those counties in which the county commissioners and other independently elected officials have nearly equal power. However, as previously described, in a number of commission counties, a county judge, county clerk, or the chairman of the board of county commissioners can help unify administration by assuming a strong leadership role. In this instance, defenders of the commission form may claim this as evidence that it does provide executive leadership. Detractors, however, may state that the emergence of a very able, experienced official should be viewed as an opportunity to change the form of government and elect this able leader as county executive.

The effectiveness of the commission form of government may also depend on the cohesiveness of party leadership in the county. A strong, cohesive party leadership can unify county administration if the county commissioners and other elected county officials are of the same party. Advocates of the commission form of county government may claim that this circumstance provides the necessary unified leadership. Those in opposition may point out that cooperation might break down if the strong party leader does not control all county elective offices. Furthermore, there is concern about unifying the government under a party boss who may not be an elected county official. Some would say it is far better for the party boss to unify county administration from an elective position within county government where his power would be subject to check by the public at the polls.

**Council-Administrator Forms.** It was estimated that five hundred counties, serving more than 60 million people, operated under the council-administrator forms of county government in 1975, and this number probably reached 580 by 1977.[9] By title, the county administrator is called a county manager, chief administrative officer, administrative assistant, assistant to the county board chairman, or even executive or executive director. The major difference in the forms of council-administrator government is whether the administrative officer has the basic authority of a county manager, a chief administrative officer, or an assistant to the chairman of the county board.

*Council-manager plan.* The county manager has the most extensive powers of the three types of county administrator. The manager is appointed by the county board as principal administrative officer of the county and serves at the pleasure of the county board. The board retains its legislative functions such as enacting ordinances, appropriating funds, setting tax rates, and exercising general oversight of administration. It also determines broad program policies and reviews program operations with the manager. The county manager appoints all or most of the department heads and is responsible to the board for the administration of county programs. Both the manager and the department heads make the day-to-day policy decisions on programs. The manager is also responsible for preparing an annual budget for submission to the board, drafting reports and ordinances requested by the board, and serving as staff arm to the county board. The council-manager plan was first adopted by Iredell County (North Carolina) in 1927, and by 1965 there were thirty-five counties using this form of government. Currently, manager counties vary in size from Dade County (Florida), with a population of more than 1.2 million, to Petroleum County (Montana), with a population of less than one thousand. Chart 3-2 shows a simplified version of a county manager plan.

In practice, the voters generally elect some officials such as a clerk or county judge, and the county council (rather than the county manager) may appoint other county officials. The county manager plan of government in Dade County (Florida), shown in Chart 3-3, is a vastly more complex organization than the simplified version of Chart 3-2.

*Chief administrative officer plan.* The chief administrative officer (CAO) has some, but not all, of the powers of the county manager. He or she is appointed by the county board and is generally responsible for preparing the budget for submission to the county board. Serving the board as chief of staff, the CAO drafts ordinances, prepares reports, and coordinates county programs under the board's direction. The CAO directly supervises administrative and staff services such as budgeting, purchasing, personnel, management analysis, data processing, and capital improvements.

Unlike the county manager, the chief administrative officer does not directly supervise most county departments and does not appoint most department directors. The county board retains the appointment of line department directors but gives the chief administrative officer power to coordinate county departments. The chief administrative officer plan is the most widely used form of county government in California and is the form used in the nation's most populous county, Los Angeles.

Chart 3-4 shows the county administrator plan of Alameda County (California), in which the chief administrative officer of the county is appointed by the Board of Supervisors. The functions of the Alameda County Administrator include: advising the Board of Supervisors, making budget recommendations to the Board, coordinating departmental activities, and developing plans for implementing county programs. Chart 3-4 shows the County Admini-

strator in a box just below the Board of Supervisors, indicating the close relationship between the County Administrator and the Board.

*County administrative assistant plan.* The administrative assistant is also appointed by the county board and, having many of the powers of the chief administrative officer, serves the county board by preparing drafts of ordinances and reports and following up on administrative action for the board. The administrative assistant usually does not appoint or directly supervise department directors, but may be responsible for budget preparation.

A simplified version of the county administrative assistant plan is shown by Chart 3-5. The administrative assistant may be given a number of different titles including that of county administrator.

Table 3-2 contains a comparison of the three appointed county administrator forms of government.

Chart 3-2

SIMPLIFIED COUNTY COUNCIL-MANAGER PLAN

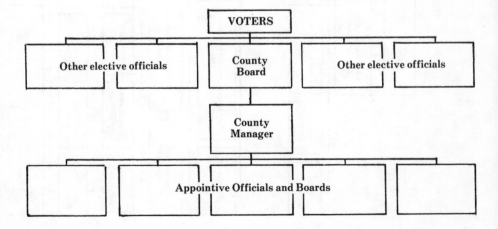

Chart 3-3

## ORGANIZATION CHART OF DADE COUNTY, FLORIDA

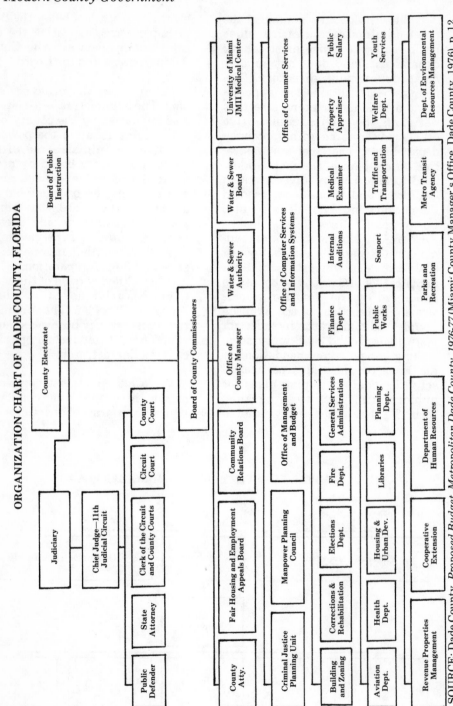

SOURCE: Dade County, *Proposed Budget, Metropolitan Dade County, 1976-77* (Miami: County Manager's Office, Dade County, 1976), p. 12.

There are a number of important advantages of the council-administrator forms of county government including:

- *"The council-administrator plan separates policy making and administration, thus removing administration from political influence.*

- *The appointed administrator, who is often recruited on a nationwide basis (unlike elected officials who must be county residents), can provide highly professional administrative leadership.*

- *The council-administrator plan is a less dramatic departure from the traditional commission plan and makes for easier transition from the commission form.*

- *The appointed administrator usually serves at the pleasure of the county board and can be replaced immediately should he or she fail to fulfill the duties of the position.*

- *The county legislature (board) under the council-administrator plan is free to spend time on policy development while the administrator handles the day-to-day business of the county government.*

- *Greater control over performances and expenditures is possible under the supervision of the appointed administrator than with the commission form."*[10]

There are three particularly significant disadvantages. The appointed administrator is dependent upon the strength and cooperative spirit of the county board, and may find it difficult to take effective action when the county board is split. The appointed administrator may also find it difficult to provide policy leadership on important issues facing the county. On the one hand, with a passive role, inaction may result. On the other hand, if the administrator becomes an agent to crystallize public opinion behind a particular issue, he or she may become vulnerable if the board takes a different stand. Nevertheless, for many counties the disadvantages of the plan are far outweighed by the advantages of unified and more effective provision of county services.

**The Council-Elected Executive Form.** In 1977, there were 142 counties, city/counties, and independent cities, with over forty-three million inhabitants, which employed the elected executive form of government.[11] The county executive is elected by the voters and heads the executive branch of government. The county board is the legislative branch of government enacting ordinances, adopting a budget, and exercising the usual oversight of administration. It has the same roles as the council in the strong mayor-council form of city government and the state legislature in state government. The county executive has the power to veto legislation passed by the county board, and the board usually has the power to override the county executive's veto with a two-thirds or greater majority.

The county executive takes general responsibility for county administration, prepares the county budget, suggests policy to the county board,

**Chart 3-4**

**COMMISSION-ADMINISTRATOR FORM OF COUNTY GOVERNMENT (ALAMEDA COUNTY, CALIFORNIA)**

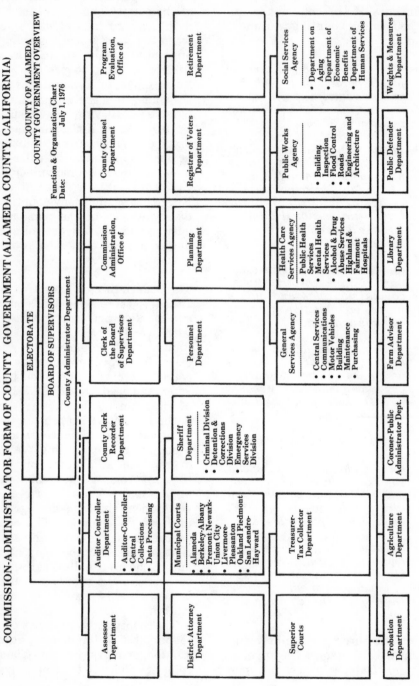

SOURCE: Sent by Loren E. Enoch, County Administrator, Alameda County, to Sydney Duncombe, February 18, 1977.

acts as spokesman for the county on ceremonial and other occasions, and sees that the acts and resolutions of the county board are executed. The county executive appoints and may dismiss department heads, usually with the consent of the county board. Under the county executive form, the voters may elect some "row" officers but not as many as in the traditional commission form of government.

Chart 3-6 shows a simplified form of the elected executive plan. One variation is the plan of Baltimore County (Maryland) where the county executive appoints a professional administrative officer to assist him in supervising county offices and departments (Chart 3-7).

Supporters of the council-elected executive form frequently cite the following advantages:

- *"The elected executive plan provides the most visible policy-making for the community through providing the public an opportunity to hear the pros and cons of each issue.*

- *The executive (particularly in urban areas) provides the needed strong political leadership for relating to diverse segments of the community. An executive elected at large is considered more dependable and less likely to resign during a crisis or crucial period of change for the county than an administrator who serves at the pleasure of the county board.*

- *The elected executive is responsive to the public will: he or she must answer to the county electorate in the next election.*

- *Greater visibility and prestige is achieved for the county with the council-elected plan. State legislators, governors, the United States Congress, and the President can focus on one individual who clearly represents the entire county.*

- *The best system of checks and balances is provided by this complete separation of powers. Through the veto, which can*

Chart 3-5

**SIMPLIFIED COUNTY ADMINISTRATIVE ASSISTANT PLAN**

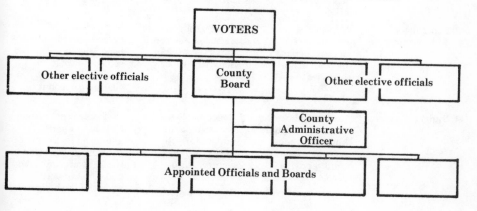

be overridden by the county board, both branches can express their commitment to their positions on various issues." [12]

One of the arguments against the council-elected executive form is that it may lead to bossism. In counties like Westchester and Nassau in New York which have used the system for nearly forty years, however, bossism has not developed. A more serious criticism is that it is difficult to find an elected executive who is both a skillful political leader and an expert administrator. Elected executive counties remedy this deficiency by providing professional administrative staff assistance for the elected executive. Under one variation of the elected executive form, the county executive appoints a professional chief administrative officer to assist him.

Critics of the form contend that conflict between the executive and the legislative body may impede county progress, but there is no evidence that this is more of a problem than conflict among the members of a county board in the commission form of government. The executive form is not the best plan for every county, but it does provide more unified administration and a better coordinated service delivery system than the commission system.

**State Action to Allow More Options.** One past criticism of county government organization was that the

Table 3-2

**TYPICAL DISTINGUISHING FEATURES OF THE APPOINTED OFFICES OF COUNTY MANAGER, CHIEF ADMINISTRATIVE OFFICER, AND ADMINISTRATIVE ASSISTANT**

|  | County Manager | Chief Administrative Officer | Administrative Assistant |
|---|---|---|---|
| 1. Appointed by | County Board | County Board | County Board (sometimes on recommendation of the chairman) |
| 2. Appointment powers | Appoints all or most department heads and staff officers | Appoints some directors of staff agencies | Appoints just members of immediate staff |
| 3. Supervision and coordination | Supervises and coordinates all or most departments and staff agencies | Supervises some staff agencies, and coordinates the work of departments | Supervises just immediate staff members. May be delegated some coordination responsibilities by chairman of county board |
| 4. Budget | Responsible for preparing annual budget for submission to the county board | Responsible for preparing annual budget for submission to the county board | Generally is not responsible for preparing annual budget but provides information to the board chairman and county board in review of the budget |

form of government was inflexible because it was established by state constitution and law. This criticism is becoming less valid as more states allow optional forms of county government organization. By 1965, eighteen states had granted counties the right to choose from optional forms of organization. By 1975, forty states permitted at least one alternative to the commission form. Counties in nine of these states gained the needed legislation between 1972 and 1974. Table 3-3 shows the forms of organization permitted in each state in 1975.

## COUNTY GOVERNING BOARDS

The county board is usually called the board of county commissioners but may also be called the board of supervisors, commissioners court, county court, fiscal court or one of several other titles. The size of the county board is often set by state law or constitutional provision and follows one of five patterns as shown by Table 3-4.

**Small Governing Boards.** The predominant type of small governing board is the county commissioner board which originated in Pennsylvania in the 1720s. The typical coun-

ty commissioner board has:

- *three or five members elected for two to four year terms;*

- *a board chairman who does not have much more legal authority than the other commissioners; and,*

- *commissioners who have administrative as well as legislative responsibilities and who do not hold a judicial or township office.*

Idaho boards of county commissioners are typical of many small boards. The three county commissioners in each Idaho county are elected by the voters of the entire county, but each must be a resident of a specific election district.[13] Elected by the board at its first regular meeting each biennium, the chairman presides over its meetings but does not have significantly greater legal powers than the other commissioners. The county commissioners in Idaho have many legislative functions, such as enacting ordinances and adopting a budget, but they also have many executive and administrative duties such as directly supervising county employees.

Chart 3-6

**SIMPLIFIED ELECTED EXECUTIVE FORM**

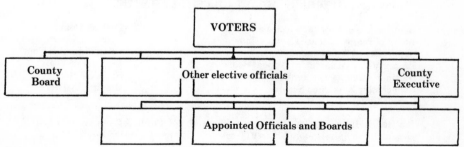

Chart 3-7
## GOVERNMENTAL ORGANIZATION OF BALTIMORE COUNTY

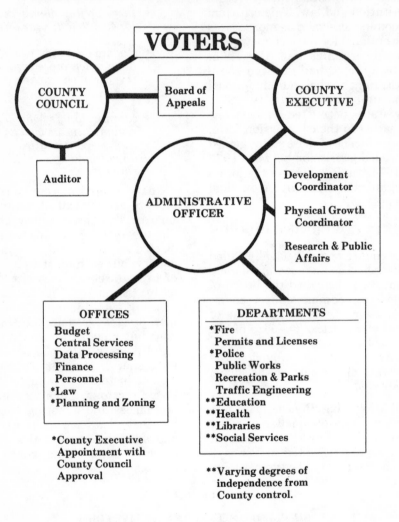

**AGENCIES NOT DIRECTLY CONTROLLED BY CHARTER:**

Board of Supervisors of Elections
Board of Liquor License Commissioners
Supervisor of Assessments
Property Tax Assessment Appeal Board
Baltimore County Revenue Authority
Cooperative Extension Service
Circuit Court

District Court
Orphans' Court
Clerk of Circuit Court
Register of Wills
State's Attorney
County Sheriff

SOURCE: Baltimore County Office of Research and Public Affairs, *Governmental Organization of Baltimore County* (Towson: Baltimore County, March 1977).

Table 3-3

**ALTERNATIVE FORMS OF COUNTY GOVERNMENT
PERMITTED AND USED IN EACH STATE**

| State | Forms Permitted | | | State | Forms Permitted | | |
|---|---|---|---|---|---|---|---|
| Alabama | C | CA |  | Missouri | C | CA | CE |
| Alaska | C | CA | CE | Montana | C | CA | CE |
| Arizona | C | CA |  | Nebraska | C | CA |  |
| Arkansas | C | CA | CE | Nevada | C | CA |  |
|  |  |  |  |  |  |  |  |
| California | C | CA | CE | New Hampshire | C | CA |  |
| Colorado | C | CA | CE | New Jersey | C | CA | CE |
| Delaware | C | CA | CE | New Mexico | C | CA |  |
| Dist. of Col. |  |  | CE | New York | C | CA | CE |
|  |  |  |  |  |  |  |  |
| Florida | C | CA | CE | North Carolina | C | CA |  |
| Georgia | C | CA | CE | North Dakota | C | CA |  |
| Hawaii |  | CA | CE | Ohio | C | CA | CE |
| Idaho | C |  |  | Oklahoma | C |  |  |
|  |  |  |  |  |  |  |  |
| Illinois | C | CA | CE | Oregon | C | CA | CE |
| Indiana | C | CA | CE | Pennsylvania | C | CA | CE |
| Iowa | C |  |  | South Carolina | C | CA |  |
| Kansas | C | CA | CE | South Dakota | C | CA | CE |
|  |  |  |  |  |  |  |  |
| Kentucky | C |  | CE | Tennessee | C | CA | CE |
| Louisiana | C | CA | CE | Texas | C |  |  |
| Maine | C | CA |  | Utah | C | CA | CE |
| Maryland | C | CA | CE | Vermont | C |  |  |
|  |  |  |  |  |  |  |  |
| Massachusetts | C |  | CE | Virginia | C | CA |  |
| Michigan | C | CA | CE | Washington | C | CA | CE |
| Minnesota | C | CA | CE | West Virginia | C |  |  |
| Mississippi | C | CA |  | Wisconsin | C | CA | CE |
|  |  |  |  | Wyoming | C |  |  |

SOURCE: Florence Zeller, "Forms of County Government," National Association of Counties and International City Management Association, *The County Year Book, 1975,* (Washington: National Association of Counties and the International City Management Association, 1975), pp. 28, 29. "C" designates counties with a commission form of government, "CA" designates a council-administrator form of government, and "CE" designates a council-elected executive form of government.

*The judge and commissioner board.* This second type of small county board is found in many counties in Alabama and Texas and a few counties in Oregon. A typical Alabama county has a five member board composed of four commissioners and a judge of probate.[14] The judge is elected at large from the entire county and the commissioners are generally elected by district. The probate judge presides over the county board, has fiscal responsibilities such as maintaining financial records and preparing the county budget, and performs judicial functions such as the probating of wills and administration of estates. With financial and judicial responsibilities, the county judge has significantly more power than the county commissioners, but the commissioners still retain some administrative responsiblities.

*The small legislative board.* This board is generally similar to the county commissioner board in structure, except that an elected or appointed executive handles all or most executive and administrative functions. Marion County (Indiana), for example, has a three-member commissioner type board as do other Indiana counties, but the Mayor of the city-county government, not the County Board, appoints and supervises the appointed county department directors.

*There are many advantages to a small board.* It is usually less costly than a large board, and the members of a small board tend to spend at least half-time on county work and become more knowledgeable of county operations. However, familiarity with county operations may lead to "meddling" in administrative detail, according to one writer.[15] Moreover, in a populous county the small county commissioner type board, without the services of a county manager, administrative officer, or administrative assistant, may find itself overwhelmed with supervisory and administrative responsibilities.

In larger urban counties, the best

Table 3-4

STATE PATTERNS IN THE NUMBER OF
MEMBERS ON THE COUNTY BOARD

| Pattern | Number of States | States |
|---|---|---|
| 2 member board | 1 | Vermont |
| 3 member board | 20 | Arizona, Colorado, Idaho, Indiana, Kansas, Maine, Massachusetts, Missouri, Montana, Nevada, New Hampshire, New Mexico, Ohio, Oklahoma, Oregon, Pennsylvania, Utah, Washington, West Virginia, Wyoming |
| 5 member board | 5 | California, Florida, Minnesota, Mississippi, Texas |
| Small boards of variable size (most under ten members) | 15 | Alabama, Alaska, Delaware, Georgia, Hawaii, Iowa, Kentucky, Maryland, Nebraska, New Jersey, North Carolina, North Dakota, South Carolina, South Dakota, Virginia |
| Large boards (many counties with ten or more members) | 7 | Arkansas, Illinois, Louisiana, Michigan, New York, Tennessee, Wisconsin |

SOURCE: Tabulated from National Association of Counties and International City Management Association, *The County Year Book, 1975*, (Washington: National Association of Counties and the International City Management Association, 1975), pp. 127-178. For a state to count as a two, three, or five member board state, all (or nearly all) of the counties had to have the same number of board members. Michigan was counted as a large board state because some of its counties had boards of twenty or more members, and many counties had ten or more members.

type of small board is one which can leave administration to an elected or appointed executive and concentrate mainly on legislative functions. Montgomery County (Ohio) and Alameda County (California) are among the many large urban counties with small county boards which have delegated much administrative responsibility to appointed county administrators.

**Large Governing Boards.** Large governing boards are the rule in all four of the states (New York, Michigan, Illinois, and Wisconsin) which extensively use the township supervisory board. As originally constituted, the township supervisory board was composed of township supervisors having the dual role of executive head of their townships and members of the county board and was a unique way of linking township and county government. By 1960, however, many populous counties with township supervisory boards were giving representation on the county board not only to a supervisor from each township but additional representation to each city in the county on a population basis.

The "one man, one vote" principle posed serious problems for county supervisory boards because although each township had one representative, there were often great population differences between the largest and smallest. In case after case, state and federal courts held invalid state laws and county practices requiring each township to have one representative on the county board.[16] As a result of court action, the Wisconsin Legislature enacted a statute requiring county boards to establish supervisory districts as nearly equal in population as practicable. Michigan now has an apportionment system in which county commissioners are elected from single member districts approximately equal in population.[17] Each Michigan county must have at least five commissioners, with the maximum varying from seven (for a county of 5,000 people or less) to thirty-five (for the state's largest counties).

The net effect of the changes is that the county boards in the more populous counties of New York, Michigan, Wisconsin, and Illinois are similar in some ways to a small state senate. Michigan counties, for example, make extensive use of the committee system, with a number of them reporting twenty or more standing committees. Formal rules and parliamentary procedures are more widely used by these larger boards. Moreover, individual members of these large county governing boards are more likely to view themselves as county legislators rather than commissioners with administrative powers.

The judge and justice of the peace system has also evolved into a large governing board (often called the Fiscal Court) in Tennessee. The judge, elected by the people, has administrative, fiscal and judicial powers with the justices of the peace having minor judicial functions. The county judge has a powerful position in Tennessee counties. It is significant that when Davidson County (1970 population 447,877) reorganized its judge and justice of the peace system to establish a Metropolitan Mayor-Council form of government, the able County Judge of Davidson County was elected Mayor of the new Metropolitan Government of Nashville and Davidson County.

On the one hand, large governing boards which are elected by district have the advantage of better representing most geographic areas and racial, ethnic, and interest groups in the county. With fewer citizens to represent, the member of a large board is likely to find it easier to have face-to-face contacts with a greater proportion of his constituents. The committee system can give the members of large boards the opportunity to specialize in various types of legislative and policy matters.

On the other hand, large boards tend to be too unwieldy for administration, leaving this responsibility to elected and appointed executives. Another disadvantage is that members elected from small constituencies may have a parochial rather than a county-wide perspective. Still another weakness is that a large board with a staff can be expensive. One writer stated that large governing boards tend "to create power blocks and special interest groups which effectively control segments of county functions."[18]

**Powers of County Boards.** County boards differ from state to state in the powers granted them by state constitutions and laws. There are important differences between commission counties, council-administrator counties, and council-elected executive counties in the powers exercised by county boards. All county boards have three types of powers commonly exercised by legislative bodies:

- *the power to enact ordinances similar in many respects to*

the ordinances enacted by city councils;

- *the power to review budget requests, appropriate funds, establish county tax levies (up to state tax limits), and incur debt (however, the incurrence of debt usually takes approval of the voters after action by the county board); and,*

- *the power to hear reports from county officers and exercise oversight of administration.*

In addition, county boards may have one or more of the following powers depending on state constitutions, state laws, and the form of government used. These include the power to:

- *appoint administrators, department directors, and members of boards and commissions;*

- *provide day-to-day supervision of administrative officials not under the supervision of elected or appointed executives;*

- *issue licenses and regulate business;*

- *adopt (and change) by resolution a comprehensive plan and adopt (and make changes in) a zoning ordinance, subdivision regulations, and housing, building, and other codes;*

- *take actions to create and finance dependent special districts;*

- *let contracts, authorize purchases, maintain buildings, pay bills, and take other ac-*

*tions needed to maintain county offices;*

- *equalize property tax assessments; and,*

- *adopt policies and regulations for a variety of county functions.*

Do county boards have adequate legal powers to meet the needs of their citizens for the many programs which county governments administer? There is no easy answer since conditions vary from program to program and state to state. Even within a state, a home rule county may have adequate powers to carry out a particular function and a non-home rule county may not. In addition to the presence or absence of a home rule charter, the adequacy of a county board's authority depends on a variety of factors.

*The provisions of state constitutions.* For example, a constitutional provision requiring an elected coroner may block the attempts of the county board to replace an unqualified coroner with an appointed professional medical examiner.

*The provisions of state law.* Very specific provisions of state law may unnecessarily hamper county boards. For example, reforms in the procedures for recording and microfilming legal documents supported by the county board, county clerk, auditor, and recorder may be blocked by specific laws requiring certain indexes and records.

*The flexibility to start new programs.* Counties are best served by laws which provide great flexibility in establishing new programs. Particularly helpful is a state law which allows counties to establish

new programs not specifically prohibited by state law.

*The form of county government.* County boards have more adequate powers to establish and make changes in programs in counties in which the administration is not split with many important programs under independently elected officials.

*The impact of the political party system of the county.* A strong, unified party system under the leadership of the chairman of the county board, for example, could enhance the power of the county board.

## ELECTED EXECUTIVES AND "ROW" OFFICERS

In commission counties, administrative responsibilities are divided between the county governing board and a number of independently elected officials. The term "row" officers is sometimes used to describe these officials because their titles appear in a long row on the organization chart of the county. There are independently elected "row" officers in council-administrator and council-elected executive counties as well, although there are often fewer of these officials and some of their powers may be diminished.

In the council-elected executive form of county government, another type of elective official is found - a county executive whose powers to supervise and administer extend generally to all county agencies not under the supervision of "row" officers. This section will describe the powers of elected officers and discuss the effect of their offices on the coordination of county programs.

**Elected Executives.** It is not far-fetched to say that an elected county executive is comparable to a governor, or even to the President of the United States, in the many demanding roles which must be filled simultaneously. The executive is the county's chief policy-maker who incorporates in a proposed budget the direction and priorities the legislative body ought to pursue.

As chief administrator, the executive is responsible for seeing that ordinances and other examples of legislative intent are actually carried out. The appointment power covers most, but not all, department heads, and there are important departments under the direction of other independently elected officials, as at the state level.

Although there may be legislators elected on an at-large basis, the county executive is not only considered a notch or two higher for the above stated reasons, but also because this official is the top elected party official on the county level.

In sum, the county executive, regardless of personal preference, is likely to be the most visible elected county official. Like a governor or the President, the executive sometimes receives blame from citizens for the actions of officials he or she does not appoint. Rightly or wrongly, it is the executive who will ultimately be responsible for public satisfaction or dissatisfaction.

The Westchester County Charter states that "the county executive shall be the chief executive and administrative officer of the county and the official head of county government."[19] Among the duties of the county executive specified by the Westchester County Charter are:[20]

- *to supervise, direct and control the administrative services and departments of the county in accordance with the county charter and local laws;*

- *to present an annual budget to the county board and to provide the county board, at least once a year, a general statement of the finances, government and affairs of the county;*

- *to present to the county board, from time to time, such other information that he may deem necessary or the board may request. To recommend measures he deems expedient;*

- *to see that county officers, boards, agencies, commissions and departments faithfully perform their duties;*

- *to make studies and investigations in the best interests of the county, to compel the attendance of witnesses, and (if necessary) to examine the books, records, or papers of county agencies to ascertain facts in connection with any study or investigation;*

- *to veto acts of the county board in a manner prescribed by the county charter;*

- *to appoint the head or acting head of county departments, offices, boards, and commissions subject to confirmation by the county board; and,*

- *to perform other duties as may be prescribed to the county executive by the county charter or acts of the county board.*

**Clerk, Court Clerk, Auditor and Recorder.** The county offices of clerk, court clerk, auditor, and recorder may be separate elective offices, or two or more of the offices may be combined. In Idaho, all four offices are combined into a single elective position. Nebraska has separate offices of county clerk, clerk of the district court, and register of deeds. Utah counties have clerks, auditors, and recorders. Although the functions may be combined or separated in different ways, the offices of county clerk, auditor, and recorder usually have the following responsibilities.

*Assistance to the county board.* An important duty of the county clerk in commission counties is often serving as secretary to the county board. In this capacity, the county clerk compiles the agenda for the board, records the action of the board, and follows up on board actions by writing letters and memoranda requested by the board. The county clerk may also help the board prepare a county budget.

*Election responsibilities.* The county clerk (or similar county officer) may be responsible for registering voters, supervising precinct election officials, publishing election notices, and handling much of the detailed work in election administration.

*Serving the court system.* The court clerk (or a deputy county clerk where the functions are combined with the county clerk) serves as an important staff officer to the main trial court having jurisdiction in the county. The court clerk is usually responsible for collecting and recording fines, forfeitures, penalties, and costs in criminal cases. Personnel in the court clerk's office keep records of court proceedings, handle judicial correspondence, type court documents, and may prepare the formal writs and process papers issued by the court.

*Recording legal documents.* The county recorder or registrar of deeds (or a deputy clerk where the functions are combined with the county clerk) plays an important role in the orderly transfer of title to property. By recording each deed, mortgage and lease, the recorder or registrar of deeds is providing a record needed for a thorough title search. The county recorder may also record, index, and microfilm other important legal documents such as marriage licenses, mining claims, wills, liens, and official bonds.

*Accounting and auditing.* A common function of the elected county auditor (or a deputy clerk or auditor) is to audit bills or other claims against the county and prepare warrants in payment of these bills. In making the audit, the county auditor will make sure that the goods or services have been actually received, that there is no error in calculating the amount of the charge, and that the agency receiving the goods or services has sufficient funds and the authority to make the expenditure. To insure that county agencies are not overspending their appropriations, it is common for the county auditor to maintain accounting records on all appropriations. The county auditor may also have responsibilities in computing and collecting property taxes.

**County Treasurer.** In Michigan, as in many other states, the county treasurer is charged with the responsibility of receiving county moneys from all sources.[21] The treasurer deposits county funds in banks and keeps records of revenues and bank balances. The treasurer may also keep records of the expenditures, revenues, and balances of county funds. In some states, the treasurer participates in the property tax collection process by sending out delinquency notices and following up on delinquent taxes.

The county treasurer generally invests funds not immediately needed for county expenses and may earn substantial amounts of interest for the county through skillful investment of these idle funds in government securities. In some states, the county treasurer also acts as public administrator of the estates of persons who die without a will. If the county treasurer has discretion in designating which banks are to receive county deposits, the treasurer's position can be politically sensitive.

**County Assessor.** The county assessor has the responsibility for appraising or setting the value of all property subject to county property taxes. The assessor has extensive maps of all parcels of property in the county and records the physical characteristics and value of all buildings. When a new building is constructed, the assessor and his staff will usually know of this from the issuance of the building permit and will make an inspection to determine the assessed valuation. The determination of assessed valuation of a home is based on a number of factors, such as the number of square feet of floor space, specific features (such as a finished basement), the location of the home, and the sales price of similar homes in the same neighborhood.

The assessor frequently is responsible for sending out notices of assessment to property owners so they may have the opportunity to challenge the assessment if they think it is excessive. This official may also send out tax notices and collect property taxes. In some counties, the assessor has non-property tax functions such as issuing automobile license plates and collecting a number of taxes and fees. Minimum qualifications for the position of assessor have been established in only a few states, but elected assessors and their deputies gain skill in assessing through experience and attending training conferences and courses.[22] Assessors are in a politically sensitive position and may be under pressure from taxpayers to under-assess their property.

**Prosecuting Attorney.** The county prosecuting attorney has two major roles. His first is to act as attorney to the county board and county officials by providing legal advice on a variety of matters and giving informal opinions on the legality of proposed action. He also represents the county in many types of cases in which the county is a plaintiff or defendant. The county attorney may, for example, represent the county in a suit in which a citizen claims injury because of the negligence of a county employee, a case relating to the bankruptcy of a creditor, or a dispute between an employee and the county involving compensation.[23]

A second role of the county prosecuting attorney is to prosecute, in the name of the state, persons suspected of crimes. In this role, the prosecuting attorney is a vital part of the criminal justice system. With an important responsibility in the preferral of charges either by grand jury or by the information system, the county attorney normally appears at the arraignment and presents the state's case at the trial.

In some counties, the roles are separated, with a county counsel serving as legal advisor to county officials and a district or state's attorney having criminal justice responsibilities.

**Sheriff.**[24] The county sheriff and his deputies serve as the county law enforcement agency patrolling streets and highways, checking the speed of motor vehicles, investigating crimes, and arresting suspected criminals. The sheriff's office also helps to enforce laws on the closing hours of taverns, illegal possession of narcotics, arson, burglary, assault, and many other crimes against persons and property. In many counties, the sheriff's office provides the largest police force in the unincorporated areas and in the small communities of the county.

As a county law enforcement officer, the sheriff is usually responsible for the county jail, the custody and feeding of prisoners, and courthouse security. In many small counties, the county sheriff maintains the only jail in the entire county. County administration of jails occurs even in the northeastern states in which towns and townships provide the primary law enforcement for the unincorporated area of the county.

The sheriff and his deputies generally serve process papers on a variety of court matters such as divorces, damage suits, and bank-

ruptcy proceedings. Under the authority of a court, they may have the task of securing, storing, advertising, and selling property to satisfy a debt. The county sheriff often acts as a court officer, attending sessions of the court and serving subpoenas, summonses, and arrest warrants. The sheriff and his deputies are often called upon to give assistance in accidents and to lead search parties in rural areas to find wrecked planes or lost hunters.

**Coroner.** Coroners were elected county officials in twenty-six states in 1973.[25] When a person has died by violence, under suspicious circumstances, or when a physician is not in attendence, the coroner is called upon to determine the cause of death. Before preparing an official report on his findings, the coroner usually examines the body, may have an autopsy performed, and may assemble a jury to conduct an official inquest. Many coroners lack medical training, and the election of county coroners has been severely criticized by some writers.

An alternative to the elected county coroner is the appointment of a physician as a medical examiner. An examiner with medical training is much better able to determine the cause of death than an elected coroner without medical training. A 1973 report states that in fifteen states the office of coroner has been abolished, and in other states the county is given the option to replace the coroner with a medical examiner.[26]

**Other County Elective "Row" Officers.** Elected county superintendents of schools have been abolished in most states but continue to provide specialized financial and program services in some states. The county surveyor's office has been abolished or stripped of most of its former land surveying duties. There are a few other elective "row" officers such as drain commissioners in Michigan. With a few exceptions, these other "row" officials play a minor role in county government.[27]

**Fragmentation of The County Executive Functions.** There is little doubt that the existence of many independently elected "row" officers fragments the executive functions of county government and makes more difficult the problem of co-ordinating county services. The problem may be particularly serious in many of the approximately 1,500 counties of 25,000 people or less, governed under a commission form of government. In these counties, all or nearly all full-time county employees may be under the direction of independently elected "row" officers.[28] If these officials refuse to cooperate on county problems, such as streamlining the property tax assessment and collection system, there is no means of forcing cooperation except the limited budget pressure at the disposal of the county commissioners. Part-time county commissioners have a difficult task in coordinating the work of full-time "row" officers. In some counties, political party leaders are able to provide an important coordinating role particularly when all county officials are of the same party.

## APPOINTED COUNTY ADMINISTRATORS

The term "county administrator" has generally been used to describe the appointed administrator in the council-administrator form of government. This official is appointed by the county legislative body and may be given the title "county manager", "administrative officer", "county administrative assistant", or a similar designation. He or she may be appointed by the county executive in the council-elected executive form of county government. The various county administrators have one common characteristic - they hold the highest administrative post in their respective counties, and they are in a key position to bring professional expertise and coordination to county government. Their skills, training, and responsibilities are of importance to a study of the operation of county government.

**Background of County Administrators.** An extensive study of county administrators in 202 counties, conducted by the International City Management Association in 1973, revealed these factors about those responding to the survey:[29]

- *the median age of administrators was 43;*

- *nearly all (99%) were men and nearly all were Caucasian;*

- *forty-four percent were registered as Democrats, 17% were independents, and 21% were registered as Republicans;*

- *the administrators were highly educated (97% had some education beyond high school, 83% had a college degree and some work toward a masters, and 35% had a masters degree);*

- *county administrators with college degrees tended to specialize in public administration (31%), political science (25%), or business administration (23%);*

- *about 62% of the respondents had participated in at least one professional institute or training program in the last three years; and,*

- *more than 95% belonged to at least one religious, fraternal, service, or community organization with 48% belonging to a service organization, 44% to a fraternal organization, and 44% to the International City Management Association.*

This profile of county administrators gives the picture of a highly trained, professional group with membership in community organizations—a group similar in many respects to city managers and school superintendents.

**Careers.** The 1973 study of county administrators revealed that most of the respondents had spent an average of nearly six years in their present positions.[30] The typical county administrator had worked most of his professional life in government with only 16% having previously been in private industry. About half of the administrators reported their most recent previous job was in municipal or county government, with many holding the position of chief administrative officer, assistant manager, or department director.

From the survey results, Larry Brown suggested that the county administrators "tend to have had substantive experience in top governmental positions and to have come to their present management position with a solid exposure to the management of local government operations."[31] Most county administrators left their previous post for career advancement, a salary increase, or a desire for a new type of experience.

In listing their career objectives, 45% of the administrators reported that they hoped to seek an administrator's position in a larger county, 16% hoped to move into private enterprise, and 14% wanted to seek a position in a county of about the same size. County administrators are an upwardly mobile group who usually advance by accepting better paying jobs in larger counties. Table 3-5 indicates that county administrators in counties of 250,000 or more people are paid salaries comparable to higher level state civil servants.

**Responsibilities.** According to the 1973 poll, county administrators do not want to exercise political leadership. Larry Brown points out that an appointed administrator "cannot become the political representative of the county without destroying the employee-employer relationship and without destroying the basis for electing the governing board."[32]

Most administrators want general supervision from the governing board, but do not want the governing board to spend its time on administrative details. They see themselves as more frequently participating in policy formulation than in initiating policies. They nearly always consult with the county council before drafting budget proposals

**64 •** *Modern County Government*

or appointing or removing department heads. They generally orient new council members on major issues and advise the council on a variety of matters, but they feel that their most frequent role is exercising administrative leadership.

The profile gives the impression of an able group of generalists working primarily in supervision, budgeting, and day-to-day administration.

The specific responsibilities of county administrators vary depending on whether the county has a council-manager, chief administrative officer, or some other council-administrator plan of government. The exact duties of the administrator are often described by the county charter (if one exists) or by an ordinance passed by the county board. The Dade County (Florida) Charter, for example, states that "The Board of County Commissioners shall appoint a County Manager who shall be the chief executive officer and head of the administrative branch of county government."[34] The Charter

gives many specific responsibilities to the County Manager, such as appointing certain department executives and recommending a county budget to the Board. In addition, it states:[35]

*"The Manager shall be responsible to the Board of County Commissioners for the administration of all units of the county government under his jurisdiction, and for carrying out policies adopted by the Board.*

*The Manager shall have the power to issue and place into effect administrative orders, rules, and regulations. The organization and operating procedure of departments shall be set forth in administrative regulations which the Manager shall develop, place into effect by administrative orders, and submit to the Board. The Board may, by resolution, modify such orders, rules or regulations providing, however, no such orders, rules or regulations creating, merging, or combining departments, shall become effective until approved by resolution of the Board. "*

Table 3-5

MEDIAN ANNUAL SALARIES OF
COUNTY ADMINISTRATORS, 1973

|  | Median Salary |
|---|---|
| Total, All Counties | $19,000 |
| Population group | |
| Over 500,000 | 40,208 |
| 250,000-500,000 | 33,830 |
| 100,000-249,999 | 26,400 |
| 50,000- 99,999 | 20,000 |
| 25,000- 49,999 | 16,900 |
| 10,000- 24,999 | 13,643 |
| 5,000- 9,999 | 14,500 |
| Under 5,000 | 11,500 |

SOURCE: Larry J. Brown, "County Administrators: Characteristics and Managerial Styles," in *The County Year Book, 1975,* (Washington: National Association of Counties and International City Management Association), p. 40.

In Alameda County (California), the basic duties of the county administrator are described, not by a county charter but by an ordinance passed by the Board of Supervisors. The Alameda County Administrator does not have the appointment powers of the Dade County Manager but has a number of important administrative functions, including:[36]

- *advising, assisting, and acting as agent for the Board of Supervisors and carrying out orders or regulations as directed by the Board;*

- *studying the proper organization of departments and recommending systems and procedures;*

- *conducting continuous research in administrative practices;*

- *reviewing the functions of departments to eliminate duplication and recommending to the Board policies for coordination and orderly conduct of departmental business;*

- *directing and performing central administrative services such as central statistical, office appliance, and clerical pools;*

- *establishing the enforcement of proper personnel policies and practices;*

- *exercising continuous control of expenditures under the supervision of the Board of Supervisors and reviewing, examining, recommending and controlling financial produres;*

- *recommending a long-term plan of capital improvements when requested by the Board of Supervisors; and,*

- *analyzing budget requests and preparing a budget for the County Board of Supervisors.*

Appointed administrators, such as the Dade County Manager and Alameda County Administrator, are able to bring unified supervision and coordination to county government thus blunting criticism that most counties lack a single chief executive.

## COUNTY POLITICS AND ORGANIZATIONAL STRUCTURE

There are three main forms of county government (commission, council-administrator, and council-elected executive) and many variations of these forms. The home rule movement has accelerated the trend toward optional forms of county government and toward voter selection of the form of government they consider best. For example, the 1971-72 Montana home rule constitutional amendment requires each county and municipality "to review its structure and submit one alternative form of government to the qualified electors..."[37]

A 1975 Montana law permits four main forms of county government and twelve structural sub-options.[38] Furthermore, the Montana law allows six types of cooperative arrangements such as county-municipality consolidation, county-municipality confederation, consolidation of two counties, and consolidation of services between cities and counties. Thus, Montana voters can choose among more than one hundred variations of organizational forms, structural sub-options, and cooperative arrangements to shape a form of government that best fits their individual needs. This trend towards more organizational options is also evident in Utah, Pennsylvania, and other states.

The organizational structure of a county is only one of a number of factors which influence how county government operates in practice. The political system of a county can bring policy coordination to a commission form of county government if all county officials are of the same party, or it can bring deeper division between officials if there is bitter strife between parties or party factions. Wearing the mantle of majority party leader in the county, a county judge, strong board chairman, or experienced county clerk may achieve nearly the powers of a county executive. Further research is badly needed to show the manner in which the party system and interest groups influence county government policies.

The political system within a county not only affects how county government operates in practice but the strength of county government in securing more adequate funding for county services and a greater measure of county home rule. The next chapter examines the role of the county and county officials in the political system.

## REFERENCES

1. Russell W. Maddox and Robert F. Fuquay, *State and Local Government*, 3rd ed. (New York: D. Van Nostrand Company, 1975), p. 439. The authors use the quotation as an introduction to the diversity of county organizational structure.

2. Hugh L. LeBlanc and D. Trudeau Allensworth, *The Politics of States and Urban Communities* (New York: Harper and Row, 1971), p. 194.

3. Florence Zeller, "Forms of County Government," National Association of Counties and International City Management Association, *The County Year Book, 1975* (Washington: National Association of Counties and International City Management Association, 1975), p. 27.

4. Henry S. Gilbertson, *The County, The 'Dark Continent' of American Politics* (New York: The National Short Ballot Association, 1917), pp. 34, 49, 50.

5. Lane W. Lancaster, *Government in Rural America*, 2nd ed. (New York: D. Van Nostrand Company, Inc., 1952), p. 54.

6. Russell W. Maddox and Robert F. Fuquay, p. 452.

7. Florence Zeller, p. 27. For further information on the plural executive and other forms of county government, see the previously cited article by Florence Zeller; also Clyde S. Snider, *Local Government in Rural America* (New York: Appleton-Century-Crofts, Inc., 1957), pp. 119-194; and Herbert Sydney Duncombe, *County Government in America* (Washington: National Association of Counties Research Foundation, 1966), pp. 9-12 and 55-59.

8. Florence Zeller, pp. 27, 28.

9. The 1975 estimate was made by Florence Zeller of the National Association of Counties staff. Ibid., p. 28. It is difficult to determine the number of counties which are operating under the council-administrator form of government because the titles of council administrator positions vary widely. Using criteria established by the National Association of County Administrators, a National Association of Counties staff member counted 587 county administrators as of January, 1977.

10. Ibid., pp. 29, 30.

11. The National Association of Counties, *NACo Fact Sheet - Elected Executives* (Washington: National Association of Counties, 1977).

12. Ibid., p. 31.

13. Michael S. Vollmer, Herbert Sydney Duncombe and Katherine D. Pell, *Handbook for County Officials in Idaho* (Moscow: Bureau of Public Affairs Research, University of Idaho, 1974), pp. 3, 9. Informally, a county board chairman of ability and long experience can greatly influence other board members.

14. James E. Thomas, *A Manual for Alabama County Commissioners* (University: Bureau of Public Administration, University of Alabama, 1975), p. 10. There are also county boards in Alabama with three, four, six, and seven members.

15. S. B. Chadman, "Organization of the County Governing Body," National Association of Counties, *Guide to County Organization and Management* (Washington: National Association of Counties, 1968), p. 120.

16. For a description of cases in New York, Wisconsin, and Michigan on this issue, see Herbert Sydney Duncombe and Clifford Dobler, "Local Legislative Apportionment," *Guide to County Organization and Management*, pp. 125, 126.

17. Kenneth VerBurg, *Guide to Michigan County Government* (East Lansing: The Institute for Community Development and Services, Michigan State University, 1972), p. II-5.

18. S. B. Chadman, p. 119.

19. Westchester County Government, *Westchester County Charter*, Article III, Section 16.

20. Ibid.

21. An excellent description of the county treasurer in Michigan may be found in Kenneth VerBurg, pp. III-3 and III-4.

22. In 1968, only California, New Jersey, Oregon, and Tennessee had statewide qualifications for assessors. For a description of the qualifications and work of assessors, see International Association of Assessing Officers, "Assessing," *Guide to County Organization and Management*, pp. 252-255.

23. For a thorough description of the types of cases which a county attorney may handle and the work of a county counsel, see Harold W. Kennedy, "Legal Functions," *Guide to County Organization and Management*, pp. 273-289.

24. For an excellent description of the work of the sheriff in Georgia counties, see Claude Abercrombie, "Sheriffs," *Guide to County Organization and Management*, pp. 258-266.

25. Statistical information on the offices of coroner and medical examiner are from National Association of Counties, 1973), p. 45.

26. Ibid.

27. One exception is the drain commissioner in Michigan counties who administers almost all aspects of the establishment and maintenance of drainage facilities in the county. Kenneth VerBurg, pp. IV-47 through IV-54.

28. In 1966, in one Idaho county, the county commissioners appointed only two full-time county employees - the courthouse janitor and the weed supervisor. In 1976, the commissioners of the same county of about 25,000 people appointed seven full-time employees out of a total of seventy. As new functions, such as civil defense, planning, parks, and solid waste, were undertaken by the county, the number of employees appointed by the county commissioners grew.

29. The study was reported in Larry J. Brown, "County Administrators: Characteristics and Managerial Styles," *The County Year Book, 1975*, pp. 34-43.

30. Ibid., p. 36.

31. Ibid.

32. Ibid., p. 38.

33. Ibid., p. 41. County administrators were asked to rank their managerial style on a scale from 1 (always) to 5 (never). Participation in policy formulation ranked lower on the scale (1.6) than initiating policies (2.4).

34. Metropolitan Dade County, *County Charter*, Section 3.01.

35. Ibid., Sections 3.04 and 4.02.

36. Alameda County, *Ordinance*, Article 5-6, and letters from County Administrator Loren W. Enoch to Sydney Duncombe, dated January 20, 1977 and February 18, 1977.

37. Montana, *Constitution*, Article XI, Section 9.

38. The four main options are the commission-executive, commission-manager, commission and commission chairman forms. For an excellent description of the many structural sub-options and cooperative arrangements, see James J. Lopach and Lauren S. McKinsey, *Handbook of Montana Forms of Local Government* (Missoula: University of Montana, 1975), pp. 122-163.

# Chapter 4

# The County in the Political System

..."The county has long been the key building block in the American political party system. Both the Democratic and Republican parties are actually confederations of state parties, which, in turn, are confederations of county and city parties. Counties are in a natural position to serve this purpose. American parties are decentralized, yet must cover all the territory within a state, and counties have this kind of geographic base. The importance of the county's political role has fluctuated through the years, but urbanization has made it increasingly powerful. When first set up, county party units were quite important, but as cities grew and assumed political power, central city politicians often dominated the party organization both within the city and the county. Now that the population has shifted to the suburbs, suburban voters in many areas outnumber city voters, and they have made it difficult for city politicians to dominate the entire county party."[1]

County party organizations are indisputably a crucial building block in the American party system, as many writers have recognized. Not as well known is the fact that national interest groups, such as the American Farm Bureau Federation, Grange, American Medical Association, and American Bar Association, are also built on a local base consisting mainly of county organizations. The key role played by county officials (such as the county clerk) in administering national-state-county election procedures also adds to the impor-tance which is explored more fully in the next three sections of the chapter. The latter part of the chapter discusses the extent to which county politics is issue-oriented, the relationship between county polit-cal leaders and county officeholders, and the political influence of associa-tions of county governments.

## THE POLITICAL PARTY
## SYSTEM AT THE LOCAL LEVEL

The political party system in the United States rests on a local base

69

where volunteers are recruited, campaign literature and yard signs distributed, small contributions collected, and ultimately where parties come into daily contact with voters during political campaigns. While there is much variation among states in party organization, it is generally recognized that the most prevalent organization is at the precinct and county level.[2] Local party organization also exists at the congressional district, state legislative district, city, town, and ward level. A state-by-state survey of political organizations in all fifty states by the author and Professor Robert Blank showed that in 1975 there were:[3]

- *county party committees in 45 states;*
- *state legislative district committees in 27 states;*
- *congressional district committees in 20 states;*
- *city committees in 20 states;*
- *ward committees within cities in 13 states;*
- *town or township committees in 13 states;*
- *judicial party districts in 3 states; and,*
- *regional party districts in 2 states.*

Party organization at the state and local levels parallels, to some extent, governmental organization, as Chart 4-1 indicates. County central committees (or county conventions) may draft platforms dealing with county issues and may fill vacancies in the party ticket for county office. While state legislative committees and congressional district committees do not parallel a unit of government, they serve specific governmental needs such as the nomination of candidates or filling of vacancies for state legislative or congressional seats. Even the precinct has its minor governmental functions in the administration of elections and as a point of citizen access to government.

**The Precinct Level.** The precinct (or election district) is the smallest area of political organization and may contain as few as a dozen voters in a sparsely settled region or more than a thousand voters in an urban area. The boundaries of each precinct are generally determined by the county governing board, and the county board is usually the body that determines whether a precinct has grown to the extent that it needs to be divided.

Precinct committeemen and women generally reach office by being elected in the primary or general elections. In some states, such as Alaska, Iowa, and Maine, they are elected by party members assembled at precinct caucuses.

The number of precinct committeepersons in each precinct varies from state to state. The study found twelve states (including Arizona, Idaho, Michigan, Nebraska, Ohio, and Texas) in which there is one precinct committeeperson.[4] In at least thirteen other states (including Colorado, Florida, Iowa, Kansas, and New Jersey) each precinct has both a committeeman and a committeewoman. More than two precinct committee officials were found in other states, with California having five to eight members depending on the party vote cast from the district and North Carolina having a precinct chairman, three vice-chairmen, and a secretary-treasurer.

There is a very close relationship between the precinct committee-persons and the county party committees. In most states, precinct committeemen and women are automatically ʹmembers of their county party committees by virtue of their office.

The work of precinct committee-men and women peaks during the election campaign and tapers off during the remainder of the year. During the general election campaign, precinct committeemen and commit-teewomen are busy contacting potential voters, organizing party workers, distributing campaign literature, raising funds, attending rallies and meetings, and arranging transportation to the polls. During the remainder of the biennium, precinct workers may spend a few hours a week contacting new voters who have moved into the area, interceding with government officials on behalf of constituents, and attending party meetings. Precinct committeemen and women are among the most active 1% of the nation in their involvement in party affairs and rank higher on the Milbrath hierarchy of political involvement than the 4% to 5% of the people in the nation who occasionally contribute time and money to political campaigns.[5]

While they may lack visiblity, committeemen and women are probably the most important participants in our political system, for they are the only party personnel who are in regular contact with the voters. This is especially important in races for state legislative, county, and local offices when voters have not followed the candidates or issues. When voters can align themselves around candidates and issues, as in presidential, state-wide and some county-wide contests, the role of the committee person is not likely to be as great.

**Sub-County Party Organization.** In almost all states, there are one or more types of party organization between the precinct and county levels.[6] In Massachusetts, Rhode Island, and other New England states, there are generally city, town, and ward political organizations. The Mid-Atlantic states of New York and Pennsylvania follow the same basic pattern. Cooke and Janosik

Chart 4-1

#### MODEL OF GOVERNMENTAL UNITS AND PARTY ORGANIZATION AT THE STATE AND LOCAL LEVELS

| Governmental Units | Party organization |
|---|---|
| State | State central committee and state chairman<br>Congressional district committee |
| County | County central committee and county chairman<br>Legislative district committee |
| City | City committees<br>Ward committees |
| Town or Township | Town or township committees<br>Precinct committees and precinct committeemen |

Chart 4-2

## ILLINOIS PARTY STRUCTURE OUTSIDE COOK COUNTY

### VOTERS ELECT AT PRIMARY

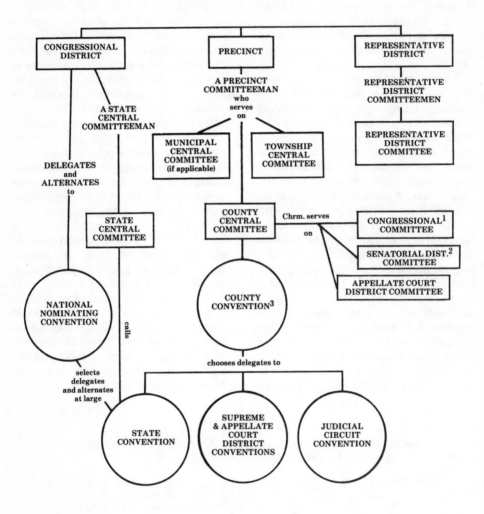

1. Composed of precinct committeemen if district lies within one county or parts of two or more counties. The State Central committeeman serves as chairman.
2. Composed of county chairman and two members of the county central committee appointed by him if district lies in one county.
3. County convention also nominates candidates for associate judges of circuit court.

SOURCE: David Kenney, *Basic Illinois Government, A Systematic Explanation* (Carbondale: Southern Illinois University Press, 1970), p. 104.

report that the political base of party organization in Pennsylvania is the election district committee, and the members of this committee serve on city, township, and borough committees.[7] In the Midwest, only Illinois and Missouri follow the New England tradition of having city, township, and ward committees. Illinois precinct committeemen serve on municipal and township committees, and there are ward committees in Chicago. The Illinois party structure, shown in Chart 4-2, also includes state representative committees and senatorial district committees.

Another type of sub-county organization is used in western states such as Idaho. There are no city, town, or ward party committees in the state, since there are no townships in the state and city elections are nonpartisan. The only sub-county party organization is the legislative district committee in those counties which have more than one legislative district. Idaho has a simple party structure, shown in Chart 4-3, in which one precinct committeeman or committeewoman is elected bien-

nially at the primary election and is automatically a member of both the county central committee and the legislative district committee.

Other patterns of sub-county organization exist in the Midwest, South, and West. Indiana has city and town party committees but no legislative district or ward committees. Louisiana has state legislative district and city party committees but no ward or town committees. In New Mexico, the ward committees form the main sub-county political organization. As the previous examples show, there is little uniformity in party organization below the county level. City committees are found in twenty states from Maine to Missouri.[8] Ward committees exist mainly in states with large metropolitan areas and city party committees. Town or township committees are found only in areas in which towns or townships are important governmental units and do not exist south of West Virginia and west of Missouri and Minnesota. State legislative district committees may be smaller in area than a county in some places and larger in area than

Chart 4-3

POLITICAL PARTY ORGANIZATION IN IDAHO

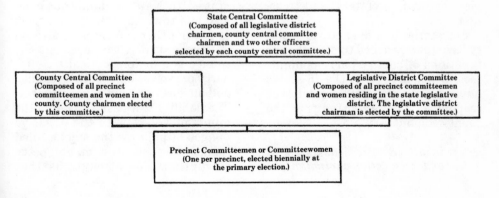

a county in other parts of the same state.

**County Committees.** The county central committee is the most common form of party organization between the precinct and state levels. County committees are found in all states except Alaska, North Dakota, and the three New England states of Connecticut, Rhode Island, and Massachusetts.[9] Alaska is divided into four regions for party purposes; North Dakota has legislative district committees in place of county committees; and the three New England states rely on city, ward, and town committees.

Despite wide differences in party organization, county party committees are surprisingly similar from state to state. In almost all states, there is a county party chairman, vice-chairman, secretary, and treasurer. In some states, there is also a county executive committee. The county party officers are almost always elected by the entire membership of the county committee. In Idaho, for example, all precinct committeepersons are automatically members of the county party committee, and this group of precinct committeemen and committeewomen elect the county party chairman, vice-chairman, secretary, and treasurer.

Secretaries of state and state party leaders were asked to describe the functions of county party committees. Officials in 38 of the 45 states having county party committees responded. They reported that the county committees:[10]

- in all 38 states assisted in general election campaigns;

- *in all 38 states raised campaign funds;*
- *in 26 states heard talks by candidates for elective office;*
- *in 20 states assisted candidates in primary campaigns;*
- *in 18 states secured signatures for candidates' petitions;*
- *in 16 states selected members to the state convention;*
- *in 14 states selected members of the state central committee; and,*
- *in 14 states approved patronage appointments.*

An indication of the importance of county political organizations is the high ranking given them by state political officials. These officials were asked to rank as "very important," "important," "somewhat important," or "not important" the various party chairmen and committees shown in Table 4-1. A ranking of very important was given the value of "3", a ranking of important was assigned a "2", somewhat important a "1", and not important a "0". If a ranking was not given, it was usually because the office or committee was not found in the state, and a ranking of "0" was assigned. Table 4-1 shows that county party committees and county party chairmen are very important in most states. In New England, however, city and town committees are more important than county committees.

Paradoxically, the fact that the county is a major political base for party organization is both a liability and an asset to county government. The liability is its association in the minds of voters with the negative images of politics: the smoke filled rooms, the spoils system, and petty corruption. The strength is that county government is responsive to popular control through the party system.[11]

## INTEREST GROUP REPRESENTATION AT THE COUNTY LEVEL

Many powerful interest groups have a local base as well as their national and state organizations. The American Farm Bureau Federation, for example, originated first on a county level as an organized group of farmers cooperating with the county agricultural extension agents.[12] The American Medical Association has a state and county base. David Truman points out that the governing arrangements of the American Medical Association are federal in character, and all but a few members of the national House of Delegates "are elected from the constituent societies, beginning at the county level."[13]

To learn more about the organization of interest groups at the local level, the author wrote forty prominent national interest groups asking for information on their local organization. A questionnaire was sent to the agricultural extension agents in a sample of thirty-five counties requesting information on agricultural interest groups in their counties.[14] The results show that the following agricultural interest groups have county organizations.

*American Farm Bureau Federation.* According to an official of the Farm Bureau, "The American Farm Bureau Federation is a federation of 49 state Farm Bureaus...Each state Farm Bureau is a federation of county Farm Bureaus. When one joins the Farm Bureau, he joins his county Farm Bureau."[15] All of the counties in the sample who replied to our questionnaire had a county Farm Bureau.

*Grange.* The Grange has a two-

Table 4-1

**Rating of the Importance of Local Party Officers and Organizations by Secretaries of State and State Party Leaders**

|  | All States | States Outside of New England | New England States |
|---|---|---|---|
| Precinct committeemen | 1.61 | 1.74 | .50 |
| County party committees | 2.19 | 2.39 | .50 |
| County party chairmen | 2.24 | 2.42 | .75 |
| Legislative district committees | .97 | .94 | 1.25 |
| Legislative district chairmen | 1.00 | .97 | 1.25 |
| City party committees | .69 | .45 | 2.50 |
| City party chairmen | .77 | .53 | 2.75 |
| Town or township committees | .47 | .26 | 2.25 |
| Town or township chairmen | .55 | .29 | 2.75 |

SOURCE: Herbert Duncombe and Robert Blank, unpublished survey, 1975. This question was answered by secretaries of state and state party leaders in thirty-eight states.

tiered organization within the counties in which it is active. In Latah County, Idaho, for example, there are seven Subordinate Granges throughout the rural areas of the county and one Pomona Grange at the county level. An official of the National Grange explains the work of the Pomona Grange as follows: "The Pomona, or county, Grange is an organization comprised of Subordinate Grange members who have taken the Fifth Degree in the Grange fraternity. The duties of the Pomona Grange are much like those of the Subordinate Grange, except that the Pomona Grange deals extensively in legislation--acting upon the resolutions which come to it from the Subordinate level. Many times the officers of the Pomona Grange are charged with working with several Subordinate Granges..."[16]

*National Farmers' Organization.* The National Farmers' Organization also has county-based local organizations. Agricultural extension agents in eleven counties of the sample stated that there were county units of the National Farmers' Organization in their counties.

*Other farm organizations.* The questionnaire returned by agricultural agents showed the following other agricultural groups organized on a county basis: wheat growers' associations, cattlemen's associations, cattle feeders' associations, dairy herd improvement associations, onion growers' associations, potato growers' associations, and sheep growers' associations.

The questionnaires from agricultural extension agents in twenty counties showed that the county was the local base of all farm organizations in their counties with the ex-

ception of the Subordinate Granges. Ninety percent of the farm organizations in the twenty-county area (with the exception of Subordinate Granges) were county-wide in area.

To learn about non-farm organizations, a second questionnaire was sent to Chambers of Commerce in thirty-five counties. The replies from national interest groups identified the following groups with county organizations.

*American Medical Association.* An official of the American Medical Association explained that the AMA "is a federation of independent state medical associations, which, in turn, are composed of county medical societies."[17] County medical societies were found in twelve of the twenty-one counties.

*American Bar Association.* County bar associations were found in thirteen of the twenty-one counties. In some of the larger counties, such as Westchester County (New York), there are also city bar associations. An official of the American Bar Association wrote that all bar associations in the United States are completely independent in their relationship to the American Bar Association so that the ABA does not have organizations at a county or local level. However, the official commented that county and large city bar associations send delegates to the American Bar Association House of Delegates, and the American Bar Association maintains contact with "about 1,000 bar associations across the country, a great many of which are county bar associations."[18]

*Chambers of Commerce.* Chambers of Commerce in the sample of twenty-one counties reported both city and county chambers. Baker County (Oregon) has a single Chamber of Commerce serving the entire county as do seven other counties. Eight of the counties reported both a city and county Chamber, with Salt Lake County (Utah) having three city Chambers in the county area. In five other counties, only cities had Chambers of Commerce or there were county, city, and town Chambers.

*Other organizations.* The questionnaires returned by Chambers of Commerce showed that the following associations were found in some counties: nurses' associations, realtors' associations, educational associations (particularly in the county operated school systems), Junior Chambers of Commerce, rifle associations, and taxpayers' associations.

A number of interest groups indicated they are not organized at the county or local level. The American Petroleum Institute has oil trade associations active at the state level but no associations at the county or local level. The American Library Association reported state associations and a few large municipal associations. The Association of Trial Lawyers of America and American Hotel and Motel Association are among a number of associations which operate almost entirely at the state and national level.

There are some groups operating at a local level, such as labor unions, which do not generally use the county as the primary geographic base. The American Legion bases its local organization on nearly 16,000 Posts. An official of the American Legion reported that most state Legions "have intermediate organizational levels between the state and the Post, usually known as Districts," and that in New Jersey and New York there are functioning county organizations.[19] The American Dental Association organizes at a district level below the state level, but there are some county dental associations in states such as California, Colorado, Hawaii, and Michigan. It is difficult to generalize about non-agricultural interest groups--some have county organizations and others do not.

The author's study yielded little information on the impact of county-based interest groups on county government policymaking. Information provided by the American Medical Association gave the impression that its Public Affairs Division is mainly interested in national and state health legislation. Information obtained from the American Bar Association stressed public service activities (such as prison reform and criminal justice) which affect county as well as the national and state governments.[20] Farm interest groups, such as the National Grange, reported having close contact with county agricultural extension agents.

The influence of lobbyists and interest groups can be measured by the number of interactions between lobbyists and legislators, perceptions by legislators as to the effectiveness of lobbying in influencing their votes, and the degree to which legislators have confidence in the information and research of lobbyists. The types of studies made by Ziegler and others, which have provided measures of lobbying effectiveness on the state level, have not been made at the county level.[21] There have not been studies of role orientations of county commissioners towards pressure groups such as have been made by Wahlke and others at the state level.[22]

Obviously, the most influential interest groups at the county level may include those which have the most to gain or lose by actions of county officials. As Susan Torrence has pointed out, land developers, builders, and home owners have much to benefit or lose from zoning decisions made by county officials.[23] Some other groups which are greatly affected by the decisions of county officials include: industries subject to air and water pollution control regulations, taxpayers facing assessment increases, and farmers dependent on agricultural services provided by the county. Interest groups with the ability to mobilize their members at the polls have great power, as Lester Milbrath has pointed out.[24] In rural counties, powerful interest groups include the Farm Bureau, Grange, and the National Farmers' Organization. In more urban counties, influential groups undoubtedly include Chambers of Commerce, Realtors' Association, County Bar Associations, labor unions, and minority groups.

Research to determine the impact of interest group pressures on the county government decision-making and agenda-setting process has been minimal. In fact, little has been done to test the applicability of results of national and state studies to the county political scene. Given the growing importance of county governments as providers of services, it is unlikely that they have remained immune to interest group pressures.

## THE COUNTY AND THE ELECTORAL SYSTEM

National, state, and county biennial elections are generally held on the same date, and the same basic electoral system is used in all three. In contrast, city, school district, and special district elections are often held at different times and are generally administered by different electoral officials.

The precinct and the county are the two most important local areas in a system which elects our President, Congressmen, state officials, and county officers. The precinct is not a unit of local government but is established (often by the county commissioners) to give voters a nearby polling place. The administration of elections within a precinct varies from state to state. In Idaho, the county clerk is responsible for appointing precinct election officials including:

- *a precinct registrar who registers voters and keeps a record of those registered;*
- *election judges, who check the voters' names against the precinct register, hand out ballots, and perform many related functions at the polling place on election day; and,*
- *election clerks who tabulate the precinct vote if paper ballots are used.*

County officials are involved in many types of electoral functions as the following state examples show.

*Alabama.*[25] The county commission establishes and sets the boundaries of precincts (called beats), determines the location of polling places, and decides what precincts are to have voting machines. Duties, such as the preparation of ballots and the list of qualified voters, are the responsibilities of other officials such as the judge of probate, sheriff, and circuit clerk. Boards of registrars in each county are responsible for registering voters.

*California.*[26] The county clerk has a key role in the California election system. It is the clerk's responsibility to divide the county into election precincts and provide maps of these precincts; handle absentee voter registration; appoint the precinct boards to count ballots in the precincts; and conduct the official canvass of election returns after the election.

*Michigan.*[27] The county board of election commissioners, consisting of the senior probate judge, the county clerk, and the county treasurer, is responsible for reviewing the recommendations of election officials regarding the preparation of ballots and election arrangements. The county board of canvassers, composed of two persons from each party selected by the board of county commissioners, is responsible for canvassing election returns and certifying the election outcome. County clerks in Michigan conduct training schools for election workers within each county. In cooperation with the board of election commissioners, the county clerk also has the responsibility for preparing and supplying the necessary ballots for elections.

*Mississippi.*[28] A five-member county election commission, elected for a period of four years, is responsible for many election functions including printing and distributing the official ballot, canvassing the returns, giving certificates of election, and making reports to the secretary of state. The county board of supervisors establishes election districts and designates polling places.

*New Mexico.*[29] The board of county commissioners is responsible for establishing, consolidating, or changing the boundaries of precincts and designating polling places. The commissioners appoint a three member board of registrations which administers much of the registration machinery along with the county clerk. The board of county commissioners serves as the county canvassing board, examines poll books of each precinct, and certifies election returns.

The political importance of county government is related to the electoral system in several ways. It is county officials who directly administer much of the election process. Since election returns are usually tabulated and canvassed on a county basis, county returns are often published.[30] The most significant compilations of voting statistics, such as *America Votes,* show county as well as state, Congressional district, and national returns.[31] Candidates for state and Congressional offices, political analysts, journalists, and the news networks carefully review past county election records. Furthermore, because county, state, and national elections are held on the same date, political parties may be encouraged to seek candidates for county office who will strengthen the party ticket.

## THE POLITICS OF COUNTY ELECTIVE OFFICE

There are no studies of county

politics comparable to the landmark regional studies of state politics of V.O. Key, Duane Lockard, John Fenton, and Frank Jonas or the studies of politics in individual states by Alan Clem, Theodore Mitau, Leon Epstein, and others.[32] Studies of state politics do provide information on county political organization and county voting trends but little data on the internal politics of county elective office. A few studies, however, do shed light on the characteristics of county officeholders and internal county politics. National studies show, for example, that about 4.1% of all county governing board members are women in 1977 and that this percent is increasing.[33]

**Who Gets Elected.** County officials who are elected to office tend to have deep roots in their constituencies. A Texas study showed that 86% of the county judges and 92% of the county commissioners were born in Texas.[34] Almost half of the commissioners in Texas served in the county of their birth. Similarly, an Idaho study showed that 55% of the county commissioners in Idaho grew up in the same county where they were elected.[35]

The predominant age of county commissioners in Idaho was 50-59 and in Texas 51-65. Noting that state representatives in Texas tended to be younger men, Davis commented that "One suspects that voters generally view the lower house of the state legislature as a body appropriate for young and inexperienced men, but reject that view for county judges and commissioners."[36]

The educational attainments of county judges and commissioners in Texas were above the state average. Seventy-two percent of the judges and 36% of the county commissioners had some college education compared to 22% of the public. Forty-seven percent of Idaho commissioners and 34% of Oklahoma commissioners were reported to have some college education.[37]

Many county officials have held prior public office. In Texas, 54% of county judges held prior public office such as another county elective position. Twenty-nine percent of Idaho county commissioners held prior public office with most having been either city councilmen or school district trustees.

Most county commissioners in Idaho and Texas came from farm or business backgrounds. Prior to their election in Idaho, 53% of the county commissioners were farmers or ranchers, 34% were businessmen, 5% were skilled workers, and 8% were semiskilled workers. Among rural county commissioners in Texas, 61% were farmers, 17% were proprietors and managers, 14% were skilled laborers, and 11% had other occupations. Among urban county commissioners, the percent of farmers was much less and the percent of proprietors and managers was much greater. As one might expect, a substantially high percentage of the county judges in Texas had legal backgrounds.

Holding public office runs in the families of many who get elected. The Texas study showed that 40% of the county judges and 27% of the county commissioners had some member of their family or a close relative who had held (or was holding) political office.

Once in public office, county

commissioners tend to be re-elected a number of times, an Oklahoma study showed. The average Oklahoma county commissioner served about nine years in office, and one commissioner had served 38 years without interruption at the time of the study.[38]

**Motivation, Expectations, and Party Allegiance.** Why do people run for county office? The three primary reasons given by Idaho county commissioners were desire for service to the county, because friends or some group wanted them to run, or because of a county issue.[39] Of lesser importance was persuasion by the county political organization. An Oklahoma study suggested that a desire to be in politics, the attraction of part-time elective office, and an annual salary of $4,000 to $12,000 were also reasons.[40]

Do county officials expect to gain higher office? This depends somewhat on the office. County prosecuting attorneys in Indiana, one study showed, expected advancement to higher political office.[41] Many Indiana county prosecutors were young, ambitious attorneys who tended to see the office as a first step in a political career. The county prosecutor has been an important office in the career pattern of U.S. Congressmen in Indiana and of lesser importance for other offices. In Texas, only 22% of the county judges and 10% of the county commissioners viewed their positions as good stepping stones to higher office.[42] While there are many county officials who try and fail in pursuing higher offices there are, of course, many who succeed. A former President (Truman) once served as County Judge in Jackson

County (Missouri); a former Vice-President (Agnew) was once County Executive of Baltimore County (Maryland); and two prominent county officials in Washington and Utah ran for Governor of their respective states in 1976.

Almost all county officials run on a ballot bearing the label of a political party, but many run without opposition. A South Dakota study showed that in that state only 42.4% of elections for county office involved more than one candidate.[43] Those county offices requiring a considerable degree of professional training (i.e. state's attorney, coroner, and superintendent of schools) were the least contested offices. The county offices most likely to be contested were those of county commissioner, sheriff, and registrar of deeds. Alan Clem stated that these more contested offices were more "likely to be the primary objects of patronage allocation between the county political organizations and the potential candidates involved."[44] Since many county officers make careers out of elective county positions in South Dakota, their continuance in office would be more difficult, according to Clem, if they were to attract the criticism of their party's county chairman or county committee.

However, county officials may not necessarily take a very active leadership role in their county party organization. An Oklahoma study reported that very rarely did county commissioners serve as county party chairmen in that state and that 95% said they held no party office.[45] The same study indicated that Oklahoma commissioners did not contribute large sums to political parties and tended to use their funds to support their own campaigns. There are, of course, some county officials who do take leadership roles in their county party organizations.

**Job-Oriented and Issue-Oriented Politics.** A distinguishing characteristic of job-oriented politics, according to John Fenton, is that "most of the people who participate in politics on a day-to-day basis do so out of a desire for jobs or contracts rather than because of a concern for public polilcy."[46] Job-oriented politicians do not neglect issues in political campaigns, but they tend to "use the issues as a means of securing support of interest groups and through them the votes to win the jobs and contracts."[47] Job-oriented politics was the way of life for most county political machines of the late 1800s and early 1900s, and the extent to which this has lingered on is difficult to document. Job-oriented politics was found in many rural county courthouses, as this description of the courthouse gangs of the 1930s and 1940s suggests:

*"This 'gang' may be described as a more or less permanent group of elective and appointive officeholders together with private individuals whose business normally brings them into contact with public officials. Among the latter will usually be found contractors interested in county road and bridge construction, printers who want county contracts and favors in the passing out of jobs too small to require competitive bidding, purveyors of various supplies used in the county buildings and institutions, lawyers in criminal and probate work, ex-officials who have grown old in party service and who have become masters of the*

*lower sorts of intrigue and so habituated to playing politics as to make residence at the county seat a psychological necessity, bankers likely to sustain close relations to the county treasurer in the not too vain hope that they may 'take care of' public funds at a profit to themselves, and a ragged company of lesser fry attracted to the county town in the hope of eking out an uncertain income by jury duty, custodial positions, and other 'pickings'. Anyone who has lived in or even visited a county seat with his eyes and ears open will readily recognize many of the dramatis personae."[48]*

Issue-oriented political leaders, in contrast, are deeply involved on a day-to-day basis with public issues because they wish to shape public policy on these issues. County officials who are issue-oriented often run for office because they feel strongly about a particular county issue or program. Issue-oriented party officials work for the party more because winning an election can result in changing public policy than because they hope for a courthouse job. To a program or issue-oriented county official, the day-to-day business of county government involves resolving disputes on public issues. Susan Torrence provides this view of issue-oriented county politics:

*"Though partisan party politics may enter in, county politics are really the means to resolve disputes concerning public issues. These conflicts may be based on geography, such as the complaint of central city residents that their county taxes are used to support services in the suburbs, or on ideology such as when the League of Women Voters proposes construction of low- and moderate-income housing in high-income*

areas, or on self-interest such as the fight of home owners' associations against high-density development. *Even seemingly technical bureaucratic decisions involve politics because technicians have differing views about the best, most efficient way to get things done, and they are constantly pressured to bend the rules to make special exceptions.*"[49]

There are no comprehensive statistical studies which show the degree to which county officials are job-oriented or issue-oriented in their approach to county politics. There are undoubtedly some counties in which party leaders and county officials take a job-oriented approach. Opposition of the Democratic Chairman to the Northampton County (Pennsylvania) Charter in 1976, for example, appears to be based partly on the concern of losing patronage.[50] However, there appear to be many counties in which county officials take an issue-oriented approach. Susan Torrence describes more than a dozen examples of an issue-oriented approach in her book on county government.[51]

As important as the question of whether county officials are job or issue oriented is the study of what guides these officials when they vote or take executive action. Using concepts developed in studies of state legislators, one can ask whether they are primarily:[52]

- *guided in their work solely by personal conscience (a trustee orientation);*
- *guided by the instructions or wishes of constituents (a delegate orientation); or,*
- *guided primarily by party leaders (a partisan orientation).*

Research on these concepts in county government is scarce. The author's own study of a sample of county officials was too small to be significant, but it did indicate that the county commissioners in the sample were more likely to see themselves first as trustees, then as delegates, and lastly as partisans. In practice, however, county officials probably combine all three roles in making many decisions.

## CASE STUDIES OF COUNTY POLITICS

The location of power in county politics varies widely. In some counties, there is a single dominant leader such as a county party chairman, congressman, state legislator, mayor, county executive, county commissioner, or some other individual. In many counties, political power may be widely shared with no single dominant individual. The following five case studies illustrate different styles of county political leadership and differing approaches to job-oriented and issue-oriented politics. The case studies are arranged by population of county.

**Latah County (Idaho)—Trustee Politics.**[53] Gerald Ingle has been the most influential man in Latah County government for the twenty years he has served on the Board of County Commissioners. Latah County (1970 population: 24,891) is a wheat and pea farming county with a county seat of nearly 15,000 people and six smaller communities. "Gerry" Ingle has lived all his life on a wheat farm near one of the smaller Latah County communities. He was elected to his local school board at age twenty-six and served twenty-eight years on the school board in his area. Active in agricultural groups, he was master of two local granges, Grand Master of the Pomona Grange which served the entire county, and a member of the County Fair Board. In 1955, he became President of the Latah County Chamber of Commerce.

In 1956, Ingle ran for a two-year term as county commissioner and won by only seventy-five votes. He had been urged to run by a state legislator from his local community; but it was an issue, replacing the obsolete county courthouse built in 1887, that was uppermost in his mind. In the next twenty years, he continued to run because he saw the need for a new nursing home, a county weed control program, a modern jail, county planning and zoning, a uniform building code, and other county programs. He was the most influential member of the Board of County Commissioners for years because he was the most experienced and had the ability to obtain needed grants and gain support for new county programs.

With power in the Latah County Democratic Party traditionally divided among the county chairman, the incumbent state legislators, and other prominent leaders, party officials have made few attempts to influence county decisions. Ingle explained that he attended the Democratic Central Committee meetings regularly and explained the county budget to party members, but he never brought county issues to the Democratic Central Committee for recommendations prior to a county vote on these issues. When a former Democratic Party Chairwoman was elected to the Board of County Commissioners, she found she had no more influence than the other Commissioners.

The politics within the Latah County Board of Commissioners for most of the past twenty years can best be described as trustee politics. Most Latah County Commissioners saw their role as doing what they thought best for the county. "We had many discussions of what was best before we voted," Ingle explained, "but when we took action as a commission we generally all stood behind the decision."

**Vigo County (Indiana)--Job Oriented Politics.** The political climate of Vigo County (1970 population, 114,528) contrasts sharply with that of Latah County. Containing the City of Terre Haute and surrounding residential and farm areas, Vigo County has been characterized as having "old-style patronage politics."[54] One party leader was quoted as stating that "our organization is geared to knocking on doors, registering people, and voting them absentee."[55] In the past, patronage employees in most city and county offices were expected to contribute about two percent of their salaries for campaign expenses. There is great competition for political jobs, and in the past, some have been lucrative plums. Local franchises for the issuing of state auto and other licenses are valuable since the licensing agent receives a fifty cent fee for each license issued.

County officials are among the most powerful county political leaders. A former County Democratic Chairman served sixteen years as County Prosecuting Attorney. The

County Clerk ran for Mayor against the incumbent and won, and the ousted Mayor was appointed to the vacant position of County Clerk by the Governor. The County Treasurer has run unsuccessfully for the Mayor's Office, while the County Republican Chairman runs the Vigo County License Bureau. In the job-oriented politics of Vigo County, a county elective position provides an important base for patronage and political power.

**Jackson County (Missouri) Metro-politics--A County In Transition.**[56] Jackson County is the most populous (654,558) of seven counties in the Kansas City metropolitan area. From the 1890s through the 1930s, the Pendergast machine dominated the politics of Jackson County and its county seat, Kansas City. Tom Pendergast supported some able men (such as former County Judge Harry S. Truman) and some reform causes such as a new charter and council-manager government for Kansas City. However, politics under the Pendergast machine was basically job-oriented politics.

After Pendergast was jailed for a year in 1939, the strength of the machine was broken, and the next three decades saw a struggle for reform. A Missouri constitutional provision enabled any county with a population of at least 85,000 to develop a county charter and submit it to the people of the county for approval. In 1946, a home rule charter movement was begun in Jackson County with the support of two leading newspapers of the county, the League of Women Voters, and a prominent trade union. The charter was defeated in 1949,

with opponents charging that the charter would result in increased taxes and domination by Kansas City representatives.[57] After St. Louis County successfully adopted a county charter, a second attempt to pass a Jackson County charter was made in 1958. Again the charter was defeated, with opponents claiming the charter would under-represent the rural areas and allow the Board of Supervisors to levy taxes such as an earnings tax.[58]

The county reform movement gained more success after 1962 when Charles Curry was elected Presiding Judge of Jackson County, and the Committee for County Progress was organized to support reform candidates and causes. A key election occurred in 1966 when the Committee for County Progress scored a major victory by winning eight of nine elective offices and controlling all three positions on the county governing body.[59] The Committee for County Progress platform stressed the need for a full-time professional administrator, a systems and procedures department, a planning and research function, a centralized data processing unit, a merit system in county employment, and home rule powers to permit reorganization of county government. Judge Curry, in his campaign, also stressed inadequacies in child care programs, medical care for the needy, and the condition of the Home for the Aged. The 1966 campaign was issue-oriented, but it soon had an effect on old style political patronage.

One of the first acts of the reform county administration was to induce James Kunde, Assistant City Manager of Dayton, Ohio, to become the first County Administrator of

Jackson County. The reform administration also acted to terminate the jobs of more than two hundred patronage county employees, most of whom did little or no work. For example, the reform administration fired half of the eighty-two employees in the Building Director's Office at a saving of $90,000 a year.[60]

The reform administration was more issue-oriented than its predecessor. A comprehensive study of juvenile care at the time recommended that emphasis should be shifted to rehabilitation instead of institutional care in sub-standard facilities. A reform judge of the county court, who was a medical doctor with a law degree, led the fight for improved administration of the detention home. Similarly, the reform administration was deeply involved in passage of a $102 million bond issue which provided funds for a sports stadium, roads, hospitals, parks, juvenile facilities, and other improvements. A third important issue was the improvement in the assessment and collection of taxes through the use of data processing.

The charter movement continued and achieved victory in 1970 when Jackson became the second county in Missouri to approve a county charter.[61] The new charter became effective in 1972 and established an elected county executive with a four year term and the power to veto legislation and appoint department directors. A fifteen-member county legislature was also established by the charter, and the charter abolished the elective positions of public administrator, clerk, treasurer, assessor, collector of taxes, recorder of deeds, circuit court clerk, highway engineer-surveyor, and coroner. The charter further provided an employment merit system to replace the partial merit system previously in operation. The trend away from the job-oriented politics of the Pendergast machine, which began when Charles Curry became Presiding Judge of Jackson County, has continued since the new charter became effective in 1973.

**WestchesterCounty(NewYork)--New Style Political Leadership.** Westchester County (1970 population, 894,406) borders New York City on the north. About 75,000 of its residents take commuter trains daily into the city.[62] Southern Westchester has large cities such as Yonkers, New Rochelle, Mt. Vernon, and White Plains which have their own commercial and industrial centers providing work for many residents.

For more than six decades, the Republicans dominated Westchester County. But the Democrats have steadily gained strength since the post World War II expansion of county population. Two decades ago, Republican party members in Westchester outnumbered Democrats by a five to two margin. Over the past twenty years, the Republican advantage has narrowed and one columnist has estimated that there are 175,000 registered Republicans, 139,000 Democrats, and 60,000 Independents who hold the balance. The new leadership in the Democratic party is issue-oriented and much more concerned with county programs than patronage positions.

The elected county executive has traditionally been a powerful figure in Westchester County politics.[63] Edward Michaelian, County Executive from 1958 to 1974, was Republican County Chairman for five years while he was county executive. During his term of office, Michaelian became a national exponent of the role of county government in solving problems of governmental fragmentation while he served on the federal Advisory Commission on Intergovernmental Relations and other national committees. Michaelian did not run for re-election in 1974.

There was an exciting race to replace him, but when the votes were counted, Alfred DelBello became the first Democratic county executive of Westchester County. The former mayor of Yonkers immediately set out to expand and improve county programs. Concerned with the need for public housing, he has made Westchester County one of eighty-four counties in the nation to participate in the Urban County Community Development Program under the Community Development Act of 1974. He has developed a comprehensive solid waste program which cost over one hundred million dollars and serves the entire county.

Under his leadership, Westchester County has developed a remarkable variety of human service programs such as senior citizen discounts at more than 1,500 stores; mobile recreation vehicles offering puppet shows, crafts projects, and other recreation services; a county art gallery; and outreach programs aimed at senior citizens, high school dropouts, and other groups.

The County Executive is a new style political leader who believes in professionalization of government rather than reserving the top

county jobs for patronage appointments. DelBello has won commendation in many quarters for the quality of his appointments. His Commissioner of Social Services had been Ohio's Director of Public Welfare; his Commissioner of Hospitals had been New York City's Health Commissioner; and his Commissioner of Corrections had been Superintendent of a New Jersey state prison. DelBello has been quoted as saying, "I've operated on the belief that if a politician is not willing to bring in the best people he can find, he is really short-changing the public."[64]

**Nassau County (New York)--Strong County Party Leadership and Able County Executive.**[65] Nassau County (1970 population, 1,428,838) is on Long Island and borders New York City on the east. Like Westchester, many of its residents commute by train to New York City, and many others work in commercial centers and industrial plants within the county.

Nassau County has had a history of strong Republican organization. J. Russell Sprague, who ran the Republican county organization from 1935 to 1959, is reported to have:

*"molded the GOP into a powerful machine run on a skillful blend of patronage, fund raising and a basic edge in enrollment. There were jobs, fees, contracts and lucrative arrangements for those willing to devote themselves to the party. Committeemen were also given a special status as the first people to see for a job. In return, they worked their election districts with a passion born of knowing where their bread was buttered."*[66]

Sprague and the men who followed him to leadership of the Nassau County Republican Committee were excellent fundraisers; however, they refused to accept very large donations which would place the party under obligation. Part of the funds were used to develop a county party headquarters which now has more than twenty full-time employees.

The current Republican County Chairman in Nassau County is Joseph M. Margiotta. He is simultaneously a committeeman from his area, Chairman of the Hempstead Town Republican Committee, and has been Chairman of the Republican County Committee since 1968. He was once a State Assemblyman from his district and thus has established access to the State Legislature. Although he is the undisputed head of his county organization, he is not a dictator. According to a political writer:

*"He constantly taps a variety of sources from executive committeemen to businessmen to incisive judges before reaching a decision. He knows how far he can go in exerting his will over his executive committee. If the vibrations to a proposal are bad, he will back off."*[67]

The inner circle of the Republican party organization in Nassau County is composed of town party and city party leaders and some state legislators and former legislators. Margiotta has revitalized the Republican Party in the county with his energy, organization, and social bonds forged through friendships and social gatherings.

The County Executive in Nassau County traditionally has been a political figure of statewide stature.

Eugene Nickerson, who was Nassau County Executive from 1962 through 1970, was a Democratic candidate for the U.S. Senate. The current County Executive, Ralph G. Caso, A Republican, has never been defeated in a county campaign in the past 25 years. Partly due to the strength and influence of the Nassau County GOP, Caso was selected as the running mate for Malcolm Wilson, Republican candidate for Governor in 1974. Wilson lost the election, and Caso has continued as County Executive.

## COUNTY ASSOCIATIONS IN THE POLITICAL SYSTEM

The role of the county in the American political system is probably affected by the success of state associations of county officials and the National Association of Counties (NACo) in representing the county point of view in state capitals and in Washington, D.C. Lobbying for county government is just one of many functions of these associations. They also conduct research, provide technical assistance to county officials, facilitate the exchange of information about county government, serve as agents of growth and change, and serve county governments in other ways.

**State Associations of Counties.** There are state associations serving county officials in forty-six states and performing some or all of the following functions.

*Publish newsletters, magazines, yearbooks, and reports.* These publications serve to keep county officials informed of state legislative and state administrative developments. The Association of County Commissioners of Georgia publishes a monthly magazine, an annual yearbook, special weekly legislative reports during the state legislative session, and research publications of various kinds.[68] The Association of Minnesota Counties has also published a manual for county officials.[69]

*Provide training for county officials.* The Association of County Commissioners of Georgia works with the University of Georgia to sponsor training programs for newly elected county commissioners.

*Technical assistance.* The Idaho Association of Counties, for example, has given assistance to county governments in preparing classification and compensation plans. State associations of counties in eight states employed human resource coordinators (with a federal grant) to provide technical assistance to counties in coordinating human resources programs.

*Sponsor annual conventions and periodic conferences.* The Association of County Commissioners of Georgia, for example, has a legislative breakfast in January, a statewide conference in October, eight district conferences, and a number of committee meetings on different county matters.

*Encourage county progress.* The Association of County Commissioners of Georgia encouraged counties to adopt a county administrator or manager form of government.

*Present the views of county officials to the state legislators and executives.* State associations have staff which devote full or part-time during legislative sessions to testifying before legislative committees

and working to influence the passage of state legislation.

Influencing state legislation is interrelated with other county association activities. For example, conferences sponsored by state associations provide opportunities for county officials to become informed on bills pending before state legislatures and to pass resolutions during the conferences urging the passage or defeat of specific bills. Newsletters keep county officials informed of the most recent legislative developments and can be used to encourage these officials to make their views known.

County associations have achieved some notable successes in influencing state action. The Association of Oregon Counties, for example, has lobbied effectively to get home rule amendments to the state constitution passed. The County Supervisors Association of California has been successful in its efforts to get a more rational county-wide approach to annexation and special district problems. In Idaho, a cooperative effort by city and county associations brought an end to a state law which caused cities and counties to operate on a deficit basis. The Oklahoma County Commissioners Association succeeded in helping defeat legislation which would have transferred road administration and funds to state government.[70]

**National Association of Counties.** The National Association of Counties (NACo) was established in 1936 to provide county governments with a voice in influencing national legislation and administrative policy affecting county government.

According to Donald H. Haider:

*"Between 1936 and 1957 the Association remained a sleepy, rural-county, paper head organization run on a part-time basis by two Washington lawyers. It had an $18,000-a-year budget based on $6 annual dues paid by 3,000 individual county officials."*[71]

The revitalization of NACo began in 1957 with the appointment of its first full-time executive director, Bernard F. Hillenbrand. Under Hillenbrand's leadership, NACo gained foundation support for research and service, acquired permanent office space, increased its staff, and broadened its membership.

In 1977, the National Association of Counties had more than 1,600 member counties, each paying dues contingent on its population. The weighted voting system at national conferences is based on population.

The officers of NACo include a President, four Vice-Presidents, and a Fiscal Officer who are all elected for one year terms at the annual conference. The Board of Directors consists of the officers: one director per state with recognized county government; 10 directors from states with largest representation in NACo; 10 at-large directors to balance race, sex or urban/rural inequities and affiliate representatives. An Executive Director is responsible for the administration of the NACo staff under the general direction of the officers and Board of Directors. NACo had a 145 member staff in 1977, most of whom worked in either research, lobbying, or information activities.

The policy positions of the National Association of Counties are recommended by twelve steering committees. These committees are assisted by the NACo staff and meet between the annual meetings to study issues and recommend policy positions on such areas as finance, manpower, welfare, health and education, community development, criminal justice and environment. The steering committee drafts are brought to the annual conference for a vote by the Board of Directors sitting as a Resolution Committee followed by a floor vote from the membership who are the final arbiters of NACo policy. Once adopted, the policy statements become part of the American County Platform and provide the direction for NACo lobbying and research activity.

NACo provides a number of valuable publications and services to county officials. It publishes a weekly newspaper, *County News*, which includes the latest information on Congressional bills and federal administrative actions affecting county officials. *County News* also has articles describing innovative county programs, the work of state associations, and the views of county officials. Included with some issues of the *County News* is *The New County Times*, a newspaper supplement devoted to topics such as regionalism and transportation. NACo also sends background papers, reports, copies of Congressional bills, staff memoranda, and much other useful information to member counties and others.

With the aid of Ford Foundation funds, federal funds, and other grants, the National Association of Counties has greatly expanded its research activities. In the past five years, the NACo staff has produced: a ten volume set of booklets on solid waste management; a series of monthly reports on county manpower programs; a comprehensive report on human services integration at the community level in six counties; action guides on highway safety, highway engineering, and air pollution control; and reports on drug abuse, alcoholism, and many other topics.

The annual conference of the National Association of Counties establishes policy and facilitates an exchange of information between county officials. The 1976 Annual Conference, held in Salt Lake City, Utah, featured workshops on topics such as juvenile justice, alcohol abuse, planning, social services, rural development, labor management, manpower, revenue sharing, regionalism, energy, and metropolitan planning organizations. The annual conference draws prominent national speakers such as the President of the United States, presidential candidates, governors, and senators.

*NACo and county modernization.* The National Association has encouraged county modernization in a number of ways. It has established, with foundation support, a unit called New County which collects information about changes taking place in county government and the results of these changes. Through a system of a-wards, the staff encourages counties to contact it with examples of innovative, successful programs. The staff is an excellent source of information on county charters and the newer forms of county organization—information which is particularly valu-

able to county officials and the academic community.

The NACo staff encourages modernization through its contract research. By means of reports and conferences, the National Association of Counties informs elected and appointed county officials of the latest professional developments and encourages program reforms within county government.

*Influencing federal action.* The National Association of Counties has twelve staff whose primary function is lobbying. These lobbyists have developed considerable expertise in their areas of specialization and are often called upon to present NACo's positions before Congressional committees and federal agencies and departments. Elected and appointed county officials often appear before Congress to offer testimony. With an excellent knowledge of bills before Congress, the staff lobbyist is able to inform the county officials most affected by a bill before Congress of its probable impact. This often results in well-timed telephone calls, telegrams, and letters which may influence legislation.

NACo has also used the mass public rally to influence the course of legislation. Concerned about the possible failure of Congress to extend federal revenue sharing when the legislation expired, the officers called a rally on November 18, 1975 in Washington, D.C. More than 1,700 county officials came to Washington and spent the day describing their need for revenue sharing to seventy-four senators and more than three hundred members of the House of Representatives.[72] County officials from forty-six states attended the rally, and Texas alone was represented by two hundred and forty persons.

The officers and lobbying staff of the National Association of Counties have actively supported bills to extend revenue sharing and countercyclical assistance, reform the aid to families with dependent children program, provide additional funds for water pollution control and law enforcement planning, amend a number of existing federal statutes. NACo has cooperated with other public interest groups in many lobbying efforts and has been at the forefront of legislative coalitions to preserve revenue sharing and adequately fund air pollution control and community development.

NACo has worked closely with the National League of Cities on many issues. The Director of the National Association of Counties once commented that on any given day in Congress a NACo supported bill can be defeated and on another day a National League of Cities bill can be defeated, but it is seldom that a bill supported by both groups is not enacted.[73]

The influence of county officials and NACo upon Congress depends, in part, on the significant strides made by counties in expanding their services and resolving areawide problems. NACo has benefitted also from unified, dynamic leadership. Donald Haider assesses the growth of county influence in Congress as follows:

*"NACo's emerging prominence among Washington lobbying organizations is in part a function of several factors. The federal government has accorded counties a greater role in intergovernmental programs through single and multiple county planning and operational grants. State and municipal governments are making greater use of counties to overcome problems of scale and organization for service delivery and consolidation of areawide functions. Also, as the National Journal maintains, 'The best thing the nation's counties have going for them in Washington is Bernard F. Hillenbrand. (His) name and hustle have become synonymous with the county cause at the White House and on Capitol Hill.'"[74]*

The influence of county officials in Washington also results from the use of the county as a geographic base for political parties and interest groups. Noting that counties are the building blocks for the local, state, and national political structure, Haider states:

*"County politicians play a major role in nominating, financing and electing members of Congress. They tend to be far more tied in to local congressmen and their activities than a mayor who may be outside the structure...Where governors have overlapping constituencies with senators and have the same coterminous political boundaries, many county officials share the identical constituency and boundaries with congressmen. In the counties' situation, control of the local party structure is by far the most important factor, and here county officials can be much more effective in influencing a congressman than a governor or his state's senators.'"[75]*

## OUR FEDERAL POLITICAL SYSTEM

The American political system is federal in nature, but it has three centers of power--located in Washington, D.C., the state capitols, and at the local level. County chairmen, county party committees, and county-based interest groups play a key role as the local base of our federal political system. County officials have important responsibilities in the administration of the federal election system.

The political influence of county officials, expressed mainly through state associations of counties and the National Association of Counties, is felt in state capitols and the halls of Congress. The President, Congress, federal administrative officials, and their counterparts in state government exercise extensive influence in county courthouses through the laws, executive orders, and regulations which they pass and the funds which they provide. This influence and the role of the county in the federal governmental system is explored in the next chapter.

## REFERENCES

1. Susan W. Torrence, *Grass Roots Government* (Washington: Robert B. Luce, Inc., 1974), pp. 17, 18.

2. For example, Daniel R. Grant and H.C. Nixon, *State and Local Government in America,* 3rd ed. (Boston: Allyn and Bacon, 1975), pp. 165, 166 wrote "The most prevalent local committee unit for the whole country is the county, but use is also made of such units as town, city, ward, precinct and district, and sometimes including the congressional district." Hugh Bone states that "The key figure in the local organization is usually the county chairman." Hugh A. Bone, *American Politics and the Party System,* 4th ed. (New York: McGraw-Hill Book Company, 1971), p. 148.

3. The unpublished survey by Herbert Duncombe and Robert Blank was conducted in 1975, and responses were received from the Secretary of State and/or party officials in all fifty states. If either party in a state listed the use of a particular type of local party committee, the state was shown as having that type of committee.

4. Ibid.

5. Lester W. Milbrath, *Political Participation* (Chicago: Rand McNally & Company, 1965), p. 18. At the top of Milbrath's hierarchy of political involvement are those holding public and party office. This includes precinct committee-persons.

6. Exceptions include Alabama, Nevada, and Wyoming. Much of the information in this section is from Herbert Duncombe and Robert Blank, unpublished survey, 1975.

7. Edward Cooke and Edward Janosik, *Pennsylvania Politics,* Revised Edition (New York: Holt, Rinehart and Winston, Inc., 1965), pp. 51, 52. An election district is a geographic area within which electors vote at one polling place.

8. Herbert Duncombe and Robert Blank, unpublished survey, 1975.

9. Ibid.

10. Ibid.

11. The advantages of the responsiveness of county government to popular control have been well described by Bernard Hillenbrand, "County Government is Reborn," *Readings in State and Local Government*, Joseph F. Zimmerman, ed. (New York: Holt, Rinehart and Winston, Inc., 1964), p. 263.

12. David B. Truman, *The Governmental Process*, 2nd ed. (New York: Alfred A. Knopf, Inc., 1971), pp. 90-92, has an excellent description of the development of the American Farm Bureau Federation from a county base. Truman states that "In setting the conditions under which extension work could be organized in a county, most State Legislatures required the establishment of an organized group of farmers as a cooperating body. Some of these specified that such groups should be known as a farm bureau. By 1916 these local groups were generally called county farm bureaus.", pp. 90, 91.

13. Ibid., p. 121.

14. The counties were part of a small national sample drawn by the author. Replies were received from twenty counties. The questionnaires were sent to agricultural extension agents because they were considered to be well informed about farm organizations within their own counties.

15. Norwood D. Eastman, Director, Field Services Division, American Farm Bureau Federation, letter to Sydney Duncombe, May 19, 1975.

16. John W. Scott, National Master, National Grange, letter to Sydney Duncombe, May 12, 1975.

17. Richard G. Layton, Assistant Director, Public Affairs Division, American Medical Association, letter to Sydney Duncombe, May 22, 1975.

18. Alan E. Kurland, Staff Director, State and Local Bar Services, American Bar Association, letter to Sydney Duncombe, May 22, 1975.

19. C.W. (Pat) Geile, Director, Internal Affairs, the American Legion, letter to Sydney Duncombe, May 5, 1975.

20. American Bar Association, "American Bar Association: A Profile," (Typewritten.)

21. See particularly Harmon Zeigler, "The Effects of Lobbying: A Comparative Assessment," Norman R. Luttbeg, ed., *Public Opinion and Public Policy* (Homewood, Ill.: The Dorsey Press, 1968), pp. 184-205.

22. John Wahlke, Heinz Eulau, William Buchanan, and LeRoy Ferguson, *The Legislative System* (New York: John Wiley and Sons, 1962), pp. 311-342.

23. Susan W. Torrence, pp. 57-63. The clash between suburban dwellers and subdividers and its effect on county planning and zoning is also documented in Theodore Lowi and Benjamin Ginsberg, *Poliscide* (New York: Macmillan Publishing Co., 1976).

24. Lester Milbrath, "The Impact of Lobbying on Government Decisions," Robert H. Salisbury, ed., *Interest Group Politics in America* (New York: Harper & Row, 1970), p. 423.

25. For further information on the role of county officials in the Alabama election process, see James D. Thomas, *A Manual for Alabama County Commissioners* (University: Bureau of Public Administration, the University of Alabama, 1975), pp. 84-86.

26. West Publishing Co., *West Annotated California Codes* (St. Paul: West Publishing Co., 1975), Vol. 29 and 29a.

27. Kenneth VerBurg, *Guide to Michigan County Government* (Lansing: Michigan State University, 1972), pp. IX-8 through IX-10.

28. Dana B. Brammer, *A Manual for Mississippi County Supervisors* (University: Bureau of Governmental Research, University of Mississippi, 1973), pp. 192, 193.

29. James O. Grieshop, *The New Mexico County Commission* (Las Cruces: Cooperative Extension Service, New Mexico State University, 1974), pp. 95-99.

30. After the results are certified, county election returns are normally sent to the secretary of state who is often responsible for publishing the official state results. In many states, the secretary of state publishes the county as well as state totals for each candidate.

31. The most comprehensive set of county election statistics may be found in the eleven volume set, *America Votes: A Handbook of Contemporary Election Statistics,* compiled and edited by Richard M. Scammon (Washington: Congressional Quarterly, 1955-1975).

32. Those interested in county politics in a particular state should begin by reading one or more of the following books: Vladimir O. Key, *Southern Politics in State and Nation* (New York: A.A. Knopf, 1949); John Fenton, *Politics in the Border States* (New Orleans: The Hauser Press, 1957); John Fenton, *Mid-West Politics* (New York: Holt, Rinehart and Winston, 1966); Frank H. Jonas, *Politics in the American West* (Salt Lake City: University of Utah Press, 1969); Duane Lockard, *New England State Politics* (Princeton: Princeton University Press, 1959); Edward F. Cooke and Edward C. Janosik, *Pennsylvania Politics,* revised edition (New York: Holt, Rinehart and Winston, Inc., 1965); Leon D. Epstein, *Politics in Wisconsin* (Madison: University of Wisconsin Press, 1958); Alan L. Clem, *Prairie State Politics* (Washington: Public Affairs Press, 1967).

33. National Association of Counties, *Survey of Women on County Governing Boards - 1977 Update* (Washington: National Association of Counties, 1977). According to the National Roster of Black Elected Officials, published by the Joint Center for Political Studies in Washington, D.C., there were 267 black members of county governing boards in May, 1975. This would be approximately 1.6% of the total number of county board members.

34. The Texas study referred to in this section is Edwin S. Davis, "Shedding Light on the Dark Continent: County Officials in Texas", *Public Service,* Vol. 3, No. 2 (May, 1976) n.p. The study describes the differences between the characteristics of county commissioners and judges in Texas. County judges preside over the commissioners' court while in session, have fiscal responsibilities such as maintaining financial records and preparing the county budget, and have judicial responsibilities such as the administration of estates.

35. H. Sydney Duncombe, "County Government in Idaho", Glenn W. Nichols, Ray C. Jolly and Boyd A. Martin, ed., *State and Local Government in Idaho: A Reader* (Moscow: University of Idaho, 1970), pp. 203-208, is used as a source for the Idaho study.

36. Edwin S. Davis, n.p.

37. Bertil L. Hanson, "County Commissioners of Oklahoma," *Midwest Journal of Political Science,* 9 (November, 1965), 393 and H. Sydney Duncombe, "County Government in Idaho," p. 205.

38. Bertil L. Hanson, p. 391.

39. H. Sydney Duncombe, "County Government in Idaho," p. 206.

40. Bertil L. Hanson, p. 389.

41. Kan Ori, "The Politicized Nature of the County Prosecutor's Office, Fact or Fancy - The Case in Indiana," James B. Kessler, ed., *Empirical Studies of Indiana Politics* (Bloomington: Indiana University Press, 1970), pp. 172, 173.

42. Edwin S. Davis, n.p.

43. Alan L. Clem, *Prairie State Politics, Popular Democracy in South Dakota* (Washington: Public Affairs Press, 1967), p. 63.

44. Ibid., pp. 63, 64.

45. Bertil L. Hanson, p. 397.

46. John H. Fenton, *Midwest Politics,* p. 115.

47. Ibid., p. 116.

48. Lane Lancaster, *Government in Rural America,* 2nd ed. (New York: D. Van Nostrand Company, 1952), pp. 57, 58.

49. Susan W. Torrence, p. 16.

50. The *Bethlehem, Pennsylvania Globe Times* editorial of April 21, 1976, stated that the County Democratic Chairman "does not want Home Rule mandating merit hiring in county jobs because he wants a say on them."

51. Susan W. Torrence's coverage of planning and zoning issues is particularly good.

52. See definitions of "trustee," "delegate," and "partisan" by Thomas R. Dye, *Politics in States and Communities* (Englewood Cliffs: Prentice Hall, 1969), p. 132. The terms trustee and delegate were used in John C. Wahlke, Heinz Eulau, William Buchanan and Leroy C. Ferguson, *The Legislative System,* pp. 280-286.

53. The case study was prepared by the author from an interview with Mr. Gerald Ingle in August, 1976. Gerald Ingle retired as county commissioner in 1977 having served twenty years. He is past President of the Idaho Association of County Commissioners and Clerks.

54. David S. Broder, *The Washington Post,* June 15, 1975, p. A-4.

55. Ibid. Voting persons absentee is a perfectly legal part of the electoral process. The county official handling the absentee ballots just had an opportunity to persuade some voters to vote as he suggested.

56. This case study was prepared largely from Thomas P. Murphy, *Metropolitics and the Urban County* (Washington: Washington National Press, Inc., 1970) and reflects the situation as of the 1970 publication date with additional data supplied by Professor Murphy in 1976.

57. Ibid., p. 92.

58. Ibid., p. 98.

59. Ibid., p. 121.

60. Ibid., p. 130.

61. Information on the 1973 Jackson County Charter was provided by Thomas Murphy, letter to Sydney Duncombe, November 22, 1976.

62. Milton Hoffman, "Westchester's Emerging Two-Party System," *Empire State Report*, March, 1976, p. 58-62, has an excellent description of the characteristics of Westchester County and the growth of its two-party system.

63. The description of the leadership of Michaelian and DelBello is based largely on an article in *The Washington Post*, June 14, 1975.

64. *The Washington Post*, June 14, 1975.

65. Alan Eysen, "Margiotta's Well-tuned Nassau Machine," *Empire State Report*, July, 1975, pp. 250-253 and pp. 270-272, was used as the primary source of material for this case study.

66. Ibid., p. 251.

67. Ibid., p. 253.

68. The information on the Association of County Commissioners of Georgia was provided by Hill R. Healan, Executive Director of the Association, letter to Sydney Duncombe, November 19, 1976.

69. Association of Minnesota Counties, *An Introductory Manual, Minnesota County Government* (St. Paul: Association of Minnesota Counties, 1975).

70. Bertil L. Hanson, p. 399.

71. Donald H. Haider, *When Governments Come to Washington* (New York: The Free Press, 1974), p. 32.

72. The rally is described in *County News*, (Washington), November 24, 1975, p. 3.

73. Bernard F. Hillenbrand, speech to National Association of Counties, Salt Lake City, Utah, June 28, 1976.

74. Donald H. Haider, p. 37.

75. Ibid., p. 38, 39. Donald Haider quotes Bernard Hillenbrand as stating that "The political strength of NACo in terms of getting something done in Washington comes basically from the fact that NACo membership corresponds to the makeup of Congress."

# Chapter 5

# The Role of County Government in the Federal System

"Just as President Nixon's New Federalism was beginning to take hold, a new theory of domestic affairs emerged on the scene, referred to in this paper as the 'New Structuralism.' It calls for action by the federal government to 'reform' the structure of state and local government in order to 'improve' their capacity, presumably to take advantage of revenue sharing funds and other similarly broadened federal grants-in-aid. This new theory of domestic affairs is beginning to pick up themes and theorists on a basis which suggests that major issues of the future will be cast in terms of the New Federalism versus the New Structuralism."[1]

How do New Structuralism and New Federalism affect county government?[2] Both concepts are, in part, responses to prior theories of federalism. One prior theory is what Michael Reagan called "old style federalism." It is a "legal concept, emphasizing a constitutional division of authority and functions between a national government and state governments, with both levels having received their powers independently of each other from a third source—the people."[3] The much criticized "layer cake" federalism—with separate layers representing national, state, and local government—is similar in some respects to "old style federalism." Both of these concepts of

federalism are static notions which leave out the interdependence and sharing of functions between the national, state, and local governments. Both envision a minor role for counties and other units of local government.

The concept of Cooperative Federalism, developed during the 1930s, recognizes the close interrelationships between federal, state, and local units of government which had developed in the financing and administration of many New Deal programs. Our federal system was pictured by Morton Grodzins as a "marble cake" in which some functions are primarily national, some mainly state, some local, and many functions

99

are shared by government at all three levels.[4]

Cooperative Federalism has brought counties and other units of local government into a closer relationship with national and state government, but at the same time it has tended to diminish the importance of local elective officials. The important relationships are the functional relationships among professional personnel at all levels of government (in highway engineering, public health, and other fields), and there is a danger that local elective officials could be by-passed.

Creative Federalism of the 1958-1968 period was, in some ways, a logical extension of the cooperative model of federalism. The number of federal grant programs expanded greatly from an estimated forty major programs prior to 1958 to 160 major programs in 1968, with "1,315 different federal assistance activities, for which money figures, application deadlines, agency contacts, and use restrictions could be identified."[5] The vast machinery of federal aid, with its national policy guidelines and restrictive provisions, was used to lead the nation toward the "Great Society" goals such as an urban-metropolitan emphasis and attention to disadvantaged persons. Policy direction came from the national level, and local elective officials were by-passed.

**The New Federalism.** The concept of New Federalism emerged as a reaction against the centralizing tendency of creative federalism, the by-passing of local elected officials, and the mushrooming growth of narrowly restrictive categorical grants. President Nixon described it, in

1969, as a "cooperative venture among governments at all levels... in which power, funds, and authority are channeled increasingly to those governments which are closest to the people."[6] Responding to the official pronouncements about the purpose of the New Federalism, the Executive Director of the National Association of Counties stated in 1974:

*"The New Federalism is intended to be a response to the discovery that local units of government are better equipped to understand the needs and demands of the people in their locale than is a federal bureaucracy thousands of miles away in a Washington office building. Prior to this revelation, the Federal government had provided financial assistance to other governmental units to execute programs designed and controlled by the federal government."[7]*

Five objectives of New Federalism benefit county governments.[8]

*Curbing the growth of categorical grants-in-aid.[9]* The restrictive provisions of these narrow grants-in-aid were seen to be inhibiting to the ability of state and local governments to shape their programs to best fit state and local needs.

*Special revenue sharing programs.* Combining narrow grants into broader "block" grants was one means to provide state and local government with funds without unduly restricting their discretion.

*General revenue sharing.* The $30 billion general revenue sharing program, passed during the Nixon administration, provided federal funds over a five year period with few provisions which inhibited state and local uses of these funds.

*Decentralization and streamlining.* The federal field office structure was to be reorganized into ten regions. The Federal Assistance Review Program was to explore ways of streamlining the administration of categorical grants.

*Strengthening general purpose units of state and local government.* Greater discretion was to be given to state and local officials—partiularly the politically accountable elective officials of general purpose state and local governments. The general purpose units of local government to be strengthened included counties, cities, villages, towns and townships but not single purpose districts such as special districts and school districts.

Administration of the New Federalism under the Nixon administra-- tion did not mean, however, that there would be a tendency to delegate all types of national government functions to state and local governments. President Nixon stated in 1970:

*"Under the New Federalism, major aims are to define more clearly functional responsibilities among levels of government institutions at all levels.- Welfare, for example, is appropriately a national responsibility."*[10]

As Richard Nathan has pointed out, the New Federalism was to result in "sorting out and rearranging domestic functions."[11] The national government was to take a strong role in income security programs such as transfer payments to individuals through Social Security benefits, cash assistance to the aged and disabled, food stamps, and health insurance. The national government was also to have a strong role in natural resources areas, particularly where there were spillovers from one political unit to another as in the case of air and water pollution control and energy policy.

The fields of human resource services and community development, however, were designated as fields in which there was to be decentralization of some national policy-making and administrative functions to state and local government. Through general and special revenue sharing, the federal government was to continue its role in financing these programs.

**The New Structuralism.** The Nixon Administration generally shied away from intervention by the federal government in the structure of American local government. However, Nathan pointed out that there is a viewpoint which asserts:

*"Yes, the federal government should decategorize, but if we are going to do this, we need to be sure that state and local governments have the organizational and structural capacity to respond to this challenge."*[12]

Nathan's view is that:

*"Advocates of the New Structuralism differ on the way in which, and the degree to which, the federal government should determine what is a 'proper' structure for state and local governments. But fundamentally what is involved is the use of federal clout to bring about preferred organizational arrangements of local governments, especially in metropolitan areas."*[13]

According to Richard Nathan, the most explicit and fully developed version of New Structuralism was the proposal by the Advisory Commission on Intergovernmental Relations that "Umbrella Multi-Jurisdictional Organizations" (UMJOs) be established in all geographic areas.[14] The UMJO would be based on councils of governments or substate districts, such as economic development districts, and would be a general purpose unit of government covering a multi-county area. Councils of governments, economic development districts, and other regional groups are described further on pages 115-117.

One of the main functions of each UMJO would be to review and approve certain types of federal grant applications.[15] A second function would be to resolve inconsistencies between applications for federal grants and officially adopted regional plans or policies. As Nathan pointed out, the UMJO idea rests on an approach which emphasizes federally encouraged regionalism.[16]

There are hazards in this approach for county government, as a Director of Planning in one Indiana County observed.[17] The UMJO staffs could become the grant-writers and planners for the multi-county region and build their own planning staffs with federal funds at the expense of city and county planning organizations. In time, a new tier of local government might develop which could increase governmental costs and undermine the capacity of existing local governments to administer their own programs.

County government, like other units of local government, has been influenced in the past (and will be influenced in the future) by concepts such as Creative Federalism, New Federalism, and New Structuralism. The county position on the proper role of federal, state, and local government is best expressed in the following statement from *The American County Platform*:

*"Leave to private initiative all the functions that citizens can perform privately; use the level of government closest to the community for all public functions it can handle; utilize cooperative intergovernmental agreements where appropriate to attain economical performance and popular approval; reserve national action for residual participation where state and local governments are not fully adequate and for the continuing responsibilities that only the national government can undertake."*[18]

## FEDERAL/COUNTY RELATIONSHIPS

Under older concepts of federalism, there was no direct federal-county relationship. The U.S. Constitution divided the formal powers of government between the national government and the states and did not mention units of local government. One writer of the early 1950s stated that contacts between national and local government should legally take place through state government, since local units of government were the creations of the states.[19] Under newer concepts of federalism, however, there is a more direct relationship between local and federal governmental agencies. Many of these relationships also involve state agencies and some by-pass the states.

**Fiscal Relationships.** The most important types of federal-county relationships are fiscal. Most federal grants, such as those for aid to families with dependent children and maternal and child health care, pass through state agencies before reaching county governments. There are some federal grants, however, such as those for airport construction, which go directly to the counties.

*Categorical grants.* Specific categorical grants have been a mixed blessing for counties. They have provided funds to stimulate program innovation and have enabled counties to finance much needed projects, such as sewage treatment plants, airport construction, and park expansion. However, as Michael Reagan pointed out, "the awarding of funds on the basis of competitive proposals places a premium on 'grantsmanship'."[20] He was concerned also that "relative capability in manipulating language to please federal administrators may become more important than relative objective need in determining which communities receive the most aid."[21]

Another problem is the lack of coordination among categorical federal grant programs which may cause conflicts and confusion if there are separate agencies administering the grants at the local level. Professor Reagan cited the example of approval by one agency of an urban renewal development location through which another agency planned to build a freeway.[22]

An even more serious problem with categorical grants is the disruption they cause in county priorities and the time they take from county personnel. As Bernard Hillenbrand pointed out:

*"The result of categorical aid was confusion among local governments as to which of their projects could receive federal aid and from whom. Often one federal agency's prerequisites were contrary to another's. A county would frequently be confronted with the necessity of altering local priorities in order to receive federal aid. In an attempt to manage a comprehensive system of services to their citizens, county officials spent more and more time, not to mention money, pulling together dozens of federal programs and filling out federal forms for programs which only partially filled citizens' needs."[23]*

*Revenue sharing.* Special revenue sharing (often called block grants) and general revenue sharing have brought a different type of federal-county relationship. The block grants are large, general purpose grants which give counties greater flexibility in spending the funds where they are most needed. General revenue sharing is a federal program with minimal restrictions which provides funds to states, counties, cities, and other general purpose units of local government.[24] General revenue sharing funds can be spent for all necessary capital expenditures authorized by law and many types of operating and maintenance expenditures. The effect of general and special revenue sharing on county governments will be analyzed in depth in Chapter 9.

**Non-Fiscal Relationships.** Not all federal-county relationships result in receipt of federal funds by county government.

*Informational relationships.* Federal agencies, such as the Bureau of the Census, provide valuable statistical information to county officials on county finance and local government organization. The *Uniform Crime Reports* of the Federal Bureau of Investigation are widely used by county sheriffs and police forces. Counties can get valuable information on pollutants, air and water quality standards, and solid waste disposal systems from the Environmental Protection Agency.

*Advisory and training relationships.* Federal agencies have assisted counties by giving expert advice in a variety of areas from airport construction to water quality problems. Federal agencies also have provided training for local officials. County law enforcement agencies have received the benefit of the fingerprint files and criminal laboratory facilities of the Federal Bureau of Investigation.

*Comments on proposed federal regulations.* The U.S. Office of Management and Budget Circular A-85 provides county officials (as well as other local and state officials) with an opportunity to review and comment on major proposed regulations, rules, standards, procedures, guidelines, and interagency agreements concerning federal programs affecting them. The National Association of Counties receives the federal regulations and disseminates them to interested county officials for review and comment.[25]

*Clearance of federal grant applications.* The U.S. Office of Management and Budget Circular A-95 has "as its objective providing state and local government with opportunity to influence the award of Federal assistance under those programs affecting state, areawide, or local development."[26] The federal grant programs included under the 1976 revision of the A-95 program include "virtually all programs having an identifiable impact on area or community development."[27] The federal grant proposals are reviewed by state clearinghouses (usually state planning agencies) and areawide clearinghouses which are generally areawide planning agencies covering one or more counties. The recommendations of the state and areawide clearinghouses are advisory in nature and do not bind the federal agency administering the grant program to accept or reject the grant. County officials participate in areawide clearinghouses as members of the boards of councils of governments or other areawide planning agencies. Thus, county and other local officials have the opportunity to provide their comments on federal grant proposals submitted by other units of local government in their area.

*Exchange of personnel.* Under the mobility section of the Intergovernmental Personnel Act, federal employees may be placed on loan from three months to a year in a particular county. For example, the Allegheny County Health Department has a federal epidemiologist assigned to its staff. County personnel may also be assigned to federal agencies under this Act.

*Enforcement of federal laws.* There are many occasions in which county officials are enforcing federal laws and regulations as well as state laws and county ordinances. Perhaps the best known example is the county sanitary engineer who enforces federal and state water quality standards.

*Training of foreign officials.* The U.S. State Department has arranged to have local government officials from foreign nations assigned to some counties for three months to a year. The purpose of the program is to allow these foreign officials to gain familiarity with local government management techniques in the United States so they may apply these techniques in their own countries.[28]

The federal-county relationship is generally a one-way relationship with federal funds, information, advice, and regulations coming down to county governments. There is need to make this more of a two-way relationship with more input from county and other local government officials used in the formulation of federal programs, budgets, and regulations. The A-85 review process is a significant means of channeling county views to federal agencies. However, it has not always been followed by federal agencies, as the Executive Director of the National Association of Counties pointed out in this comment.

*"The counties are pleased with the A-85 process. However, neither the spirit nor the letter of the A-85 process has been followed by federal agencies. For example, OMB announced—with no prior consultation with state and local government— that federal aid to state and local pollution control agencies would be terminated. Another surprise federal government announcement was that major airports would be required to have round-the-clock security guards as an anti-highjacking measure. Local governments are consulted, if at all, only after the proposed regulations are virtually in final form. Almost no pre-consultation occurs at an early stage of program design and regulation preparation so that states and localities may make their views known before federal agencies are committed to a certain point of view."[29]*

One NACo staff member has suggested that the basic problem with the A-85 review process may not be with the procedure itself but with the absence of sanctions to encourage cooperation by federal officials.[30] A report of the Advisory Commission on Intergovernmental Relations commented that agencies often use the A-85 process at the time they submit a draft of the regulations for publication in the *Federal Register,* thus discouraging early consultation with affected local governments.[31] Among public interest groups, only the National Association of Counties and International City Management Association have consistently responded to drafts of regulations submitted to them through the A-85 process.[32]

## COUNTY-STATE RELATIONSHIPS

The basic powers of counties, cities, and other units of local government are derived from state constitutions and state laws. Local units of government have no formal means to block constitutional amendments inimical to their interests like states which can block federal constitutional changes through failure to ratify amendments proposed by Congress. State constitutions and constitutional amendments are ratified by state legislatures and/or state voters rather than through action of local legislative bodies and conventions.

**State Constitutions.** In many states, county government is constitutionally established, and thus it is impossible to abolish county government without amending the state constitution.[33] The provisions of many state constitutions prescribe the manner in which counties may be formed or consolidated, establish county elective offices, and list the terms and manner of election of county officials. By requiring the election of certain county officials and not permitting the election of other officials, state constitutions may be denying the people of counties the opportunity to choose the county executive plan or other newer forms of county government.

**State Laws.** Within the framework of the state constitution, state laws control county government. These laws often prescribe in detail the duties of county officials. They limit the services which counties may provide, set county tax limits, establish a system of county funds, and may even prescribe detailed county procedures and forms. To secure additional powers and funds, county officials are largely dependent upon the state legislature.

The special legislative act, common many years ago, is one of the methods for dealing with a specific county. This enabled the legislature to be flexible in providing for the individual needs of each county. However, it also greatly increased the number of bills before the legislature, facilitated discrimination against certain counties, and resulted in legislators from the entire state acting on matters of concern to just one county.

General laws are now the most common form of state legislation affecting counties. These laws reduce favoritism and discrimination by treating all counties alike. However, it is an inflexible system which may require large, urban counties and small, rural counties to provide the same services. Another approach is to classify counties by population as a basis for making variations in county services and the salaries of county officials. This approach provides more flexibility, but still leaves the decision-making on vital local questions to the state legislature rather than to the citizens of the county.

**The Dillon Rule.** Do local governments have inherent power independent of the state constitution and state law? Judge Thomas M. Cooley in 1871 stated that local governments have inherent and inalienable rights of self-government.[34] However, the most widely accepted judicial view is that local governments derive their powers from state government and have no inherent powers apart from those granted by state constitutions and laws. Judge John F. Dillon expressed the most widely accepted legal viewpoint on local government powers in the following quotation, which applies to county as well as city government. The powers described in the quotation are those granted by state constitutions and laws.

*"It is a general and undisputed proposition of law that a municipal corporation possesses and can exer-*

cise the following powers, and no others: First, those granted in express words; second, those necessary or fairly implied in or incident to the powers expressly granted; third, those essential to the declared objects and purposes of the corporation—not simply convenient, but indispensable. Any fair, reasonable, substantial doubt concerning the existence of power is resolved by the courts against the corporation, and the power is denied."[35]

The effect of the Dillon Rule is to greatly reduce the discretion of city and county officials in exercising their powers and make them dependent upon authority conferred in specific terms by state laws, implied by these laws, or essential to the operation of local government.

**Judicial and Administrative Influences.** State constitutions and laws are not the only form of state influence on county government. State courts can invalidate the ordinances and administrative actions of county officials, and opinions of state attorney generals may also affect county actions. In addition, state administrative agencies may have an influence by providing:

- *training for county officials (for example, state tax commissions provide training courses for county assessors that influence the techniques they use to assess local property);*

- *technical assistance such as the assistance provided by state planning agencies to county planning commissions;*

- *informational reports and guides such as curriculum guides and educational reports of state departments of education;*

- *administrative regulations such as the detailed requirements on county programs of aid to families with dependent children;*

- *requirements that county agencies prepare and submit financial and other reports. (In some states, the financial reports must be reviewed by the state auditor or some other audit agency); and,*

- *state aid which requires compliance with state regulations and standards.*

Counties have benefitted from information, technical assistance, training, and financial aid from the state, but state controls and regulations have tended, in many cases, to block rather than facilitate progress in county government.

**Home Rule.** County home rule is a reform movement directed at freeing county government from excessive legal restrictions imposed by state laws and the strict construction of those laws in accordance with the Dillon Rule. Home rule is not absolute since counties and other units of local government are created by state government and will always be affected by state law in areas of state concern. However, the adoption of home rule charters does provide county governments with greater flexibility in organization, function, and finance.

*State permission needed.* Constitutional provisions for the adoption of county home rule charters vary from state to state.[36] In California, counties first elect a charter board. After a charter is drafted, it is placed on the ballot and, if the voters approve by a simple majority, it goes to the Legislature for approval or rejection as a whole without power of amendment. The Maryland Constitution provides for a two-step process. Based on a petition bearing the signatures of 20% or more of the registered voters in the county, a charter board of five registered voters is created. The charter board has twelve months to draft a charter and submit it to the voters of the county. If approved by a simple majority of the voters, the charter is adopted. The South Dakota Constitution permits any county or city to provide for the adoption or amendment of a home rule charter if approved at an election by a majority of the voters. The Constitution permits ten percent or more of those voting in the last preceding gubernatorial election to initiate the question of whether to adopt a home rule charter. In most states where charters are permitted, the state constitution generally authorizes the adoption of a home rule charter and leaves some of the detailed implementation of the provision to state law.

*Differing authorities granted.* The powers provided by home rule constitutional provisions also differ from state to state. One of the most sweeping constitutional home rule provisions is found in the South Dakota Constitution.

*"A chartered governmental unit may exercise any legislative power or perform any function not denied by its charter, the Constitution or the general laws of the state. The charter may provide for any form of executive, legislative and administrative structure which shall be of superior authority to statute, provided that the legislative body so established be chosen by popular election and that the administrative proceedings be subject to judicial review. Powers and functions of home rule units shall be construed liberally."*[37]

The net impact of the South Dakota provision is to diminish greatly the restriction of the Dillon Rule and to allow counties and cities to exercise powers not specifically authorized by state law so long as they do not conflict with the State Constitution, state laws or home rule charters.

The Constitutions of California and Florida have provisions with similar effects. When a California county has adopted a home rule charter, it has the power to make and enforce within its limits, police, sanitary, and other regulations not in conflict with general laws. The Florida Constitution provides that "counties operating under county charters shall have all powers of local self government not inconsistent with general law, or with special law approved by vote of the electors."[38]

The real impact of county home rule charters depends, not only on the constitutional provision, but also on the implementing state legislation and the wording of the charter adopted by the county. This impact will be discussed further in the concluding chapter of the book. It is important, at this point, to make clear that home rule is not a panacea for

ounty government. It does not as-
ure adequate financing of county
ervices, more efficient procedures,
r more effective and responsible
orms of county organization. How-
ver, it does allow a greater range
f discretion to counties, as Clyde F.
nider has remarked:

*". . .It is ordinarily not possible
or a home-rule county, under exist-
ng constitutional provisions, to exer-
ise a completely free hand in re-
amping even the structure of its
overnment. Nevertheless, the range
f discretion conferred has enabled
harter counties to effect substantial
mprovement in their governmental
nachinery. In shortening the ballot,
ntegrating administrative respon-
ibility, and inaugurating the merit
ystem and scientific budgeting,
ounties strike at the very heart
f long-standing weaknesses in tradi-
ional organization; and a majority
f the home-rule charters have in-
luded most or all of these reforms.* "[39]

## LOCAL INTERGOVERN-
## MENTAL RELATIONSHIPS

Counties, cities, villages, bor-
ughs, towns, townships, school dis-
ricts, special districts, and public
uthorities are separate legal en-
ities, but they do not exist in com-
lete isolation from each other. With-
n most counties, there are almost
laily contacts among local govern-
nent officials. County governments
re involved in relationships with
ther units of local government with-
n the county in many ways: (1) as
enior units of local government in
elationships with townships and
pecial districts; (2) as vendors or
urchasers of services; (3) as partici-
ants in informal cooperative ar-

rangements; (4) as creators of dependent districts and subordinate
taxing areas; (5) as participants in
city-county agencies; (6) as participants in city-county consolidated
governments; and (7) as participants
in bi-county and multi-county agencies.

**The Senior Unit of Local Govern-
ment.** As the largest general purpose unit of government within a
county area, county government
has sometimes been given responsibility by the state legislature to
act as its legal and fiscal arm in re-
lation to smaller units of local government. In Michigan, for example,
the State Legislature granted counties the power to establish an equalization department to review the assessments made by city and township assessors.[40] After examining
information on the sales prices of
property and the assessed values set
by city and township assessors,
the county equalization department
computes a factor used to equalize
assessments throughout the county.
Therefore, Michigan is relying on an
agency of county government to
bring greater equity to the assessment of city and township property.

Boards containing county officials may also play a significant
role in setting tax rates of local governments within a county area. In
Michigan, the Legislature has granted power to set tax rates, within a
fifteen-mill limit, to a seven-member tax allocation board consisting
of two county officials, the superintendent of a school district, a school
board member, a citizen of a municipality, a township board member,
and a member who has no official
connection within any governmental

## 110 • Modern County Government

unit.[41] The tax allocation board conducts hearings on the financial needs of local units and decides (within the limits set by state law) the amount of mills each local governmental unit may levy without a vote of the people.[42] The allocation of tax levies among units of local government is a politically significant action. The use of a tax allocation board, containing members of the units affected by the allocations, is a good means of adjudicating this decision at the local level.

The state legislature may delegate certain functions in the creation of special districts to county boards. In Idaho, for example, county commissioners have the power to approve or dismiss petitions for the formation of a recreation district.[43] If the petition is approved, they have the authority to conduct an election to determine whether the district will be established. In California, city and county officials are appointed to a commission which has the power to determine whether new cities or special districts can be created within the county.

**Counties as Vendors of Services.** In many parts of the nation, units of local government have purchased services from county government. Cities in Kansas which cannot afford expensive road equipment have rented it from counties, while townships in Wisconsin, Minnesota, and Nebraska have contracted with counties to maintain township roads.

Los Angeles County has the most extensive system of service contracts in the nation.[44] Thirty cities within Los Angeles County contract with the county to provide most of their municipal services. In 1954,

the City of Lakewood incorporate and became the fifteenth largest cit in California. Immediately followin, incorporation, the Lakewood Cit Council, rather than establish it own departments, requested th county to continue to provide mos of the municipal type services with in the city. The legal authorizatio for Los Angeles County to provid services to cities by contract is cor tained in a California law which state that the board of supervisors of county may contract with any cit within the county for any municipa type service requested by the city.

In March, 1977, Los Angeles Cour ty was providing at least one servic on a contract basis to each of the 7 cities in the county.[45] These service included: general services agree ments (75 cities); emergency am bulance services (73); services o the District Attorney in prosecut ing city misdemeanors (59); traffi signal maintenance (53); and stree light maintenance (48). The mor than seventy services provided b contract also included personnel engineering, planning and zoning parks and recreation, animal contro microfilm storage, library services bridge maintenance, enforcement o city health ordinances, and a variet of law enforcement services admini stered by the County Sheriff.

The service contracts are initiatec at the request of the city and are ap proved by the County Board of Super visors. The rates charged are devel oped to recover actual costs of pro viding the service. Most of the stand ard contracts are written for a one year or five-year period and may either be renewed or are self-renew ing. The use of service contracts ir Los Angeles County has been creditec with improving the organization and service of county departments.

**Informal Intergovernmental Arrangements.** Counties enter into a number of cooperative agreements with cities and other units of local government that do not involve the sale of county services. These include:

- *meetings in which county and city officials meet on a regular basis to exchange information and discuss common problems;*

- *routine cooperation of county law enforcement agencies, city police departments, and state police in exchanging information about suspects, establishing road blocks to capture fleeing criminals, and training police personnel;*

- *exchange of equipment and services on an emergency basis as in flood control and snow removal;*

- *coordination of traffic signals, pavement markings, and traffic light synchronization on county roads, city streets, and state highways within the county;*[46]

- *sharing of the costs of facilities such as public safety buildings, swimming pools, and expensive communications equipment;*[47]

- *cooperative purchasing programs in which the county buys standard products such as gasoline and rock salt for its own use as well as for cities and school districts within the county; and,*

- *county subsidization or financial support of city or special district operations. (For example, Los Angeles County has used revenue sharing funds to subsidize seven municipal bus lines and the Southern California Rapid Transit District.).*[48]

A number of states have adopted laws facilitating intergovernmental cooperation. A common provision authorizes counties, cities, and other local governments to cooperate with other units of government in the exercise of any power or function that each unit has the authority to exercise on its own.

**Creators of Subordinate Taxing Areas.** County subordinate taxing areas are districts which provide a specific improvement or service within a particular area of the county. They are not independent entities like special districts but are created by county government and have no governmental structure of their own. In California, a county service area may be initiated by request of two of the five members of the county board of supervisors or a petition signed by ten percent or more of the voters in the area. The county government is reimbursed for the costs of providing services by taxes levied by the county service area on its residents. The county board serves as the governing body of the county service area, and county employees are often used as staff of the service area.

County service areas provide the same functions as special districts such as fire protection, streets or street lighting, road construction and maintenance, water and sewer facilities, and flood control. Robert Smith pointed out that "the advantage to the county of the taxing area over the special district is that policy making for the area remains with the county officials who are thus able to blend it into a comprehensive picture of the needs of the county."[49] In 1972 there were 6,283 subordinate taxing areas in 669 counties. California and Iowa had 1,758 and 1,663 of these areas, respectively.[50] Metropolitan counties like Los Angeles and San Diego had the largest number. The League of California Cities felt that if annexation would not meet the needs of a developing area, city incorporation and the creation of a county service district were the two next best choices.

The Los Angeles Flood Control District, created after a 1914 flood caused serious damage to the Los Angeles area, is one of the larger subordinate taxing areas in California.[51] The governing body of the district is the Los Angeles County Board of Supervisors, and county officers, such as the county counsel and purchasing officer, provide services for the district. It covers about two-thirds of the county and taxes property only within the area of its district. Through the district, the county is able to provide flood control, channel improvements, and similar services for that area without taxing other county citizens.

**Counties As Participants in City-County Agencies.** Counties cooperate with cities in forming joint city-county agencies. There are many city-county planning commissions such as the Warren County-Bowling Green, Kentucky, Planning Commis-

sion described in Chapter 8. These have the advantage of being able to plan for the entire county including both the major city in the county and the unincorporated area. Forsyth County and Winston-Salem, North Carolina, have formed a joint city-county tax collecting department. The department is operated by the county, but the city pays a proportionate share of the cost. Joint city-county agencies are also found extensively in the fields of assessing, fire protection, industrial development, libraries, sewage disposal, water supply, and zoning.

**City-County Mergers.** There are two types of mergers of city and county government that have been used in the United States. Under city-county separation type, the urban area of a county separates from the remainder of the county. In the urban area of the county, the city and county governments merge and perform both city and county functions. City-county separation was used in the 1850-1910 period to form the city-county governments of Baltimore, San Francisco, St. Louis, and Denver. However, the urban area has expanded beyond the early boundaries of these city-counties, leaving areas with many metropolitan problems outside the service jurisdictions. City-county separation has been used recently, mainly in Virginia, to create independent cities.[52]

*City-county consolidation.* A better solution to resolving urban problems is city-county consolidation by which the governments of the county and major city within the county combine. This plan was used in New Orleans, Boston, Philadelphia, and New York in the 1800s and

Honolulu in 1907. For more than forty years, there were no further consolidations. Interest was revived in city-county consolidation with the success of the Baton Rouge-East Baton Rouge Parish consolidation in 1947 and the Nashville-Davidson County consolidation of 1962. From 1962 to the present, there have been ten other city-county consolidations:[53]

> *Virginia Beach-Princess Anne*
> *County, Virginia*          *1962*
> *South Norfolk-Norfolk County,*
> *Virginia*                  *1962*
> *Jacksonville-Duval County,*
> *Florida*                   *1967*
> *Juneau-Greater Juneau*
> *Borough, Alaska*           *1969*
> *Indianapolis-Marion County,*
> *Indiana*                   *1969*
> *Carson City-Ormsby County,*
> *Nevada*                    *1969*
> *Columbus-Muscogee County,*
> *Georgia*                   *1970*
> *Sitka-Greater Sitka Borough,*
> *Alaska*                    *1971*
> *Suffolk-Nansemond County,*
> *Virginia*                  *1972*
> *Lexington-Fayette County,*
> *Kentucky*                  *1972*

A study of six city-county consolidations showed that some smaller cities in these counties were not brought into the consolidation of the county and major city. The study showed that the mayor-council form of government is being used in all but one of the city-counties, and the mayor-president-council form is used in the other.[54]

One of the primary features of city-county consolidation in Davidson County, Tennessee and Duval County, Florida was the establishment of two taxing districts. The general services district encompasses the entire county, and residents of this district pay for countywide services. The urban services district includes only the more urban areas of the county, and its residents pay additional taxes for the urban services which only they receive. This arrangement tends to insure that residents outside the urban area of the county are not charged for services they do not receive.

Two frequently cited benefits of city-county consolidations are the promotion of greater efficiency in the provision of services and the promotion of economy of scale and coordination of services.[55] Former Mayor Beverly Briley of Nashville-Davidson County supports this contention and demonstrated it by producing a lower effective tax rate in his county than in counties of comparable size in Tennessee.[56] He was able to reduce taxes after consolidation and to maintain the tax rate for a number of years until inflation forced an increase.

A third benefit of city-county consolidation is a reduction in the amount of governmental overlap and fragmentation. Mayor Hans Tanzler of Jacksonville-Duval County, Florida, described the problems which preceded the consolidation there: "We were crippled here with the duplication of services and the overlapping of responsibility and the inability of either of those governments to address itself to the needs."[57]

City-county consolidation has also permitted an area to combine financial resources to deal with matters such as sewage disposal, better fire protection, and more adequate law enforcement. City-county consolidation has reduced or eliminated the need for the creation of special districts. It has also created a responsive form of government that is flexible enough to meet future needs. As former Mayor Richard Lugar of Indianapolis-Marion County, Indiana stated: "Our objective was to provide a better form of government, in which popular expression might come to the fore, in which neighborhood groups might have some faith in the democratic process."[58]

**Multi-County Administrative Agencies.** County governments have participated as partners in the governance and financing of a number of multi-county administrative agencies. One of the earliest was the Washington Suburban Sanitary commission, established in 1918 by the Maryland General Assembly.[59] The Commission is charged with providing water and sanitary sewer services within a district which includes almost all of Montgomery and Prince George's Counties in Maryland. The Commission is directed by a board of six commissioners—three appointed by the County Executive and confirmed by the Council in Montgomery County and three appointed in Prince George's County. The costs of the Commission's programs are financed by the sale of revenue bonds, water and sewer rate charges, federal and state grants, and other charges on home owners and developers.

Montgomery and Prince George's Counties also participate in the governance of the Maryland-National Capital Park and Planning Commission established in 1927.[60] The bi-county Commission is headed by a ten-member Board with five members representing each county. The objective of the agency is to prepare comprehensive land use and transportation plans for the Maryland suburban area and develop a park system for the two counties. The Board members of each county meet separately and make most of the decisions involving their county. The capital improvements program developed by the Commission for each county must be submitted to the County Council for approval.

In the field of health services, there are a number of multi-county health agencies. Henry, Louisa, and Jefferson Counties in southeastern Iowa, for example, operate a three-county mental health program.[61] The Agency is run by a Board of Directors composed of one county supervisor from each county plus five citizens appointed by the three county supervisors. The Center provides psychotherapy, marriage counseling, reconcilation services in divorce cases, and other types of mental health services and is financed from federal aid and payments made by the participating counties.

*The government consortium.* Multi-county agencies have also served a useful purpose in manpower, solid waste disposal, criminal justice, and other fields. One of the means of administering the manpower programs funded through the federal Comprehensive Employment and Training Act is a consortium of local governments. County officials participate in the governing bodies of manpower consortia such as the Northeast Florida Manpower Consortium operated by Jacksonville-Duval County (city-county) and the county governments of Baker and Nassau Counties.[62]

In areas where a single county does not have sufficient population to operate its own solid waste disposal system, multi-county agencies have been developed. In southeastern Iowa, for example, Appanoose, Lucas, Monroe, and Wayne Counties cooperatively formed the Chariton Valley Regional Services Agency to manage a multi-county system.[63] Multi-county agencies have also been used to build a regional jail in northeastern North Carolina, to operate correctional centers in Minnesota, and to engage in law enforcement planning in South Dakota and in many other areas of the nation.[64]

*Project construction and program operation.* Multi-county agencies are a useful administrative device in cases in which one county is too small to support construction of a particular facility (such as a correctional center) or operation of a particular program (such as a mental health program or solid waste disposal system). More populous areas (such as Montgomery and Prince George's Counties) have found them useful for planning and operating programs in which coordination between two or more similar counties is essential.

## COUNTY GOVERNMENT AND REGIONAL COUNCILS

The relationship between county governments and regional councils is becoming sufficiently important and complex to be described at length. Regional councils are basically voluntary associations of local government officials within regions.

Such councils share the following basic characteristics:[65]

- *"They are multijurisdictional in scope (i.e., they encompass more than one local government, usually several). Most often they are multicounty operations, although some councils are composed of a single county and several cities.*

- *Their prime purpose is to achieve local government cooperation across legal jurisdictional boundary lines in order to deal with mutual problems which a single city or county cannot handle adequately.*

- *Their programs are multifunctional. Rather than approaching a single problem (like the special purpose district), regional councils deal with a variety of public issues, such as transportation, health, public safety, and environmental quality.*

- *Regional councils are advisory in nature and (with few exceptions) lack the normal governmental powers of taxation, regulation, and direct operation of public facilities.*

- *They have legal status and exist through the agreement of member local governments."*

**Types of Regional Councils.** The earliest type of regional council was the regional planning commission. The Boston Metropolitan Improvement Commission in 1902 had some regional planning functions, but the first metropolitan planning commission was established in Los Angeles County, California in 1922 as an advisory body to the Los Angeles County Board of Supervisors.[66]

*Comprehensive planning.* The number of regional planning commissions grew slowly until the 1930s and 1940s, although the federal government gave some impetus to regional approaches during the 1930s by requiring coordinated planning for some public works projects.[67] After Congress passed the Housing Act of 1954, which provided urban planning assistance to metropolitan areas, the number of regional planning commissions doubled in five years. These planning commissions are helpful in developing a mechanism for interlocal cooperation and in involving citizens in the regional planning process. The commissions are advisory in nature and depend upon city and county governments to implement their decisions. For county planning officials, regional councils furnish a useful means of extending the land-use planning process to a multi-county area, although the plans are limited in scope, and it does not include most types of human resources planning.

*Economic and local development districts.* These are a second form of regional cooperation. Economic development districts were established as a result of the Public Works and Economic Development Act of 1965, and local development districts derived their authority from the Appalachian Regional Development Act of the same year. Both acts were designed to provide aid to sections of the nation experiencing high unemployment, low income, and out-migration. The purposes of both types of districts are "to promote economic progress and to coordinate public and private planning and development efforts in multi-county target areas."[68] The governing boards of the more numerous economic development districts are required to have a majority of the members to be elected local officials. It is a common practice for each county and major city in the district to name an elected official to represent it on the governing board. Economic development districts are involved in planning, A-95 review, and programs of economic development.

*Councils of governments.* A third form of regional council is the council of governments (COG), which has been described as "multi-functional voluntary regional associations of elected local officials or local governments represented by their elected officials."[69] The governing body of a COG is composed mainly of elected officials of counties, cities, and other units of local government within a multi-county area. The first of the COG's was the Supervisors' Inter-County Committee of the Detroit Area which was founded in 1954 by Edward Conner, President of the Wayne County Board of Supervisors, and supervisors from neighboring counties.[70] The Committee was established because of concern over water supply, sewage, waste disposal, and regional transportation needs in an area of rapidly expanding population. The Committee served as a forum for discussion and was instrumental in the initiation of needed studies of airport, sewage, drainage, and other projects. The Committee was also successful in getting many of the bills it recommended passed by the Michigan Legislature, including a bill to develop a metropolitan-wide plan for major expressways and thoroughfares.

The Supervisors' Inter-County Committee of the Detroit Area was followed by COG's in the New York City; Puget Sound, Washington; Mid-Willamette Valley, Oregon; Washington, D.C.; San Francisco; Southern California; and Atlanta areas.[71] The COGs were viewed "as an organizational device for bringing together, at regular intervals and on a voluntary basis, representatives of the local governments within a given area to discuss common problems, exchange information, and develop consensus on policy questions of mutual interest."[72] The early COGs had no operating responsibilities and no power to compel participation by local government or force constitutent local governments to back their decisions.

**County Involvement in Regional Councils.** County governments have been involved in establishing regional councils, providing members for their governing boards, and contributing to the revenues of these councils. However, the following examples show the diversity of county relations with regional councils.

*Detroit.*[73] The Supervisors' Inter-County Committee was composed exclusively of representatives chosen by the boards of supervisors in the six counties in the area with each county getting equal representation. Counties contributed most of the financial support of the Committee in its first decade. In 1968, the Committee merged with the Detroit Metropolitan Area Planning Commission to form the Southeastern Michigan Council of Governments. The membership of the COG was broadened to include representatives from cities, villages, townships, and school districts as well as counties. Funding sources in the late 1960s included federal grants, a Ford Foundation grant, and fees from local government members.

*San Francisco.*[74] Initiation of the Association of Bay Area Governments (ABAG) came jointly from city and county officials. During the Spring of 1959, the State Legislature considered creating a Golden Gate Transportation Authority for the San Francisco Bay Area. Partly in opposition to this, representatives from eighty-one cities were invited to a meeting sponsored by the Alameda Mayor's Conference to consider formation of a metropolitan council. County officials met to consider a similar organization, and both cities and counties cooperated to establish the Association of Bay Area Governments (ABAG). Membership in ABAG is open to nine counties and about ninety cities and, in 1972, seven counties and eighty-four cities were members.

The General Assembly of ABAG meets twice a year and consists of one representative from each city and county, with each having one vote. City and county votes are tabulated separately, and a majority of the quorum of county representatives and a majority of the quorum of city representatives are required to approve policy recommendations. An Executive Committee meets more frequently. It consists of city and county representatives and provides representation roughly on the basis of population. Funds for ABAG come from regular assessments of the members, special assessments levied by the General Assembly, and from federal grants.

*Atlanta.*[75] The Atlanta Regional Planning Commission was organized by a special Act of the Georgia Legislature in 1947. This two-county planning commission was expanded to the five-county Atlanta Regional Metropolitan Planning Commission in 1960, and other regional agencies such as the Metropolitan Atlanta Council for Health were established. The Atlanta Regional Commission was established by legislative act in 1971 and assumed the powers of a number of prior Atlanta metropolitan agencies. In 1972, the Atlanta Regional Commission was composed of twelve public members and eleven members at large. The public members included the chairmen of the boards of county commissioners of the five counties in the area, the Mayor and an Alderman from Atlanta, and five other mayors each selected within the five counties. The members at large are elected by popular vote from districts within the region. The Atlanta Regional Commission is financed from a charge to counties and cities based primarily on population and receives federal and state grants. The functions of ARC include reviewing and evaluating applications for federal and state grants by agencies within the area, reviewing and recommending changes in area plans, engaging in research on matters affecting land use, transportation, waste disposal, drainage, parks, criminal justice, social services, and other matters.

The initiation of these regional commissions came from different sources. In the Detroit area, it was county officials who spearheaded the first COG in the area; in the San Francisco Bay area, the impetus was from both city and county officials; while in the Atlanta area, Georgia legislators took a significant role in the establishment of the Atlanta Regional Commission. The systems of representation in the three regional councils and the methods of financing also differ to some degree.

**Federal Intervention and the Rapid Growth of Regional Councils.** From 1966 on, the monetary incentives of federal grants and the requirements of federal clearance influenced the growth of regional councils.[76] Congress encouraged areawide clearance through the passage of the Demonstration Cities and Metropolitan Development Act of 1966 and the Intergovernmental Cooperation Act of 1968. Section 204 of the former Act required that there be a regional planning agency in each metropolitan area charged with reviewing and commenting upon local government applications for thirty-nine types of federal aid. The latter Act directed the President to establish regulations governing federal programs which would foster orderly community development in urban and rural areas. The Office of Management and Budget in 1969 issued circular A-95 which extended the project review process of section 204 of the 1966 act to many additional federal programs. Regional councils became an essential element in the process of review of federal grant applications at the local level.

Since the 1960s, the primary source of revenue has shifted from local resources to federal grants. In 1971, regional councils received $33 million in federal funds. Of that amount, $14 million came from HUD comprehensive planning grants, and a total of $10 million was received from mass transportation planning, law enforcement planning, and highway planning act.[77] In 1971, 66% of all regional councils received more than half their funds from the federal government.[78] Only 26% of the regional councils received half or more of their funds from local government, and only 9% of the regional councils received half or more of their funds from state government. Melvin Mogulouf has contended that, "It is Federal money, Federal staff assistance, and Federal policy that is largely responsible for the health and/or weakness of the COG."[79]

With the incentives of federal grants and requirements for areawide clearance, it is not surprising that the number of councils of governments increased from 30 in 1965 to 223 by 1970.[80] Carl Stenberg estimated that there were more than 600 councils of governments and regional planning commissions by 1974.[81]

**Advantages of Regional Councils.** One frequently cited advantage of regional councils is that they utilize, rather than replace, existing units of local government. Walter A. Scheiber presented a number of traditional arguments for COGs in 1968 when he stated:

*"The council device has a good deal to offer the urban county official. It is a metropolitanwide organization which is built upon, rather than replacing, his government. Its multi-purpose character gives him latitude to move against those regional problems which are of concern to him. The county and its counterpart governments control the activities of the council. A council is relatively easy to organize since its creation requires no legislative action and generally arouses no adverse public reaction. Finally, under the provisions of the Housing and Urban Development Act of 1965, councils of government are eligible for two-to-one federal matching grants to support their programs. Thus, every county dollar invested in a council of governments can triple its value in the fight against regional problems."*[82]

Other justifications for regional councils stress the advantages of regional government for the survival of local government. Eugene T. Gualco, past President of the National Association of Regional Councils and a County Supervisor of Sacramento County, California, stated:

*"The stakes on the regional table are much higher than the economic value of regional programs...the very future of local government is on the line. Local elected officials must come to understand that citizens want solutions to areawide problems like air and water pollution, traffic congestion, urban sprawl, and crime. And in this complex and mobile world of today, areawide problems like these simply cannot be solved within the boundaries of a single county or municipality.*

*Our constituents are still looking to local governments to do the job. But if local elected officials fight among themselves and fail to produce solutions to recognized multijurisdictional problems, then the public will simply turn to the state capitol or to Washington for solutions to their problems."*[83]

The strength of local government depends on its political strength and ability to deal effectively with federal agencies and state government. Regional councils are a means by which local government officials create their own solutions to regional problems and present a united front before state legislatures and state executive agencies in supporting these solutions.[84] The alternative can be for state government to make the decisions on programs and the location of facilities within the region. As a Georgia state legislator, Gerald T. Horton, pointed out:

*"Such decisions of location of facilities within a region are too often made by state government without regard to the planning or desires of the individual units of local government. A regional organization could and should assume the responsibility of location decisions within a multi-county area."*[85]

**Problems and Dangers.** The traditional criticisms of regional councils stress their lack of power. Scheiber, for example, pointed out that because they are voluntary in nature, individual local governments can withdraw from these councils if they disagree with policies. He comments that "this very fact frequently inhibits the council from taking bold action on a matter for a fear of offending some member."[86] He also criticizes the lack of legislative power or executive authority on the part of regional councils to implement their own decisions. The result may be that the regional council becomes "a toothless tiger whose presence lulls its members into thinking they can do an adequate job when, in fact, its weaknesses make this impossible."[87]

The "toothless tiger" arguments against regional councils have been heard much less frequently since regional councils have become major recipients of federal funding and have been given federal powers for reviewing and commenting on local applications for federal aid. Some county officials are now concerned that regional councils may become a means by which the federal government by-passes local officials. Arch Lamb, a County Commissioner from Lubbock, Texas, resigned from the Southern Plains Association of Governments in Texas because he felt that with so many controls and so much authority centered in Washington, it was difficult to accomplish the objectives of Councils of Governments. He commented that:

"... the regionalism movement is primarily a result of federal guidelines which have required certain areawide procedures in order to receive federal monetary support. This process removes much of the local autonomy from the cities, towns, and counties; and therefore should be closely watched by elected officials."[88]

Some county officials favor the voluntary council of governments approach but are concerned about federal agencies forcing operating functions on regional councils or imposing a single regional structure on the entire nation. Bernard Smith, a Sioux County (Iowa) Commissioner, believes that councils of governments are helpful in providing technical services to local government, but he is concerned that the federal government may force operating responsibilities on regional councils in the next decade.[89] Francis Francois, a Vice-President of the National Association of Counties, and former President of the National Association of Regional Councils, also favors the voluntary regional council approach in which local, city, and county officials constitute a majority of the governing body. He believes, however, that:

"... the worst thing we can do is try and impose a single regional organizational structure model on all local governments, in all of our 50 states. This flies in the face of the great diversity in government structures, objectives and styles found in our nation. And yet, to a great extent that is what we have done in America over the past 15 years."[90]

**The Regional Council—An Opportunity or A Threat?** The implications for county government of regional councils and substate districting will be discussed further in Chapter 10. There are obvious opportunities for counties and other units of local government in having a forum for discussion of areawide problems—particularly when the metropolitan area spans two or more counties.

here are many other advantages in
A-95 review, research, and other
functions of regional councils. How-
ver, there is also a threat that the
New Structuralist philosophy might
be used in Congress or executive of-
ices to justify undercutting existing
units of local government through
regulations and federal aid which encourage regional councils to admini-
ter operating functions.

## THE RIGHT OF LOCAL
## SELF-DETERMINATION

The role of county government is
hat of the senior unit of local gov-
rnment in the federal system where
he two principal sources of power
ie at federal and state levels. The
government has had an increasing
nfluence on county programs
hrough grant-in-aid provisions,
general and special revenue sharing,
and through advisory, training,
clearance, and other relationships.
The federal influence may grow
stronger, particularly if the New
Structuralists persuade the President
and Congress that federal aid requirements should include provisions
for the restructuring of county government. State constitutions, laws,
and the regulations of state administrative agencies also have a significant influence on county programs.

The right of county officials and
their constituents to determine the
organization, functions, and method
of financing of county government is
limited by restrictive state constitutions and laws. The right to greater
self-determination is strongly supported by the National Association
of Counties' 1976-77 *American County Platform* which states that: "We
in county government believe that
home rule, or the right of local self-
determination, is the keystone of
our American democracy."[91] Home
rule, as advocated by the National
Association of Counties, involves:

- *the flexibility for counties "to
devise their own internal organizational structure either
under charter or under general law;"*[92]

- *the flexibility to employ alternative means of county finance rather than the traditional and inadequate property tax; and,*

- *the flexibility "to determine
the scope and the extent of
the governmental service
each (county) will render, subject to the recognized need for
some uniformity in the standard of delivery of services of
national or statewide im-
port."*[93]

The role of the state in requiring
counties to provide certain services
and the growth of newer services
in which county officials have a
greater measure of local self-determination are described in the next
chapter.

## REFERENCES

1. Richard P. Nathan, "The New Federalism Versus the Emerging New Structuralism," *Publius,* Summer, 1975, p. 111.

2. New Federalism is a term associated with the attempts of the Nixon administration to define more clearly functional responsibilities among all levels of government and provide additional funds and fiscal flexibility to state and local governments.

3. Michael D. Reagan, *The New Federalism* (New York: Oxford University Press, 1972), p. 3.

4. Grodzin writes, "The federal system is not accurately symbolized by a neat layer cake of three distinct and separate planes. A far more realistic symbol is that of the marble cake. Wherever you slice through it you reveal an inseparable mixture of differently colored ingredients." Morton Grodzin, "Centralization and Decentralization in the American Federal System," Robert A. Goldwin, ed., *A Nation of States* (Chicago: Rand McNally & Company, 1961), pp. 3, 4.

5. Deil S. Wright, "Intergovernmental Relations: An Analytical Overview," in *Intergovernmental Relations in America Today,* Richard H. Leach, ed., (Philadelphia: American Academy of Political and Social Sciences, November, 1974), p. 10.

6. Quoted in Thomas J. Graves, "IGR and the Executive Branch: The New Federalism," *Intergovernmental Relations in America Today,* Richard H. Leach, ed. p. 41. Graves describes the New Federalism as "a deep-seated commitment to bringing government closer to its citizens, to restoring faith and credibility to government at all levels, and to strengthening state and local governments in ways that will foster the wise and responsible local level leadership which gave the nation so much strength and vitality in the earlier days of the republic."

7. Bernard F. Hillenbrand, "Counties: The Emerging Force," in *Intergovernmental Relations in America Today,* Richard H. Leach, ed., p. 92.

8. The writer is indebted to David B. Walker, "How Fares Federalism in the Mid-Seventies?" *Intergovernmental Relations in America Today,* Richard H. Leach, ed., p. 19 for his description of the major elements in the New Federalism.

9. A categorical grant-in-aid is a federal grant for a very specific and limited purpose. For example, the Public Health Service provides a grant limited to the collection, analysis, and furnishing of information on the causes of Sudden Death Syndrome among infants. The grants can be used to counsel families affected by this illness but cannot be used for other categories of disease. U.S. Office of Management and Budget, *1976 Catalogue of Federal Domestic Assistance* (Washington: U.S. Government Printing Office, 1976), pp. 176, 177.

10. Quoted in Richard P. Nathan, p. 112.

11. Ibid. The writer is indebted to Richard P. Nathan, pp. 112, 113 for many of the ideas expressed in this paragraph.

12. Ibid., pp. 117, 118.

13. Ibid., p. 118.

14. Ibid.

15. Ibid. For a full description of Umbrella Multi-Jurisdictional Organizations see Advisory Commission on Intergovernmental Relations, *Regional Decision Making: New Strategies for Substate Districts*, (Washington: U.S. Government Printing Office, 1973), p. 348.

16. Richard P. Nathan, pp. 118, 119. Nathan used the phrase "Regionalism Federally Powered."

17. The Director of Planning saw the staff of a regional council increasing rapidly as it wrote and received additional federal grants. He saw federal funding being funneled particularly into areawide wastewater and other regional plans and was concerned about his inability to get federal funds to prepare needed land use plans within his growing county. The result, he felt, was an undermining of county land use planning. The large increase in expenditures for areawide planning did not diminish his need for expenditures for county land use planning, zoning, and subdivision controls.

18. National Association of Counties, *The American County Platform* (Washington: National Association of Counties, 1976), p. 5.

19. Lane Lancaster, *Government in Rural America* (New York: D. Van Nostrand Company, 1952), p. 331.

20. Michael Reagan, p. 86.

21. Ibid., pp. 86, 87.

22. Ibid., p. 88.

23. Bernard F. Hillenbrand, "Counties: The Emerging Force," *Intergovernmental Relations in America Today*, Richard H. Leach, ed., p. 92.

24. Among the few revenue sharing requirements are the prohibitions against discrimination in any program funded by revenue sharing and the requirement that the receiving unit of government must hold public hearings on the proposed use of revenue sharing funds.

25. See National Association of Counties and National Association of County Development Coordinators, *A Guide to Grantsmanship for County Officials* (Washington: National Association of Counties, 1973), p. 26.

26. U.S. Office of Management and Budget, *A-95: What It Is - How It Works* (Washington: U.S. Government Printing Office, 1976), p. 29.

27. Ibid., p. 6.

28. The writer is indebted to Thomas P. Bruderle, of the National Association of Counties staff, for the description of this program.

29. Bernard F. Hillenbrand, "Counties: The Emerging Force", *Intergovernmental Relations in America Today*, ed., Richard H. Leach, p. 95.

30. Thomas P. Bruderle monitored the A-85 process in 1973 while on the staff of the Advisory Commission on Intergovernmental Relations. He has commented that federal officials may have comfortable relations with functional specialists that they wish to preserve and may be unwilling to include locally elected or appointed county officials in the rule-making process. In the absence of sanctions encouraging cooperation, it is easier for federal officials to rely on comments of functional specialists who agree with their views.

# 124 • *Modern County Government*

31. Advisory Commission on Intergovernmental Relations, *Annual Report on Operations Under Office of Management and Budget Circular A-85* (Washington: Advisory Commission on Intergovernmental Relations, 1976), p. 8. The report listed other problems such as the fact that agencies rarely respond to major changes in regulations suggested by public interest groups.

32. Ibid., p. 3.

33. There are, of course, many administrative and political reasons why county governments have not been abolished by state legislatures as well as a constitutional reason.

34. The views of Judge Cooley and the theory of state-local relations of Judge Dillon are described well in John H. Baker, *Urban Politics in America* (New York: Charles Scribner's Sons, 1971), pp. 28-33.

35. John F. Dillon, *Commentaries on the Law of Municipal Corporations*, 4th ed. (Boston: Little, Brown and Company, 1890), Vol. I. Sec. 87, p. 145.

36. For a more extensive description of provisions for adoption of county home rule charters see New County, National Association of Counties, *From America's Counties Today* (Washington: National Association of Counties, 1973), pp. 51-59.

37. South Dakota, *Constitution*, Article IX, Section 2.

38. Florida, *Constitution*, Article VIII, Section 1.

39. Clyde F. Snider, *Local Government in Rural America* (New York: Appleton-Century-Crofts, 1957), p. 111.

40. Kenneth VerBurg, *Guide to Michigan County Government* (East Lansing: Michigan State University, 1972), pp. VIII 12-15.

41. Ibid., pp. VIII 15-17. One of the county officials is the treasurer; the second is the chairman of the board of auditors (if there is one) or the chairman of the county finance committee. A mill is one thousandth of one dollar; therefore a fifteen mill tax levy on $1,000 of valuation would bring in $15 in taxes.

42. In some Michigan counties, the voters have approved a fixed millage allocation system in which different procedures are used.

43. Michael S. Vollmer, Herbert Sydney Duncombe and Katherine D. Pell, *Handbook for County Officials in Idaho* (Moscow: Bureau of Public Affairs Research, University of Idaho, 1974), p. 24.

44. For further information about the Lakewood Plan from a county official's point of view, see L.S. Hollinger, "The Lakewood Plan" in National Association of Counties, *Guide to County Organization and Management* (Washington: National Association of Counties, 1968), pp. 49-58.

45. Stanley R. Steenbock, letter to Sydney Duncombe, April 29, 1977.

46. Los Angeles County, California has taken the leadership role in securing greater uniformity of traffic signals, pavement markings, and traffic light synchronization within the county. Stanley R. Steenbock, Director, Information Services Section, Los Angeles County, letter to Sydney Duncombe, December 30, 1976.

47. The county government, three cities, and a school district contribute to the costs of operating a swimming pool in Payette, Idaho. Ada County, Idaho and the City of Boise are among many counties and cities sharing the costs of a city-county law enforcement building. Nancy Weller, *Idaho Interlocal Cooperation Inventory* (Moscow: Bureau of Public Affairs Research, University of Idaho, 1975), pp. 37, 55.

48. Stanley R. Steenbock, letter to Sydney Duncombe, December 30, 1976.

49. Robert G. Smith, "County Service Districts and Special Districts" National Association of Counties, *Guide to County Organization and Management*, p. 83.

50. U.S. Bureau of the Census, *1972 Census of Governments*, Volume 1, *Governmental Organization* (Washington: U.S. Government Printing Office, 1973), pp. 12, 301,302. Many county subordinate taxing areas provide urban-type services such as water, sewage disposal, fire protection, or streets for the unincorporated urban fringe around cities.

51. This district is described more fully in John Bollens, *Special District Governments in the United States* (Los Angeles: University of California Press, 1957), pp. 233-235. More recent information was supplied by Stanley R. Steenbock, letter to Sydney Duncombe, April 29, 1977.

52. An independent city is a form of government found mainly in Virginia which performs both city and county functions.

53. National Association of Counties, *From America's Counties Today*, p. 60.

54. Ibid., p. 61. The mayor-president-council form is used in Baton Rouge-East Baton Rouge Parish. The mayor-council form is used in Nashville-Davidson County (Tennessee); Jacksonville-Duval County (Florida); Indianapolis-Marion County (Indiana); Juneau-Greater Juneau Borough (Alaska); and Columbus-Muscogee County (Georgia).

55. Ibid., p. 59.

56. See National Association of Counties, *Consolidation: Partial or Total* (Washington: National Association of Counties, 1973), pp. 6, 7.

57. Ibid., p. 5.

58. Ibid., p. 7.

59. Montgomery County Government, *Recommended Capital Improvements Program, Montgomery County Government*, Fiscal Years 1977-1982, Vol. 2 (Rockville: Montgomery County, 1976), pp. 5001-5003.

60. Ibid., p. 4001.

61. Information obtained from interviews with the Center personnel June 24, 1976.

62. Information obtained from a letter and material from Suzann E. Dutton, Planning Supervisor, Jacksonville-Duval Manpower Division, dated April 30, 1976.

63. Kay Stouffer, "Garbage No Longer a Local Worry" in *County News*, (Washington), June 23, 1975.

64. Particularly significant are programs established in Minnesota under the Minnesota Community Corrections Act which provides financial incentives for the development of

# 126 • *Modern County Government*

multi-county corrections programs. For a description of this Act see Association of Minnesota Counties, *The Minnesota Community Corrections Act* (St. Paul: Association of Minnesota Counties, 1974).

65. National Service to Regional Councils (now called the National Association of Regional Councils), *Regionalism: A New Dimension in Local Government and Intergovernmental Relations* (Washington: National Service to Regional Councils, 1971), p. 4.

66. Advisory Commission on Intergovernmental Relations, *Regional Decision Making: New Strategies for Substate Districts* (Washington: U.S. Government Printing Office, 1973), pp. 53, 54.

67. Ibid., p. 54.

68. Ibid., p. 71.

69. Ibid., p. 50.

70. Edward Conner, "The Detroit Metropolitan Area Inter-County Plan," National Association of County Officials, *The Urban County Congress* (Washington: National Association of County Officials, 1959), pp. 40-46.

71. Advisory Commission on Intergovernmental Relations, *Regional Decision Making: New Strategies for Substate Districts*, pp. 64-69 contains excellent short case studies of the establishment of these COGs.

72. Ibid., p. 50.

73. Ibid., pp. 63, 64 and Citizens Research Council of Michigan, "Southeast Michigan Regionalism," Kent Mathewson, ed., *The Regionalist Papers* (Detroit: Metropolitan Fund, 1974), pp. 56-65.

74. Victor Jones, "Bay Area Regionalism," Kent Mathewson, ed., *The Regionalist Papers*, pp. 122-145 was the primary source of information used in describing ABAG. See particularly pp. 134-136.

75. Robert McArthur, "The Atlanta Regional Commission," Advisory Commission on Intergovernmental Relations, *Regional Governance: Promise and Performance* (Washington: U.S. Government Printing Office, 1973), pp. 37-42.

76. Advisory Commission on Intergovernmental Relations, *Regional Decision Making: New Strategies for Substate Districts*, pp. 74-77.

77. Ibid., p. 90.

78. Ibid., p. 89.

79. Melvin Mogulouf, quoted in Ibid., p. 88.

80. National Service to Regional Councils, p. 6.

81. Carl Stenberg, "Counties Should be the Regional Answer," *County News* (Washington), June 24, 1974, p. 6.

82. Walter A. Scheiber, "Regional Councils of Governments," National Association of Counties, *Guide to County Organization and Management*, p. 96.

83. Eugene T. Gualco, "Maintains Local Control," *County News* (Washington), June 24, 1974, p. 8.

84. This has been a strength of Councils of Governments since their inception. One of the major accomplishments of the first Council of Governments organization, The Supervisors' Inter-County Committee, was in getting bills needed by area governments passed by the Michigan Legislature.

85. Gerald T. Horton, "Holds State Accountable," *County News* (Washington), June 24, 1974, p. 9.

86. Walter A. Scheiber, p. 96.

87. Ibid., p. 97.

88. Arch Lamb, "Bypasses Local Control," *County News* (Washington) June 24, 1974, p. 8.

89. Interview with Bernard Smith, September 16, 1976 in Boston.

90. Francis B. Francois, "Counties and Intergovernmental Relationships Facing the Third Century," A paper prepared for the Symposium on the Future of County Government, Boston, September, 1976, p. 16.

91. National Association of Counties, *The American County Platform*, p. 5.

92. Ibid., p. 6.

93. Ibid.

# Chapter 6

# County Services

"Counties perform two types of functions—those which the state requires of them and those which it permits but does not require them to perform. Most of them are in the first category. Thus, the mandatory functions nearly everywhere include at least some responsibility for the maintenance of law and order, the administration of justice, the care of prisoners, the relief of paupers, the care of dependent and neglected children, the conduct of elections, the laying out and upkeep of roads, the recording of deeds and certain other documents, the settlement of estates, the advancement of agriculture and the assumption of some phases of public school administration. The extent to which the state assigns these functions to the counties rather than carrying them out directly varies widely from state to state."[1]

The traditional functions of county government, however, are being supplemented by more urban type services which in the past have been considered functions of municipal government. Increases in population density and population migration to the suburbs have resulted in a variety of new service needs—garbage pick-up and disposal, air and water pollution control, emergency medical care, urban renewal, housing, mass transit. The county has assumed these responsibilities as part of its new role."[2]

What services do counties provide? The first quotation, by Paul Wager in 1950, stresses the state-mandated functions of county government. Wager commented that most county functions are required by the state, but he described in later paragraphs, a number of optional functions a county might perform; for example, the establishment of hospitals, the supervision of garbage and sewage disposal, and the provision of parks, recreation, and zoning. The second quotation, written in 1973, stressed the newer, urban functions which have become increasingly important since 1950. The difference in the two statements represents the shift which has occurred in the past quarter century from state-mandated, traditional services to optional, more modern urban services performed by counties.

## DEFINING THE TERMS

Terms, such as "mandatory," "optional," "traditional," and "urban," used to describe county services are the means some writers have used to classify county functions in order to make generalizations about them more meaningful. Other writers have used "basic," "newer," and "modern" to describe differing county services. Before listing the services which counties now provide, it is useful to examine the meaning of these terms and their use in describing county functions.

**Mandatory and Optional Functions.** Mandatory functions are those which counties are required to perform by state law or state constitution. Optional (or permissive) functions are those which county officials are permitted to perform by state law. For example, Idaho Law provides that:

*It is the legal duty of the sheriff to preserve the peace and to "arrest and take before the nearest magistrate for examination all persons who attempt to commit or have committed a public offense."*[3]

*The board of county commissioners may purchase, lease, or obtain by gift*

*or grant property for use for park or recreation purposes.*[4]

The first example is a function that the sheriff is mandated to perform; the second is an action the county commission is permitted to take if it chooses.

The functions which are mandatory in one state may not be mandatory in another. For example, property tax assessment is a mandatory county function in Alabama and Idaho but not in Michigan. The best means of determining whether county functions are mandatory or permissive is a careful reading of the state constitution and laws. However, even this may not be enough. For example, Washington law specifically requires county health departments to provide communicable disease control, although the law is silent on what, if any, maternal and child health programs the county is required to provide.[5] It may be necessary to read state health department regulations to determine if a specific health program is a required function of local health departments. Another complication is the degree to which the administration of a particular function is state-mandated. A state law may simply require that the function be performed and leave the details of administration to county officials; on the other hand, the law may specify detailed procedures and even the design of records and forms.

Table 6-1 shows the state-mandated functions found by a review of the law in Idaho, Alabama, and Michigan.

**Traditional and Modern Services.**
Maddox and Fuquay have noted that
state-mandated functions tend to be
traditional functions while the optional services are the newer functions. They state:

*"Of the many functions per-
formed by the county some are
required by state law, while others
are optional; some are traditional,
while others are new. Considered
generally, those required by state
law are the traditional functions,
while optional activities are the
newer ones. In the former category
belong such duties as law enforcement, administration of justice,
public welfare, construction and
maintenance of roads and highways,
assistance to agriculture, and
responsibility for phases of public
education, a particularly important
function in certain parts of the country."*[6]

To be more precise in using the
terms "traditional" and "modern"

county services, the writer has
adopted a somewhat arbitrary definition. A traditional county service
is one which was widely performed
by county government prior to the
mid-1920s—fifty years ago. The
mid-1920s was selected because it
came a decade before the sweeping
changes in county functions brought
about by the New Deal social
programs. Several excellent books
and articles were written during the
1920s which provide information on
county services of the period and the
generally slow rate of change in
them.[7]

Establishing a benchmark date
does not eliminate all problems of
differentiating traditional from
newer services. Some county functions, such as libraries, parks, and
hospital administration, pre-date
1920 but were just coming into extensive use by mid-decade. A re-
searcher must use whatever
historical evidence is available to
determine whether most counties

Table 6-1

STATE-MANDATED FUNCTIONS OF COUNTY GOVERNMENT
IN IDAHO, ALABAMA, AND MICHIGAN
FUNCTIONS FOUND MANDATORY IN TWO OR MORE OF THE STATES

| Function | Idaho | Alabama | Michigan |
|---|---|---|---|
| Property tax assessment | x | x | |
| Property tax collection | x | x | |
| Law enforcement - Patrol | x | x | x |
| County courts | | x | x |
| Clerical assistance to the court | x | x | x |
| Criminal prosecution | x | x | x |
| Public health | | x | x |
| Election administration | x | x | x |
| Recording of deed | x | x | x |

SOURCE: *Idaho Code, Alabama Code,* and *Michigan Compiled Law Annotated.* This table
lists only functions found to be mandatory in at least two of the three states. It is important
to note that some counties may be performing a function in a state even though it is not mandatory they do so.

did or did not provide a specific service in the mid-1920s.[8] Using the best information available, the writer has compiled the following list of traditional county functions:

- *property tax assessment and collection;*

- *recording of deeds and other legal instruments;*

- *election administration;*

- *judicial administration (this includes county courts, probate courts, other county-based courts, and the work of the county court clerk);*

- *criminal prosecution;*

- *law enforcement (including the work of the sheriff and coroner);*

- *maintenance of a county jail;*

- *certain types of public school administration;*

- *construction and maintenance of rural roads and bridges;*

- *certain types of welfare and social services such as the provision of what used to be called poor relief;*

- *certain health functions such as vital statistics and communicable disease control; and,*

- *certain agricultural functions such as cooperative extension services and provision of county fairs.*

It is important to note that the list of traditional services is similar, with some exceptions, to the list of state-mandated services in Table 6-1.

**Urban Services.** The term "urban" services has been used to identify those which city governments have traditionally provided and which county governments are now supplying. Among the urban services commonly listed are: parking, public housing, air and water pollution control, enforcement of building and housing codes, water supply, sewage disposal, mass transit, the provision of metropolitan airports and park systems, and the operation of convention centers, stadiums, and museums.[9]

Why have counties become the provider of services commonly considered municipal services? The two most common reasons are the financial squeeze many cities have felt and, in many densely populated unincorporated areas, the lack of any other government unit capable of providing these services. These two reasons are described more fully by the writer in his 1966 book which dramatized the "urban cycle" in this oversimplified fashion:

> *"Through no fault of city officials, many cities are becoming victims of what might be termed 'the urban cycle.' In the first stage of the urban cycle in the 1800's, most of these cities were able to keep expanding through annexation so that city limits nearly kept pace with the limits of the urbanized areas. In the second stage in the 1900's, annexations slowed, and satellite suburban cities and villages grew around the central city.*
>
> *As the 1900's progressed, more and more of the upper and middle income business and professional men moved outside the central city to the suburbs. These new suburbanites*

tended to resist annexation for many reasons such as their fear of higher taxes or loss of their status as suburbanites. The cities lost, not only many able leaders, but also an important tax base. The poorer people who remained in the cities tended to require higher cost health, welfare, and other services. The suburbanites continued to work in the cities and to utilize city services usually without paying any city taxes. Compounding the financial problems of the cities were restrictive state tax and debt limits.

After World War II, there was an increased movement of both shopping centers and industry to suburban communities. The deterioration of downtown business districts, traffic congestion, and the need for airport runway expansion, new parks, and urban renewal added to city problems at a time of financial strain.

The third stage of the urban cycle has begun. It begins usually in a single functional area. The city airport is losing money and needs to expand its runways to provide jet service. It is physically outside the city limits, and it receives proportionately greater use from suburban businessmen (who pay no city taxes) than from city dwellers. When the financial pinch is greatest, city officials may request the county to take over operation of the airport. This is more equitable for the city dweller since he now pays only part of the taxes needed to extend the airport runways for jet service.

The same cycle may be repeated in the park program. As the city becomes densely populated, it tends to purchase land for larger parks outside the city limits where large blocks of land are much less costly. These parks are closer to suburban dwellers who tend to make extensive use of them without paying any fees or city taxes. When the city needs to expand its park system, city dwellers may be unwilling to pay the cost of more parks for use by suburbanites. The stage is set for city officials to turn again to the county or some metropolitan authority to take over the larger city parks and run an area-wide park system.

At the same time as counties (and other units of government such as metropolitan districts) are assuming area-wide functions from cities, the suburbanites are having their governmental problems. They moved to suburban areas to escape city living and taxes, but they frequently find population density rising in their areas to the point where they must have urban water, sewer and other services. Often the suburbanite lives in an unincorporated area, and he may first try a piecemeal solution to his problem through the use of single-purpose special districts. This may provide a partial solution to his problems at a relatively high cost.

Suburban dwellers may also form small incorporated communities and try to provide urban services in this manner. In many areas, suburbanites are finding that small special districts and satellite cities are not large enough to offer the economies of mass purchasing, a professional staff, and effective use of expensive equipment. These suburbanites may ask counties to perform urban functions for them.

Thus counties have been requested to undertake 'urban' functions by both city officials and suburbanites . . .'[10]

## THE MOST RECENT SURVEY OF COUNTY SERVICES

In November, 1975, the Joint Data Center of the National Association of Counties and the International City Management Association mailed a questionnaire to the nation's counties requesting information on the services they provided. The cover letter stated: "We are interested in knowing which services are available to residents of your county for which your county has full or partial responsibility, regardless of how the services are provided."[11]

By April, 1976, 1,153 questionnaires had been returned, and computer listings and tabulations were prepared from the questionnaires for use in the *1976 County Year Book,* and in this book. Table 6-2 shows that there are nineteen services which more than 80% of all the

## 134 • Modern County Government

reporting counties provide. Many of these are called "basic" services by Susan W. Torrence in her study of county government.[12]

**Area of Service Within the County.** One of the myths of county government is that it serves just the residents of the rural or unincorporated areas of the county. Table 6-3, which lists the 102 county services in functional groups, shows that a high proportion of county services are provided on a county-wide basis rather than just to residents of unincorporated areas.[13] The services most likely to be provided by the county to unincorporated areas include: police patrol, investigation, fire protection, road construction and maintenance, planning, zoning, subdivision control, and building code enforcement. The "other" column includes services provided by counties in special service districts of the county, by multi-county agencies, and in other ways.

**Population.** Table 6-4 has divided counties into ten population categor-

ies and calculated the percent of counties in each group providing the 102 county services. The data in Table 6-4 indicates that for many general functions (such as manpower), the percent of counties responsible for the function is greatest among counties of 100,000 or more people. For a few functions (such as property tax assessment and collection), counties of less than 10,000 people are the most likely to provide this service.[14]

The tendency for the percent of counties undertaking a particular function to increase with the population group of the county is shown on Graph 1. This trend is particularly significant with urban functions and least evident with the most traditional county services. The variation in percents between group A (over one million) and group B (500,000-999,999) is not particularly significant because of the small number of counties in the two groups.

**Metropolitan Status, Region, and Form of Administration.** Using statistics from the Joint Data Cen-

Table 6-2

### SERVICES MOST FREQUENTLY PROVIDED BY COUNTIES IN 1975

| Service | Percent of Counties Providing | Service | Percent of Counties Providing |
|---|---|---|---|
| Land Records | 97.2% | General jurisdiction courts | 89.2 |
| Election administration | 96.8 | Detention Facilities | 89.1 |
| Property tax collection | 95.6 | Criminal prosecution | 88.2 |
| Patrol (law enforcement) | 93.1 | Road maintenance | 87.0 |
| Property tax assessment | 92.5 | Road construction | 84.8 |
| Criminal records | 91.1 | Vital statistics | 84.7 |
| ·Detective investigation | 90.5 | Limited jurisdiction courts | 83.2 |
| Disaster preparedness | 90.3 | Forensic investigation | 82.3 |
| | | Juvenile/family court | 81.4 |

SOURCE: Carolyn B. Lawrence and John M. DeGrove, "County Government Services" in *The County Year Book, 1976* (Washington: National Association of Counties and International City Management Association, 1976), pp. 92, 94.

ter of the National Association of Counties and International City Management Association, the author related the number of services provided by counties to:[15]

- *whether or not the county is located in a metropolitan area;*

- *the region of the nation in which the county is located; and,*

- *the form of government of the county.*

As Table 6-5 shows, counties located in metropolitan areas provide 52% of the 102 services while non-metropolitan counties provide 44%. Non-metropolitan counties are slightly more likely to provide traditional services than metropolitan counties, but metropolitan counties are almost twice as likely to provide the more urban services than are non-metropolitan counties.

There are some variations by region of the nation in the numbers of county services. Western counties provide 50% of the 102 services, southern counties 47%, north-central counties 44% and northeastern counties 43%. The most

Table 6-3

**PERCENT OF RESPONDING COUNTIES HAVING RESPONSIBILITY FOR VARIOUS SERVICES**

| | County Responsibility | County-wide | Unincorp. Areas Only | Incorp. Areas Only | Other |
|---|---|---|---|---|---|
| **Finance** | | | | | |
| Property tax assessment | 92.5 | 88.1 | 2.0 | .4 | 2.0 |
| Property tax collection | 95.6 | 88.2 | 4.5 | .4 | 2.5 |
| **Police protection/corrections** | | | | | |
| Patrol | 93.1 | 65.2 | 24.7 | 1.7 | 1.5 |
| Detective investigation | 90.5 | 68.7 | 18.7 | .9 | 2.2 |
| Forensic investigation | 82.3 | 67.3 | 11.4 | .6 | 3.0 |
| Criminal records | 91.1 | 79.5 | 8.7 | .6 | 2.3 |
| Central emergency number | 48.0 | 41.3 | 2.5 | 1.0 | 3.2 |
| Detention facilities | 89.1 | 83.0 | 2.7 | .8 | 2.6 |
| Work release program | 43.9 | 39.9 | 1.6 | .2 | 2.2 |
| Adult probation program | 57.0 | 52.3 | 1.2 | .2 | 3.3 |
| Juvenile probation program | 75.8 | 70.8 | 1.2 | .3 | 3.5 |
| **Judicial** | | | | | |
| General jurisdiction courts | 89.2 | 84.4 | 1.1 | .2 | 3.5 |
| Limited jurisdiction courts | 83.2 | 74.6 | 3.6 | 2.1 | 2.9 |
| Juvenile/family court | 81.4 | 77.8 | .4 | .2 | 3.0 |
| **Legal services and prosecution** | | | | | |
| Criminal prosecution | 88.2 | 84.0 | 1.3 | .1 | 2.8 |
| Legal/civil services | 52.8 | 47.5 | 1.7 | .1 | 3.5 |
| Indigent defense | 76.3 | 71.8 | .7 | .0 | 3.8 |
| **Other public safety** | | | | | |
| Fire protection | 54.5 | 31.1 | 13.3 | 2.0 | 8.1 |
| Emergency medical services | 66.0 | 58.3 | 2.3 | .8 | 4.6 |
| Disaster preparedness | 90.3 | 85.0 | 2.6 | .3 | 2.4 |

| | County Responsibility | County-wide | Unincorp. Areas Only | Incorp. Areas Only | Other |
|---|---|---|---|---|---|
| **Public health** | | | | | |
| Home health | 76.8 | 73.1 | 1.2 | .2 | 2.3 |
| Maternal and child health | 74.0 | 70.9 | .9 | .2 | 2.0 |
| Communicable disease control | 79.0 | 75.3 | 1.3 | .1 | 2.3 |
| Dental health | 38.8 | 35.5 | .4 | .1 | 2.8 |
| Mental health facilities | 49.7 | 45.2 | .0 | .2 | 4.3 |
| Mental health outpatients | 79.3 | 73.7 | .6 | .1 | 4.9 |
| Mental retardation facilities | 38.4 | 34.0 | .0 | .2 | 4.2 |
| Training of mentally retarded | 56.8 | 51.9 | .1 | .2 | 4.6 |
| Alcoholism/drug programs | 67.3 | 62.5 | .5 | .1 | 4.2 |
| Animal control | 58.1 | 48.7 | 7.1 | 2.2 | 0.1 |
| Sanitation inspection | 60.8 | 57.0 | 1.5 | .2 | 2.1 |
| Hospital care | 46.9 | 44.0 | .3 | .2 | 2.4 |
| Outpatient medical services | 43.1 | 40.4 | .5 | .1 | 2.1 |
| Homes for the aged | 42.9 | 40.1 | .2 | .3 | 2.3 |
| **Social services** | | | | | |
| Income maintenance | 45.6 | 43.8 | .3 | .0 | 1.5 |
| Emergency financial assistance | 64.3 | 61.5 | .2 | .1 | 2.5 |
| Food stamps | 72.9 | 6.0 | .4 | .0 | 3.5 |
| Family social services | 64.7 | 60.8 | .3 | .1 | 3.5 |
| Individual social services | 55.8 | 53.5 | .2 | .0 | 2.1 |
| Services to the aging | 67.4 | 61.9 | 1.1 | .5 | 3.9 |
| Child welfare services | 77.2 | 73.8 | .3 | .2 | 2.9 |
| Day care services | 42.9 | 39.1 | .6 | .3 | 2.9 |
| Human resources planning | 46.2 | 43.2 | .5 | .0 | 2.5 |
| **Manpower** | | | | | |
| Job training | 53.2 | 48.6 | .9 | .2 | 3.5 |
| Work experience programs | 59.7 | 54.5 | 1.5 | .3 | 3.4 |
| Public service employment | 76.2 | 69.5 | 3.3 | .2 | 3.2 |
| **Transportation** | | | | | |
| Road maintenance | 87.0 | 59.2 | 24.0 | 1.2 | 2.6 |
| Road construction | 84.8 | 57.4 | 24.0 | 1.3 | 2.1 |
| Public parking facilities | 25.1 | 16.2 | 4.2 | 2.2 | 2.5 |
| Mass Transit | 13.3 | 9.6 | 1.1 | .3 | 2.3 |
| Airports | 42.4 | 36.6 | 2.2 | 1.1 | 2.5 |
| Highway safety | 40.9 | 32.6 | 5.9 | .2 | 2.2 |
| Bikeways | 18.7 | 11.5 | 5.6 | .2 | 1.4 |
| **Public utility** | | | | | |
| Water supply | 22.2 | 10.8 | 4.2 | 2.0 | 5.2 |
| Power supply | 6.4 | 4.8 | .2 | .5 | .9 |
| Sewage treatment | 26.3 | 12.3 | 5.0 | 3.0 | 6.0 |
| **Natural Resources** | | | | | |
| Flood/drainage control | 52.4 | 39.1 | 8.9 | .4 | 4.0 |
| Irrigation | 10.5 | 7.2 | 1.0 | .1 | 2.2 |
| Soil conservation | 63.0 | 52.0 | 5.7 | .0 | 5.3 |
| Coastal zoning | 10.4 | 7.3 | 2.2 | .0 | 0.9 |
| Energy conservation | 22.7 | 19.9 | 1.3 | .0 | 1.5 |
| Energy management | 15.1 | 12.3 | 1.8 | .2 | 0.8 |
| Solid waste collection | 49.0 | 35.0 | 10.4 | 2.4 | 1.2 |
| Solid waste disposal | 70.5 | 58.4 | 9.0 | 1.3 | 1.8 |
| Water pollution control | 32.9 | 27.9 | 2.4 | .9 | 1.7 |
| Air pollution control | 23.8 | 20.7 | 1.5 | .2 | 1.4 |
| Noise control | 11.0 | 8.7 | 1.3 | .4 | 0.6 |

|  | County Responsi-bility | County-wide | Unincorp. Areas Only | Incorp. Areas Only | Other |
|---|---|---|---|---|---|
| **Land use** | | | | | |
| Comprehensive land use planning | 66.9 | 48.0 | 16.8 | .5 | 1.6 |
| Zoning | 63.2 | 38.2 | 21.4 | 1.8 | 1.8 |
| Growth management | 46.7 | 29.7 | 15.2 | .6 | 1.2 |
| Open space control | 33.9 | 19.5 | 13.2 | .2 | 1.0 |
| Subdivision control | 68.0 | 41.0 | 24.1 | 1.2 | 1.7 |
| **Community development/housing** | | | | | |
| Building code enforcement | 48.7 | 25.8 | 19.0 | 2.8 | 1.1 |
| Housing code enforcement | 32.7 | 16.4 | 12.8 | 2.6 | 0.9 |
| Conventional public housing | 18.1 | 11.2 | 3.5 | 2.5 | 0.9 |
| Leased public housing | 13.9 | 8.9 | 2.4 | 2.0 | 0.6 |
| Rural housing programs | 16.1 | 11.7 | 2.8 | .6 | 1.0 |
| Industrial development | 43.6 | 34.8 | 6.5 | 1.7 | 0.6 |
| **Parks** | | | | | |
| Park acquisition | 52.2 | 35.2 | 14.4 | 1.4 | 1.2 |
| Park development | 53.7 | 35.6 | 14.5 | 1.3 | 2.3 |
| Park maintenance | 54.2 | 35.5 | 14.6 | 1.6 | 2.5 |
| Neighborhood parks | 29.4 | 17.7 | 7.7 | 1.8 | 2.2 |
| County parks | 56.6 | 43.8 | 10.4 | .5 | 1.9 |
| **Culture and recreation** | | | | | |
| Recreational services | 45.3 | 36.6 | 4.9 | 1.6 | 2.2 |
| Fairgrounds | 49.1 | 43.9 | 1.8 | .6 | 2.8 |
| Stadiums | 8.9 | 7.3 | .6 | .1 | 0.9 |
| Convention centers | 6.0 | 5.3 | .2 | .0 | 0.5 |
| Marinas | 5.7 | 4.6 | .8 | .1 | 0.2 |
| Swimming pools | 15.8 | 12.2 | 1.6 | 1.3 | 0.7 |
| Museums | 24.2 | 22.4 | .6 | .3 | 0.9 |
| Performing arts | 8.7 | 7.4 | .5 | .2 | 0.6 |
| **Education** | | | | | |
| Pre-school | 18.5 | 16.8 | .2 | .4 | 1.1 |
| Elementary and secondary | 23.9 | 21.4 | .8 | .4 | 1.3 |
| Community college | 11.6 | 10.4 | .0 | .1 | 1.1 |
| Vocational technical | 24.9 | 22.4 | .4 | .2 | 1.9 |
| **Miscellaneous** | | | | | |
| Land records | 97.2 | 93.5 | .4 | .3 | 3.0 |
| Vital statistics | 84.7 | 80.5 | .7 | .2 | 3.3 |
| Elections | 96.8 | 92.6 | .8 | .5 | 2.9 |
| Libraries | 76.4 | 68.2 | 2.8 | 1.3 | 4.1 |
| Public information services | 32.6 | 31.0 | .6 | .0 | 1.0 |
| Consumer protection services | 15.2 | 14.5 | .3 | .1 | 0.3 |
| Cable television | 13.4 | 8.4 | 3.8 | .4 | 0.8 |

SOURCE: Tabulation runs provided in 1976 by the Joint Data Center of the National Association of Counties and International City Management Association. The data shows the percent of counties responding to the questions about particular services. The left hand column shows the percent of the responding counties having responsibility for each function or service. The four right hand columns show the percent of the responding counties which provide the service either county-wide or within some area of the county. The sum of the four right hand columns adds to the column on the left.

significant difference is in the performance of traditional functions. Fewer northeastern counties provide traditional services since towns and townships are responsible for some of these.

Counties with a county administrator (executive, manager, or administrative officer) tend to provide more services than counties without a county administrator. Counties with a county administra-

Table 6-4
PERCENT OF COUNTIES HAVING RESPONSIBILITY FOR COUNTY FUNCTIONS
BY POPULATION GROUP

|  | A | B | C | D | E | F | G | H | I | J |
|---|---|---|---|---|---|---|---|---|---|---|
| All 102 county functions | 87 | 66 | 71 | 67 | 60 | 59 | 57 | 56 | 55 | 54 |
| Fifteen traditional county functions | 94 | 84 | 88 | 84 | 88 | 88 | 88 | 89 | 87 | 87 |
| Twenty urban functions | 67 | 41 | 42 | 33 | 23 | 20 | 16 | 14 | 10 | 8 |
| Functional groups | | | | | | | | | | |
| Property tax assessment and collection | 85 | 74 | 87 | 89 | 89 | 94 | 95 | 98 | 99 | 98 |
| Police protection/ corrections | 89 | 88 | 88 | 82 | 75 | 77 | 71 | 68 | 71 | 66 |
| Judicial | 100 | 88 | 85 | 86 | 80 | 90 | 85 | 85 | 78 | 72 |
| Legal services and prosecution | 94 | 86 | 83 | 80 | 70 | 67 | 71 | 69 | 75 | 72 |
| Other public safety | 76 | 61 | 68 | 65 | 65 | 70 | 72 | 74 | 72 | 79 |
| Public health | 86 | 66 | 70 | 69 | 68 | 59 | 56 | 49 | 45 | 39 |
| Social services | 90 | 69 | 69 | 69 | 68 | 59 | 59 | 51 | 51 | 32 |
| Manpower | 100 | 88 | 86 | 92 | 75 | 60 | 58 | 45 | 43 | 45 |
| Transportation | 85 | 61 | 55 | 55 | 41 | 45 | 41 | 40 | 39 | 37 |
| Public utilities | 40 | 37 | 37 | 25 | 18 | 18 | 14 | 17 | 11 | 11 |
| Natural resources | 65 | 36 | 45 | 44 | 34 | 35 | 29 | 27 | 26 | 24 |
| Land use | 71 | 65 | 71 | 74 | 59 | 56 | 46 | 38 | 44 | 43 |
| Community development/ housing | 59 | 41 | 43 | 38 | 32 | 31 | 26 | 23 | 15 | 12 |
| Parks | 86 | 73 | 82 | 74 | 56 | 51 | 44 | 36 | 23 | 23 |
| Culture and recreation | 57 | 35 | 31 | 25 | 19 | 19 | 19 | 16 | 19 | 18 |
| Education | 18 | 24 | 18 | 21 | 19 | 24 | 21 | 17 | 9 | 11 |
| Miscellaneous | 87 | 66 | 71 | 67 | 60 | 59 | 57 | 56 | 55 | 54 |

SOURCE: Data provided in 1976 by the Joint Data Center of the National Association of Counties and International City Management Association. The population classes used in the study are designated as follows:

A - One million or more people     F - 25,000 - 49,999
B - 500,000 - 999,999     G - 10,000 - 24,999
C - 250,000 - 499,999     H - 5,000 - 9,999
D - 100,000 - 249,999     I - 2,500 - 4,999
E - 50,000 - 99,999     J - under 2,500

The 15 traditional functions were selected from a number of functional groups. They are: property tax assessment, property tax collection, land records, (i.e. recording of deeds, etc.), elections, general jurisdiction courts, limited jurisdiction courts, criminal prosecution, police patrol, criminal records, jail or detention facilities, road construction, road maintenance, vital statistics, communicable disease control, and fairgrounds. The urban functions were also distributed to include a number of functional groups and include: parking, mass transit, airports, bikeways, water supply, sewage disposal, water pollution control, air pollution control, noise pollution control, building codes, housing codes, conventional public housing, leased public housing, neighborhood parks, stadiums, convention centers, marinas, performing arts, consumer protection, and cable television.

tor tend to be the more populous ones. It is also possible that county administrators are more likely to be employed in counties in which coordination of many county services is necessary. County boards may be more likely to initiate new services when they have a county administrator to take responsibility for the services.

## CASE STUDIES OF TRADITIONAL AND MODERN COUNTY SERVICES

County services range from traditional, state-mandated functions which counties have been furnishing for more than two centuries to newer types of services which counties have established within the past decade in response to the needs of their citizens. The following three case studies provide illustrations of one of the most traditional county functions, a service generally furnished by counties only in this century, and one of the newest county responsibilities.

**Property Tax Assessment and Collection.** County governments have been assessing and collecting property taxes for more than two centuries although some of the techniques now used (such as data processing) are modern. The property tax system involves all units of local government (not just the county). Tax rates may be set by action of city, village, town, school district, and other local governing boards, and these other units depend on revenue collected by county officials from the property tax. County gov-

ernments are involved in the property tax system through:

*Assessing property.* County governments assessed property in 92% of the counties in a national sample, and in 88% of the reporting counties they assessed property throughout the entire county.

*Levying taxes for county functions.* Cities, towns, school districts, and other units of local government levy taxes for their own functions.

*Collecting property taxes for all units of local government.* As Table 6-3 shows, county governments collected property taxes in 95.6% of the reporting counties.

There are three types of property which are taxed. Most property taxes are levied on real property—i.e. land, buildings, and other permanent structures. Taxes are also levied on personal property (equipment, store inventories, and other types of property not fastened to the earth or the floor of a building; intangible property—stocks, bonds, etc.—may also be classified as personal property); and on utility operating property (railroad tracks, freight cars, pipe lines, electric generating plants, etc.).

The real property tax assessment and collection process can be pictured as a cycle in which maintenance of an accurate property file is a first step, and the final steps include collection of taxes, distribution of funds to other local governments, and placement of up-dated information in the property file. In more than 90% of all reporting counties, the major flow of work goes through county offices, as shown by the circle in Chart 6-1. Other units of local government are involved mainly in setting tax rates and receiving tax

**Graph 6-1**
**PERCENT OF COUNTIES PROVIDING VARIOUS FUNCTIONS**

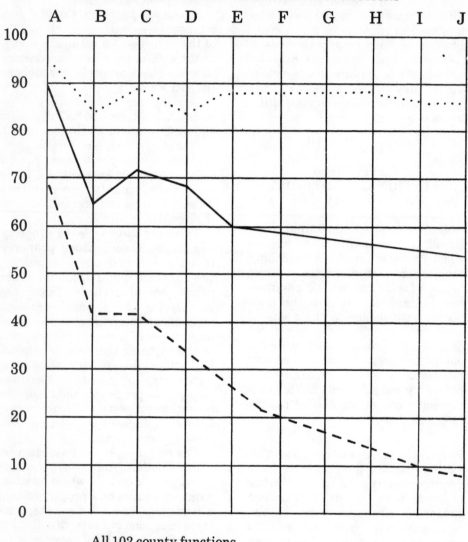

_____ All 102 county functions
............ Fifteen traditional county functions
------------ Twenty urban functions

SOURCE: Tabulations provided in 1976 by the Joint Data Center of the National Association of Counties and International City Management Association. The population classes are those shown on Table 6-4 and vary from Class A (one million or more people) to Class J (under 2,500 people). The twenty urban and fifteen traditional county functions were selected by the author.

funds distributed by county officials. Taxpayers, shown in the center of Chart 6-1, are also involved at several points in the process.

The procedure for assessing and collecting real property taxes differs from state to state but generally includes the following steps, illustrated in chart 6-1.[16]

1.  The county assessor keeps an accurate, up-to-date listing of all real property in the county with information on the location of the property, acreage, ownership, and types of buildings. The assessor

Table 6-5

## PERCENT OF COUNTIES HAVING RESPONSIBILITY FOR COUNTY FUNCTIONS BY METROPOLITAN STATUS, REGION OF THE NATION, AND FORM OF COUNTY GOVERNMENT

| | Region of the Nation | | | | Metropolitan Status | | Form of Government | |
|---|---|---|---|---|---|---|---|---|
| | North-East | North-Central | South | West | Metro. Counties | Non-Metro. | With Admin. | Without Admin. |
| All 102 county functions | 43 | 44 | 47 | 50 | 52 | 44 | 55 | 43 |
| Fifteen traditional county functions | 69 | 92 | 84 | 90 | 86 | 87 | 83 | 88 |
| Twenty modern, urban functions | 17 | 14 | 22 | 30 | 31 | 17 | 35 | 16 |
| Functional groups | | | | | | | | |
| Property tax assessment and collection | 60 | 95 | 97 | 97 | 90 | 95 | 95 | 91 |
| Police protection and corrections | 83 | 72 | 72 | 76 | 82 | 72 | 74 | 77 |
| Judicial | 88 | 92 | 81 | 78 | 87 | 84 | 86 | 78 |
| Legal services and prosecution | 78 | 82 | 62 | 75 | 76 | 71 | 74 | 66 |
| Other public safety | 45 | 58 | 82 | 77 | 66 | 72 | 68 | 77 |
| Public health | 50 | 56 | 60 | 60 | 66 | 54 | 53 | 67 |
| Social services | 64 | 61 | 59 | 56 | 67 | 57 | 54 | 74 |
| Manpower | 80 | 52 | 68 | 65 | 80 | 57 | 58 | 78 |
| Transportation | 39 | 45 | 41 | 53 | 51 | 42 | 42 | 50 |
| Public utilities | 14 | 12 | 25 | 18 | 27 | 15 | 13 | 33 |
| Natural resources | 28 | 27 | 36 | 38 | 39 | 31 | 29 | 45 |
| Land use | 42 | 52 | 47 | 83 | 67 | 51 | 49 | 76 |
| Community development/ housing | 16 | 21 | 37 | 37 | 36 | 26 | 23 | 44 |
| Parks | 43 | 44 | 50 | 59 | 67 | 43 | 42 | 70 |
| Culture and recreation | 20 | 16 | 20 | 27 | 25 | 19 | 17 | 29 |
| Education | 16 | 8 | 35 | 8 | 20 | 20 | 15 | 32 |
| Miscellaneous | 43 | 44 | 47 | 50 | 52 | 44 | 43 | 55 |

SOURCE: Tabulations provided in 1976 by the Joint Data Center of the National Association of Counties and International City Management Association. The Northeast includes states north and east of Pennsylvania and New Jersey; the South extends from Maryland through Texas; the North-Central states range from Ohio to the Dakotas and Kansas; and the West includes all states west of the Dakotas, Kansas, and Texas. Metropolitan counties are those in metropolitan areas. Counties with administrators are those with council-administrator and council-elected executive forms of government.

Chart 6-1

Simplified Diagram of the Real Property Tax System

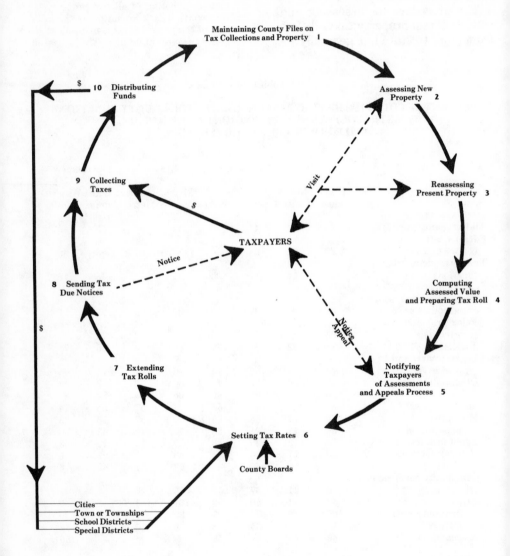

NOTE: The numbers listed on the diagram refer to the steps in the property tax process described in the next paragraph.

keeps up with changes in ownership of property by following the recording of deeds.

2. When a new building or structure is built or remodeled, the county assessor's office will usually learn of it because the owner is required to file an application for a building permit. The assessor will visit the location and record the characteristics of the building such as the number of square feet of floor space, number of rooms, whether the basement is finished, and type of inside walls. The assessor will then apply numeric factors (generally developed by the State Tax Commission) to compute the market value of the building.

3. Periodically both land and buildings are reassessed. The county assessor or a deputy will again visit the home, farm, or business and use the form to recompute the true value. In some cases, aerial photographs, soil conservation records, and farm production records have been used to reassess farm land.

4. The assessed value of real property is computed in the county assessor's office by multiplying the true or market value by a percent set by the county or state. The assessment percents vary from under 10% to nearly 100%. After making this computation, a listing of property tax owners and assessments (often called a real property tax roll) is prepared.

5. The taxpayer is then notified of his property tax assessment and has an opportunity to appeal, first to the assessor, then to the county governing board, and finally to the courts.

6. County tax rates are set by the county governing body. The tax rates of cities, towns, school districts, and other local governmental units are set by their governing boards, with notification sent to the county.

7. County personnel go through a process (often called extending the tax roll) in which they multiply the assessed valuation of the property of each taxpayer by the property tax rates to compute the tax due each unit of local government. This

extension is generally done by machine accounting or data processing equipment which produces, at the same time, a notice to be sent to the taxpayer.

8. A notice of tax due is then sent, and payment can generally be made in installments or deducted by the bank holding the taxpayer's mortgage.

9. The taxpayer or his bank makes payment. If property tax payments are delinquent, penalties may be assessed and, as a last resort, the county may take and sell the property to recover the taxes.

10. Funds received from the property tax are distributed to the county, cities, towns, school districts, and other local government units levying these taxes. In some states (such as Pennsylvania) the property owner makes payment directly to the city, town, or school district.

The assessment and collection of taxes on other types of property follow different patterns. Personal property taxes for mobile homes and travel trailers are usually collected by the assessor when they are licensed for the year. Machinery, tools, and fixtures are often listed by the owners of businesses and periodically checked by the assessor. Valuation of utility property often requires specialized skills, and frequently the State Tax Commission will either directly assess this property or provide technical assistance to the county assessor. Certain types of personal property (such as home furnishings) and intangible property (such as stocks and bonds) are often exempt from taxation.

There are significant economies of scale in assessing and collecting property taxes. Counties such as Lane County (Oregon) and Ventura County (California) have used computers effectively in maintaining property files and computing assessments.[17] The process of extending tax rolls and sending assessment notifications and tax notices can be most efficiently administered by machine or data processing methods, and smaller townships and cities which attempt this process frequently must rely on time-consuming typing and hand computation methods. County administration also tends to stimulate a more uniform assessment on a county-wide basis. Small city, village, and town assessors are frequently the most poorly trained and most likely to apply uneven assessment methods. Cities and townships still engage in assessment and collection of property taxes in some areas of the nation, but the trend is toward county administration.

**Libraries.** Libraries are neither a traditional county function nor a very recent one. County libraries were first authorized by state law in Indiana in 1816, but only one state (California) had more than a dozen county libraries by 1923.[18] Most county libraries have been established since the end of World War II.

There are nearly twenty-six thousand libraries in the United States, according to the 1974-75 American Library Directory.[19] Libraries are operated by counties, cities, towns, school districts, library districts, regional library systems, colleges and universities, federal and state agencies, hospitals, corporations, religious and other organizations. Although less than a quarter of all libraries are county libraries, twelve of the thirty-six largest library systems are, and five are city-county systems.[20] County

governments have the following important roles in furnishing library services.[21]

*Providing library service to the entire county.* Fairfax County (Virginia), for example, furnishes library service to a county with a 1970 population of 455,021 through a system of fourteen branch libraries.

*Supplying library service to part of the county.* The Cuyahoga County (Ohio) library system serves more than 600,000 county residents in areas not served by city library systems. The county system has twenty-seven branch libraries.

*Jointly operating city-county library systems.* The public library of Cincinnati and Hamilton County is a joint city-county library system as are library systems in many consolidated city-county governments such as Indianapolis and Marion County (Indiana).

*Operating in association with a larger regional system.* Hancock County (Kentucky) (1970 population 7,090) has one librarian, a bookmobile, and about 18,000 books. Its library gains additional resources by associating with the Green River Regional Library system which includes Davies, Henderson, Ohio, and Union Counties.

*Furnishing a law library for judges, court personnel, and attorneys in the county.* Baltimore County (Maryland), for example, has a law library associated with the Circuit Court.

Counties have often established library systems because existing small libraries were inadequate. Chesterfield County (Virginia) had a system of small, inadequate subscription libraries located in the cities and villages of the county in the 1960's.[22] The impetus for change came from women's clubs, and the result was the formation of a Committee for Library Action and the establishment by the County Board of Supervisors of a county-wide library system in 1965. In Montgomery County (Maryland), a county-wide library system was created after a Library Advisory Committee found in 1949 that existing independent libraries were inadequate to meet county needs.[23] The Montgomery County Library began operating in 1951 with seven formerly independent libraries and has expanded to seventeen branch libraries. One of the advantages of a county-wide library system with a number of branches is that it can provide a larger number of volumes and more specialized services.

Libraries can provide valuable assistance for programs aiding the blind, deaf, senior citizens, and the unemployed. Among the county library systems which have provided innovative specialized services for these residents are:[24]

- *The Montgomery County (Maryland) Library is one of many county libraries which provide Braille books, talking books, large print books, and tapes for the blind.*

- *The San Bernardino County (California) Library has involved its senior citizens in library programs as volunteers and offers direct mailing of books, pictures, and recorded materials to the homebound.*

- *The Prince George's County (Maryland) Library system has installed a teletype machine for direct communication with a number of deaf people in the county who rent or own similar machines. Deaf people use their teletype to get library information or order books.*

- *The Forsyth County (North Carolina) Library system has a program designed particularly to aid the unemployed, the economically disadvantaged, and adults 55 years of age and older. The Library has a central information referral and counseling center which maintains a directory of course offerings. It also provides counseling service for those who wish to find a particular course that will help them develop a new job or gain new types of knowledge.*

**Consumer Protection.** Consumer protection is one of the newest county services. It has developed as the consumer rights movement has gained national prominence in the past decade. In a 1971 message to Congress proposing a "Buyer's Bill of Rights," President Nixon stated:

*". . . In today's marketplace, however, the consumer often finds himself confronted with what seems an impenetrable complexity in many of our consumer goods, in the advertising claims that surround them, the merchandising methods that purvey them and the means available to conceal their quality. The result is a degree of confusion that often confounds the unwary, and too easily can be made to favor the unscrupulous."[25]

Federal agencies are involved in preventing misleading advertising and in setting standards for food labeling, but do not investigate individual consumer complaints. Many states provide consumer protection (sometimes through the Attorney General's Office). However, these services are not located close enough to the individual consumer to effectively answer all complaints. Local government or some quasi-public agency, such as a Better Business Bureau or Legal Aid Society, is best suited to answer the bulk of consumer complaints. In about 15% of all counties, it is county government that provides this assistance.[26]

County consumer protection services originate in a number of ways. In Orange County (California) a number of departments of county government reported in 1971 an increasing number of consumer complaints and inquiries which were beyond their jurisdiction.[27] County citizens who felt that they had been treated unfairly in the market place were unable to voice their complaints effectively since, in most instances, there was no clear violation of law and therefore their complaints were not within the jurisdiction of the District Attorney or the local police department.

In November, 1971, the Orange County Board of Supervisors established an Office of Consumer Affairs. The main function of this office was to receive, investigate, and mediate complaints of unfair or deceptive business practice. The Office officially opened its doors on March 1, 1972, and since that time has received more than 20,000 complaints. Typical of the investigations conducted by OCA was the case of a woman who complained that she had not received a pair of shoes for which she had paid forty dollars. An OCA investigator found that the man promising the shoes had moved to Massachusetts. Through contact with police departments in two Massachusetts cities, the man was traced and the woman received a full refund. In another case, a man whose car was damaged turned his claim over to his insurance company but did not receive payment. An investigator was able to get the claim paid in full.

The Office of Consumer Affairs has recovered over $1,500,000 for Orange County citizens since beginning its operation. Although investigating and mediating complaints is the Office's main function, it has other functions which include:

- *Reporting violations of law to the appropriate agency.*

- *Representing the interests of consumers before administrative and regulatory agencies. For example, the Orange County staff noted the tendency of household moving and storage companies to deliberately underestimate the cost of moving home owners. Staff members appeared before the California Public Utilities Commission, and this Commission established new procedures designed to preclude these unlawful procedures.*

- *Conducting programs of consumer education and information. The Orange County programs included lectures at college and high school classes and the development of hand-outs and bulletins on consumer problems.*

The county's Office of Consumer Affairs has established cooperative relationships with state consumer agencies and with Legal Aid Societies.

A different approach is taken by the Nassau County (New York) Office of Consumer Affairs, which has made supermarket practices, misleading advertising, home improvement problems, and consumer education part of its program.[28]

The Office guided the enactment of two local laws to protect food shoppers: one requires supermarkets to continue marking prices on items regardless of the Universal Product Code system; the other requires a freshness expiration date on all perishables. The Office conducts surveys of food prices and supported Congressional action to investigate high retail prices. It polices food stores for mislabeling, short weight, and excess fat content in ground beef.

In addition to resolving consumer complaints, the Nassau County Office of Consumer Affairs reviews and investigates misleading advertising and unfair business practices, and licenses more than five thousand home improvement contractors. Its education program includes personal presentations to students, a library of audio-visual aids, and an in-service course for teachers of consumer education.

Related to consumer protection are landlord-tenant relations programs. Montgomery County (Maryland) has an Office of Landlord-Tenant Affairs which resolves disputes between tenants and landlords.[29] This Office uses a conciliation process as a first step in resolving landlord-tenant disputes. If the landlord and tenant can resolve their differences with conciliation, a consent agreement is signed by both parties setting forth the terms of the conciliation. Violation of the consent agreement may result in a $1,000 fine. If the tenant and landlord cannot resolve their differences during the conciliation process, the case may go to the Montgomery County Commission on Landlord-Tenant Affairs which can then make a final decision subject to appeal to the courts. This Commission is composed of three landlord representatives, three tenant representatives, and three members of the public at large who are neither landlords nor tenants. The conciliation process is a quicker, less costly alternative to court action on landlord-tenant disputes.

In the three counties cited in this section, the consumer protection and landlord-tenant relations programs provide service to the entire county. The county programs are, of course, one of a number of consumer protection services of governmental agencies, better business bureaus, legal aid societies, and other groups which help the consumer and tenant protect their rights.

## COUNTY STAFF SERVICES

Budgeting, purchasing, and personnel are among the many functions of county government (usually called staff services) which do not directly serve the public but which

**148** • *Modern County Government*

are essential for the internal operation of county government. Data processing, accounting, maintenance of county buildings, and the operation of duplicating centers are other essential staff or operating services in a large county. In counties of 200,000 or more people, there are often specialized units performing data processing, budgeting, accounting, purchasing, and related functions.

**Budgeting.** The typical small county has a budget process which begins several months before the fiscal year with each elected official making an estimate of the department's annual needs. The county governing board in small counties with a commission form of government often does not have the assistance of a trained budget officer to review departmental requests. The county board reviews the budget requests, holds one or more public hearings, and passes an appropriation ordinance. The amount appropriated to each county office is recorded on the central accounting records (usually kept by the county auditor), and expenditures are checked against this record to be sure the county agency has sufficient funds to cover them. A typical small county has a line item budget, which is adequate for control purposes but does not provide needed information for program planning, coordination, and evaluation.

More populous counties usually have a budget officer or budget unit. Westchester County (New York) has a budget staff of more than a dozen persons responsible for budget analysis, budget control, and the preparation of special studies.[30] The Fairfax County (Virginia) Office of

Table 6-6

PURCHASING PRACTICES IN COUNTIES OF VARIOUS CLASSIFICATIONS IN 1975

| Classification | Percent Having Central Purchasing | Percent Permitted to Conduct Cooperative Purchasing | Percent Having Purchasing Manual | Percent Having a Full-time Purchasing Officer |
|---|---|---|---|---|
| All counties | 40 | 68 | 14 | 22 |
| Population group | | | | |
| Over 500,000 | 93 | 97 | 59 | 93 |
| 250,000-500,000 | 92 | 94 | 44 | 92 |
| 100,000-249,999 | 63 | 80 | 30 | 49 |
| 50,000- 99,999 | 50 | 72 | 16 | 25 |
| 25,000- 49,999 | 32 | 65 | 9 | 6 |
| 10,000- 24,999 | 21 | 56 | 3 | 4 |
| Form of government | | | | |
| With administrator | 72 | 86 | 41 | 52 |
| Without administrator | 33 | 64 | 6 | 14 |

SOURCE: Adapted from James T. Carter and Ronald Welf, "Purchasing Practices in Counties," in *The County Year Book, 1975* (Washington: National Association of Counties and International City Management Association, 1975), pp. 76-82. The study was based on responses from 696 counties of 2,203 counties surveyed.

Management and Budget continually reviews county programs, prepares management studies and cost-benefit analyses, and reviews all federal grant applications.[31] The Metropolitan Government of Nashville-Davidson County (Tennessee) has both a Budget Unit, which prepares the budget and analyzes the productivity of agency programs, and an Administrative Analysis Unit, which makes comprehensive studies of county programs.[32] In many of the most populous counties budget and management staffs go far beyond traditional budget preparation and control functions in helping to analyze, coordinate, and evaluate county programs.

**Purchasing.** In many small counties, each county office does its own purchasing; and competitive bidding might be used only with large items such as patrol cars. The larger a county's population, as Table 6-6 shows, the more likely it is to have central purchasing, to engage in cooperative purchasing with other governmental units, and to use purchasing manuals. Central purchasing is particularly useful because it is more economical in many ways than the small scale buying of individual county agencies. A nationwide study of county purchasing (see Table 6-6) found that 93% of the sample counties in the largest population group had full-time purchasing officers as compared to only 4% of the least populous counties.

**Data Processing.** The number of counties using computers has increased rapidly in the past thirty years, according to a 1976 survey.[33] Before 1955, fewer than 5% of all counties of 10,000 or more people employed computers. As Chart 6-2 shows, computer usage by county government has expanded rapidly; 26% of all counties of 10,000 or more people had computers by 1970, and 54% of these counties had them in 1975. Utilization of computers is greatest among counties with 50,000 or more people, as is shown by Chart 6-3.

Average expenditures for electronic data processing by counties responding to the 1976 survey varied from $2.7 million a year for counties of 500,000 or more people to about $25,000 annually for counties in the 10,000 to 25,000 group.[34] Data processing is frequently used by counties to prepare payrolls and maintain accounting records, and in the assessment and collection of property taxes. In addition, Lackawanna County (Pennsylvania) uses data processing in voter registration, energy conservation, and property management.[35] Anne Arundel County (Maryland) uses data processing in its water and sewer billing, voter registration, capital projects management, and dog licensing. El Paso County (Colorado) tracks down abuses in the county's welfare program by comparing lists of welfare clients in the county's program with those in the programs of other agencies.

There are also counties, such as Middlesex County (New Jersey), which provide data processing services to cities within the county at a cost lower than charged by private service bureaus. Large and medium sized county governments tend to have their own data processing in-

Chart 6-2

### PERCENTAGE OF COUNTIES USING COMPUTERS, BY COUNTY SIZE, 1965 AND 1975

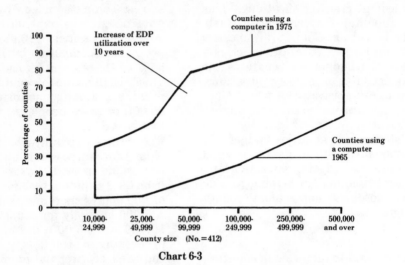

Chart 6-3

### CUMULATIVE PERCENTAGE OF COUNTIES USING COMPUTERS, BY YEAR OF ADOPTION AND POPULATION

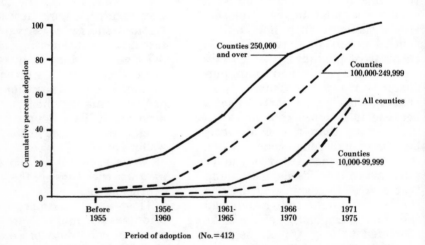

SOURCE: Joseph R. Matthews, William H. Dutton and Kenneth L. Kraemer, "County Computers: Growth, Usage, and Management," in National Association of Counties and International City Management Association, *The County Year Book, 1976* (Washington: National Association of Counties and International City Management Association, 1976), p. 134. The charts were based on a survey of 2,199 counties and responses received from 753 of these counties.

stallations; counties of less than 25,000 people which use data processing tend to rely on private service bureaus or larger public data processing centers in the area.

**Personnel and Labor Relations.** There are no national statistical studies (comparable to the studies on data processing and purchasing previously described)which show the percent of counties performing all types of personnel functions. However, information is available on county personnel practices in a number of states and counties. In North Carolina, the board of county commissioners determines the number of county employees when it approves a budget for each department and establishes a pay plan which sets the salary range for each class of positions.[36] The county board also establishes qualifications for appointive offices; determines the pay and expense allowances of employees; appoints, dismisses and supervises some groups of employees; approves the appointments made by the manager or administrator; and adopts rules and regulations governing hours, days of work, and working conditions. Approximately half of North Carolina's one hundred counties have adopted position classification and pay plans. All North Carolina counties have brought their employees under Social Security, and the employees in ninety-six counties are also under the Local Government Employees Retirement System.

Personnel practices vary in other states. Only one Michigan county (Wayne) had a civil service system in 1972, and several had personnel offices.[37] Personnel recruitment and selection activities in most Michigan counties are handled by the heads of operating departments and their deputies.[38] Several Michigan counties have recognized employee organizations and their right of collective bargaining. In Idaho, recruitment of employees is also handled by elective officials and the appointive heads of departments, but classification and compensation plans are used in more than a fourth of the state's forty-four counties.[39] In New York State, the Public Employees Fair Employment Act of 1967 granted public employees the right to organize for collective bargaining purposes. Local governments are required to negotiate with and enter into written contracts with these organizations.[40]

Perhaps the most significant development taking place in county personnel practices in the 1970s is the unionization of county employees. A 1975 survey shows that 51% of the 9.2 million state and local government employees in the nation belong to labor unions.[41] In 1970, over half the urban counties had at least one employee organization, and some had more than four employee organizations.[42] Santa Clara County (California) for example, had employees in seven unions or professional associations.

Some strikes have also occurred. Garrett County (Maryland) had a 227-day strike which resulted in recognition of a union and Charleston County (South Carolina) had a 113-day strike of its hospital employees.[43] The merits and problems of county unionization have been debated in an article in the *1976 County Year Book.*[44] To better prepare county officials to work with unions and other employee organizations, the National Association of Counties has sponsored a number of labor-management conferences for county officials.

**Public Information Services.** Public information services are furnished by 32.6% of the counties sampled in a NACo/ICMA survey.[45] Many county information staffs, like the one in San Bernardino County (California), consist of one person whose main function is to prepare news releases and publications, design exhibits, and provide service to newspapers and radio stations.[46] In Forsyth County (North Carolina), a major responsibility of two professional persons is to write news releases and prepare a monthly employee newsletter. The two receptionists who are part of this public information staff are trained in the operations of county government and able to answer many questions from citizens over the telephone as well as refer callers to appropriate county officials.

Maricopa County (Arizona) has a three-person public information staff.[47] Among the tasks of this staff are to write and distribute news releases; prepare magazine articles, pamphlets, and a small booklet on county government; and plan the county booth at the state fair. The public information office has also developed an award winning color documentary film on county government and a monthly television program.

Handling citizen complaints is sometimes a function of the county public information office and sometimes a responsibility of a separate unit. In Baltimore County (Maryland), the County Executive has established a Community Affairs Division to handle citizen complaints.[48] In its first month of operation, the new agency handled eight hundred calls, referring them to the appropriate departments on the same day they were received. After referral, the Division follows up the complaint to make sure that the county agency has resolved the citizen's problems. The time required to resolve these complaints has been reduced from an average of thirty days to five days.

**Other Staff Services.** Accounting and auditing are usually the responsibility of an elected county auditor or clerk. In Mississippi, for example, the clerk of the board of county supervisors serves as county auditor and is required to keep a ledger showing the receipts and disbursements of county funds.[49] The clerk is also required to examine, pre-audit, and settle all accounts of county officers. The post-audit of county expenditures is made in Mississippi by the State Department of Audit.

While most audits of county funds are the traditional financial audits, some counties are utilizing program and performance audits. In King County (Washington) the County Auditor uses audits to determine:[50]

- *the extent to which legislative policies are being faithfully, efficiently and effectively implemented by administrative officials;*

- *whether programs are achieving their desired objectives; and,*

• *if administrative control sytems are adequate and effective in accomplishing their objectives.*

Many county accounting systems are traditional systems which provide little cost or analytical data but excellent information on county receipts, expenditures, liabilities, and balances. Some counties have developed excellent analyses of the relationships of expenditures and budgets. Union County (New Jersey), for example, has a quarterly report which compares departmental expenditures with budget estimates on a month-by-month basis, thus pinpointing departments which are in danger of over-spending their appropriations.[51]

County governments have also been leaders in local government investment, insurance, and central receiving and disbursing systems. Forsyth County (North Carolina) is one of a number of counties which have earned substantial sums for the county through investment of idle funds.[52] The St. Clair County (Illinois) insurance plan greatly reduced county insurance at one time after a bid process.

Legal services in most counties are provided by the county prosecuting attorney. In Idaho and in most other states, the county prosecuting attorney is responsible both for furnishing legal advice to the board of county commissioners and other county officials and for representing the state in criminal justice functions. In some counties, such as San Diego (California),the county has a County Counsel who acts just as a legal adviser to county officials and other units of local government within the county.[53]

## MORE EXTENSIVE COUNTY FUNCTIONS

The county services previously described are just a few of more than one hundred county functions. The following two chapters describe most of the remaining services which can be categorized in five important groups (or systems) of services: criminal justice;, human services; transportation, utilities, and natural resources; parks, recreation, and culture; and planning and development.

## REFERENCES

1. Paul Wager, *County Government Across the Nation* (Chapel Hill: The University of North Carolina Press, 1950), p. 18.

2. National Association of Counties, *From America's Counties Today, 1973* (Washington: National Association of Counties, 1973), p. 30.

3. *Idaho Code,* Section 31-2202. The underlining is provided for emphasis.

4. *Idaho Code,* Section 63-908.

5. *Revised Code of Washington,* Section 70.05.070.

6. Russell W. Maddox and Robert F. Fuquay, *State and Local Government* 3rd ed. (New York: D. Van Nostrand Company, 1975), pp. 456, 457.

7. Particularly useful in describing county functions at the beginning of the 1920s is Herman G. James, *Local Government in the United States* (New York: D. Appleton and Company, 1921). Charles M. Kneier, "Development of Newer County Functions," *American Political Science Review* 24: February, 1930):134 was helpful in describing the development of newer county services during the 1920s.

8. It was difficult to determine whether a few county services, such as libraries, hospitals, and parks should be considered traditional or new. All three were listed as new county services by Charles M. Kneier, but counties were expanding all three services in the 1920's. Kneier stated that the laws authorizing county government to establish county libraries existed in 25 states in 1925, but no county libraries had been established in some of these states. On the basis of this evidence, county libraries were considered a newer function. Charles M. Kneier, "Development of Newer County Functions," p. 134.

9. See Susan W. Torrence, *Grass Roots Government, The County in American Politics* (Washington: Robert B. Luce, Inc., 1974), p. 29 for a similar list of urban functions. The percent of counties providing urban services may be found in Table 6-4 of this chapter.

10. Herbert Sydney Duncombe, *County Government in America* (Washington: National Association of Counties Research Foundation, 1966), pp. 74-76.

11. National Association of Counties and International City Management Association, "County Functions/Services Questionnaire," November, 1975.

12. Susan W. Torrence has used the term "basic" services to refer to eleven services that "virtually all counties-urban and rural-perform." The eleven services corresponded closely to the traditional services listed earlier in the chapter. Interestingly, disaster preparedness, which is not among the eleven basic services listed by Susan Torrence, has become a very frequently provided county function. For more information on basic services, see Susan W. Torrence, *Grass Roots Government, The County in American Politics,* pp. 26, 27.

13. The data shown in Table 6-3 was provided by the Joint Data Center of the National Association of Counties and International City Management Association. The same data was reported in a slightly different manner by Carolyn B. Lawrence and John M. DeGrove "County Government Services" in *The County Year Book, 1976* (Washington: National Association of Counties and International City Management Association, 1976), p. 92-95. The table in *The County Year Book,* for example, shows the percent of counties which are responsible for a particular service that provide the service on a county-wide basis. Table 6-3 in this chapter shows the percent of all responding counties that provide the service on a county-wide basis. The article by Lawrence and DeGrove contains excellent information on county functions and lists the source of funds for county services as well as the area of service.

14. The data on each of the 102 services, provided by the Joint Data Center of the National Association of Counties and International City Management Association, was averaged by the author to produce the 17 functional group totals shown in Table 6-4.

15. The percents for each of the 102 services provided by the Joint Data Center were averaged to produce the 17 functional group totals shown on Table 6-5.

16. For a detailed description of property tax assessment in a specific state see Michael S. Vollmer, Herbert Sydney Duncombe and Katherine D. Pell, *Handbook for County Officials in Idaho* (Moscow: University of Idaho, 1974), pp. 93-112 and James D. Thomas, *A Manual for Alabama County Commissioners* (University: University of Alabama, 1975), pp. 60-61.

17. Utilizing data fed into a computer, the Lane County Assessor is able to appraise a parcel of property without making a personal inspection. The entire real and personal property records system in Ventura County has been placed on a computer to provide rapid access to information on more than 150,000 parcels of property. National Association of Counties, *Living Library* 7th ed. (Washington: National Association of Counties, 1976), p. 34.

18. Charles M. Kneier, p. 134.

19. *The 1974-75 American Library Directory,* compiled by Helaine MacKeigan (New York: R.R. Bowker, Inc., 1974), p. xi.

20. Compiled from Madeline Miele and Sarah Prakken, ed., *The Bowker Annual of Library and Book Trade Information* (New York: R.R. Bowker Company, 1975), pp. 220, 221. Sixteen of the remaining library systems were city systems, and one was the public system of the District of Columbia.

21. Information on libraries in this section was mainly from *The 1974-75 American Library Directory.*

22. Ibid. and 1975 Achievement Award on Chesterfield County, Virginia, in the files of the National Association of Counties.

23. The Montgomery County library system covers the entire county except the city of Takoma Park (1970 population 18,455) which operates its own library system. Thus, more than 95% of the county population receives county library services. Information on this county library system comes from unpublished sources provided by the Montgomery County Department of Public Libraries.

24. The information is from county sources, county achievement awards in the files of the National Association of Counties, and Thomas P. Bruderle, "Counties Fight Unemployment with Education," *New County Times,* (Washington), May 31, 1976, p. 13.

25. Quoted in National Association of Counties, *Orange County, California, Office of Consumer Affairs* (Washington: National Association of Counties, 1974), p. 1.

26. Data provided by the Joint Data Center of the National Association of Counties and International City Management Association.

27. Information for this case study was obtained from M.S. Shimanoff, Director of the Office of Consumer Affairs of Orange County, letter to Sydney Duncombe, November 8, 1976.

28. National Association of Counties, *Nassau County, New York, Consumer Advocacy Program* (Washington: National Association of Counties, 1974) and Elaine King, Special Assistant to the Office of Nassau County Executive, letter to Sydney Duncombe, December 28, 1976.

29. National Association of Counties, *Montgomery County, Montgomery Landlord-Tenant Relations Program* (Washington: National Association of Counties, 1974) and updating information submitted by Alastair McArthur, Intergovernmental Programs Coordinator, Montgomery County, letter to Sydney Duncombe, November 24, 1976.

30. Westchester County, New York, "1976 Budget," pp. C-22, 23 provides a description of the work of this unit.

31. See Fairfax County, "Advertised Fiscal Plan, Fiscal 1975," pp. I-88-91 for a description of the work of this unit.

32. Information based on interviews with Mr. Joseph Torrence, Director of Finance, and Mr. Robert Horton of the Mayor's Office in Nashville, Tennessee, on January 8, 1976. The Administrative Analysis Unit has also made studies of solid waste management, child abuse, and flood plain zoning.

33. The statistical information used in this section is based on a study of data processing in 753 counties reported in Joseph R. Matthews, William H. Dutton and Kenneth L. Kraemer, "County Computers: Growth, Usage, and Management," National Association of Counties and International City Management Association, *The County Year Book, 1976*, pp. 133-143.

34. Ibid., p. 135. The average county in the sample spent 1.3% of its operating budget on electronic data processing.

35. Short descriptions of the Lackawanna, Anne Arundel, El Paso, and Middlesex County data processing systems may be found in National Association of Counties, *Living Library*, 7th ed., p. 32.

36. Donald B. Hayman, "Administering the County," in Joseph S. Ferrell, ed., *County Government in North Carolina* (Chapel Hill: University of North Carolina, 1975), pp. 29-39 is the source of information on North Carolina personnel practices.

37. Kenneth VerBurg, *Guide to Michigan County Government* (East Lansing: Michigan State University, 1972), pp. III-14, 17. The Wayne County civil service system provides for the classification of county positions, examinations, maintenance of a list of eligible employees, maintenance of service records on each employee, and appeals procedures.

38. Ibid., pp. III-16.

39. Idaho counties were assisted by the Idaho Association of Counties which provided personnel financed by an Intergovernmental Personnel Act grant to assist counties in preparing classification plans.

40. Clark Hamlin, *County Legislative Guide* (Ithaca: Cornell University, 1975), pp. 181, 182.

41. Reported in Charles C. Mulcahy and Dennis W. Rader, "Collective Bargaining in Public Employment: The County View" in *The County Year Book, 1976*, p. 159.

42. Reported in Susan W. Torrence, p. 111.

43. Ibid., pp. 111, 112.

44. See Charles C. Mulcahy and Dennis W. Rader, "Collective Bargaining in Public Employment: The County View" and Jerry Wurf, "Collective Bargaining in Public Employment: The AFSCME View" in *The County Year Book, 1976*, pp. 150-159.

45. See Table 6-3 of this chapter.

46. Information on San Bernardino and Forsyth Counties were provided by their information officers at a panel session of the Annual Conference of the National Association of Counties on June 28, 1976.

47. Information supplied by the Public Information Director of Maricopa County, Arizona.

48. Case study in the files of the National Association of Counties.

49. Dana B. Brammer, *A Manual for Mississippi County Supervisors*, 2nd ed. (University: University of Mississippi, 1973), p. 54.

50. King County Auditor, *The Sixth Annual Report of the King County Auditor's Office* (Seattle: King County Auditor's Office, 1976).

51. Union County, New Jersey, "1976 Budget vs. Expenditure Report, January 1, 1976-April 30, 1976." (Mimeographed.)

52. National Association of Counties, *Living Library*, 7th ed., p. 30. Forsyth County earned one million dollars in 1973-74 through investment of idle funds.

53. Case study in the files of the National Association of Counties. The San Diego County Council has established a computerized system for indexing all written opinions of the County Council since 1933.

# Chapter 7
# Criminal Justice and Human Services Systems

"Any criminal justice system is an apparatus society uses to enforce standards of conduct necessary to protect individuals and the community. It operates by apprehending, prosecuting, convicting, and sentencing those members of the community who violate the basic rules of group existence. The action against lawbreakers is designed to serve three purposes beyond the immediate punitive one. It removes dangerous people from the community; it deters others from criminal behavior; and it gives society an opportunity to attempt to transform lawbreakers into law-abiding citizens. What most significantly distinguishes the system of one country from that of another is the extent and the form of the protections it offers individuals in the process of determining guilt and imposing punishment. Our system of justice deliberately sacrifices much in efficiency and even in effectiveness in order to preserve local autonomy and to protect the individual.

"The criminal justice system has three separately organized parts—the police, the courts, and corrections—and each has distinct tasks. However, these parts are by no means independent of each other. What each one does and how it does it has a direct effect on the work of the others. The courts must deal, and can only deal, with those whom the police arrest; the business of corrections is with those delivered to it by the courts. How successfully corrections reforms convicts determines whether they will once again become police business and influences the sentences the judges pass; police activities are subject to court scrutiny and are often determined by court decisions. And so reforming or reorganizing any part or procedure of the system changes other parts or procedures..."[1]

County government is involved in all three parts of the criminal justice system—the police, the courts, and corrections. Before the systems approach was applied to criminal justice, the functions of the sheriff, prosecuting attorney, defense attorney, courts, jails, and probation officers were considered separate functions. Since county officials were responsible for only some of the criminal justice functions, there was a tendency for them to pay less attention to related criminal justice responsibilities of city, state and other governmental agencies. Looking at criminal justice as a system, it is more likely that all officials having criminal justice responsibilities will view the process as a whole. The assembly line nature of the criminal justice system is pictured in the cartoon on the following page. It is important that each agency (county, state, or other) understand its role in the capture and trial of the accused and the rehabilitation of the criminals.

There are also important interrelationships between county responsibilities in human services programs. For example, public assistance, health, manpower, and community college and vocational technical school programs may all have responsibilities in supplying the needs of an unemployed woman receiving aid to families with dependent children. The county welfare department may supply grants and the counseling of a skilled social worker; the county health department may provide free immunization through its maternal and child health programs; and the county manpower department may finance further education at the county community college to make the woman employable. Provision of services to groups (such as the unemployed) can best be accomplished and understood by using a systems approach.

In using this approach, it is important also to consider the relationships between federal, state, and local governmental agencies in policy determination, in administration, and in financing services. Intergovernmental relationships in the county welfare system are pictured in Chart 7-1. The federal. government, through laws, policies, regulations, and grant-in-aid requirements, influences state policies, which in turn influence those of the county. The federal government provides grants to states for public assistance, and these grants pass through to the counties usually with state supplements.

In states with county administration of welfare, county governments develop their own plans. These are reviewed at the state level and incorporated into the state plan which is then reviewed at the federal level. Counties are also able to exert influence on the shaping of state and national policies through state associations of counties and the National Association of Counties. At the county level, county welfare officials have many contacts, not only with the clients served by their programs, but also with community action and non-profit agencies, other local governments, and medical, business, and labor groups.

The remainder of this chapter describes about half of the functions listed in Table 6-3 of the preceeding chapter. Rather than describing each function individually, as was done

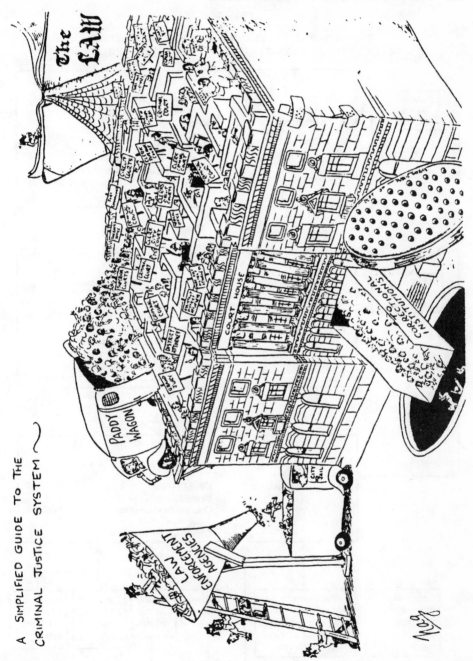

A SIMPLIFIED GUIDE TO THE CRIMINAL JUSTICE SYSTEM

SOURCE: Advisory Commission on Intergovernmental Relations, *State-Local Relations in the Criminal Justice System* (Washington: U.S. Government Printing Office, 1971), p. xvi.

Chart 7-1

## THE FEDERAL-STATE-COUNTY WELFARE SYSTEM
## IN COUNTIES ADMINISTERING FEDERAL GRANT PROGRAMS

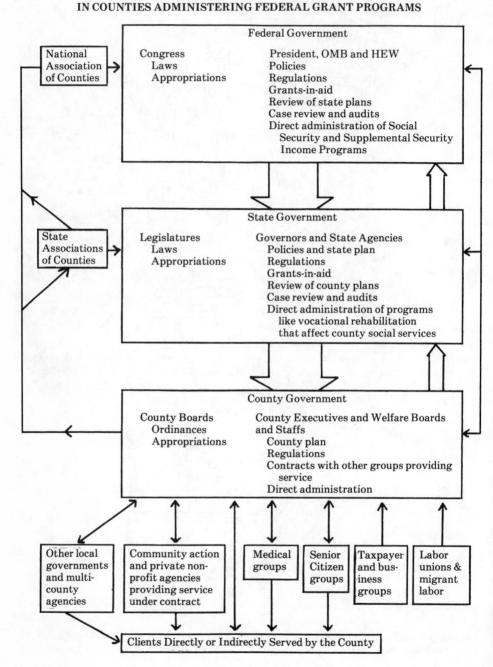

Federal Government

National Association of Counties

Congress
Laws
Appropriations

President, OMB and HEW
Policies
Regulations
Grants-in-aid
Review of state plans
Case review and audits
Direct administration of Social
    Security and Supplemental Security
    Income Programs

State Government

State Associations of Counties

Legislatures
Laws
Appropriations

Governors and State Agencies
Policies and state plan
Regulations
Grants-in-aid
Review of county plans
Case review and audits
Direct administration of programs
    like vocational rehabilitation
    that affect county social services

County Government

County Boards
Ordinances
Appropriations

County Executives and Welfare Boards
and Staffs
    County plan
    Regulations
    Contracts with other groups providing
        service
    Direct administration

Other local governments and multi-county agencies

Community action and private non-profit agencies providing service under contract

Medical groups

Senior Citizen groups

Taxpayer and business groups

Labor unions & migrant labor

Clients Directly or Indirectly Served by the County

with several specific services in Chapter 6, the services are grouped together and considered part of the criminal justice and human services systems. Public safety programs, such as disaster preparedness, emergency medical services, and fire protection, are described in this chapter because they are more closely related to criminal justice than to other service systems.

## THE CRIMINAL JUSTICE SYSTEM

The criminal justice system involves the police, the courts, correctional institutions, and other agencies in a step-by-step process which begins at the time an alleged crime is reported and ends after the criminal is captured, tried, imprisoned, and possibly paroled. The role of county government in the criminal justice system is one of an intergovernmental partner. The relationship between county, city, state, and federal agencies in the flow of a particular criminal case varies greatly depending upon which state and county the crime is committed in. Chart 7-2 shows two of the many possible patterns of relationships in a burglary committed in the unincorporated area of the county.

County agencies having important roles in the criminal justice system include: county sheriffs' offices and police departments; county courts; county prosecuting attorneys and public defenders; and county jails, correctional institutions, and probation officers. County agencies furnishing these services also provide a variety of other law enforcement, legal, and related public safety services.

**Police Protection.** County sheriffs and other county law enforcement personnel have important functions in the criminal justice system, which include:

- *preventing crimes through patrol and other activities;*

- *investigating crimes which have occurred;*

- *apprehending suspects and bringing them in for booking;*

- *testifying before magistrates and courts;*

- *recovering property and assisting persons injured in a crime; and,*

- *maintaining fingerprint files and other records.*

They have a variety of other useful functions, such as: assisting the injured in an accident, directing traffic, answering emergency calls placed to a central emergency number, maintaining friendly relationships with juvenile groups, and responding to calls about neighborhood disputes.

About two-thirds of all counties provide patrol and investigation services on a county-wide basis; other counties furnish these services just to rural parts of the county.[2] The county sheriff is responsible for police protection in most counties. Some urban counties have placed this function under the jurisdiction of a county police department with a director appointed by the county executive or county administrator.

The Advisory Commission on Intergovernmental Relations has criticized the large number of uneconomically small police agencies in the United States. The Commission found that nearly 90% of all local governments have less than ten full-time personnel and that most of these police agencies could not provide full-time patrol and investigative services for their citizens.[3] The Commission recommended that in metropolitan areas:

"...county government should be empowered to assume the police function in any metropolitan locality which fails to provide patrol and pre-

*liminary investigative services, charging the costs of such assumed police service to the affected local government.*"[4]

Where municipal police forces are large enough for full-time patrol services but not sufficiently large for specialized services, the Commission recommended that counties be encouraged to provide supportive staff and auxiliary services in single county metropolitan areas.[5] A 1974 survey of police services in counties

Chart 7-2

PATTERNS OF INTERGOVERNMENTAL RELATIONS IN TWO FELONY CASES

|  | Pattern A (An Idaho Case) | Pattern B (A Maryland Case) |
|---|---|---|
| 1. Discovery of crime by homeowner | Crime is committed in a rural area of the county and homeowner calls county sheriff. | Crime is committed in unincorporated area of county and county police are called. |
| 2. Investigation | A deputy sheriff conducts the investigation but gets a lead from a state patrolman. | County police conduct investigation with key leads from Washington, D.C. police and Rockville, Maryland police. |
| 3. Arrest | A deputy sheriff makes the arrest. | County police make arrest. |
| 4. Booking (which usually involves fingerprinting, photographing, and questioning). | Suspect brought to the county law enforcement building and booked. After arrest and booking, a complaint is executed before a magistrate. | Suspect brought to county police station and booked. |
| 5. Initial appearance before a magistrate | Suspect appears before a Magistrate who is part of the state court system but is selected by county, city, and state officials. An attorney is assigned to an indigent suspect. | Suspect appears before a Commissioner of the District Court of Maryland. |
| 6. Preliminary hearing | Preliminary hearing is before a Magistrate with office in the County Courthouse. | Preliminary hearing is before a State District Court Judge at the State District Courthouse located in the county. |

| | | |
|---|---|---|
| 7. Preferral of charges | County Prosecuting Attorney uses information system to prefer charges. | State's Attorney (a county elected official) prefers charges. |
| 8. Pre-trial activities | Suspect arraigned before State District Court. | Suspect arraigned before State Circuit Court. A state public defender, with offices in the county, defends the indigent suspect. |
| 9. Trial | Trial in State District Court with County Prosecuting Attorney presenting the state's case. | Trial in the State Circuit Court with a county official (the State's Attorney) presenting the state's case. |
| 10. Sentencing | Sentencing by the State Court Judge after presentence investigation by the county probation officer. | Sentencing by the State Circuit Court Judge after investigation by a state probation officer. |
| 11. Imprisonment | Suspect held in county jail during trial and before sentencing. After sentencing prisoner transferred to State Penitentiary. | Suspect held in county jail until sentencing and then returned to county correctional institution for up to 18 months imprisonment. |
| 12. Parole | State parole officers maintain contact with the prisoner for a year after his release. | State parole officers maintain contact with prisoner for the length of the parole period. |

SOURCE: The cases were typical of actual cases in the two counties developed as a result of contact with officials in Latah County, Idaho, and Montgomery County, Maryland. In Montgomery County, it is the County Police Department, not the County Sheriff, which provides police protection in the unincorporated area of the county.

of 250,000 or more people showed that county police agencies in these counties were usually large enough to provide adequate patrol and specialized services.[6] Eighty-eight percent of these counties had county police forces of one hundred or more employees; whereas only six percent of municipalities in the same counties had police forces this large.

The law enforcement role of most county police departments is to provide police services for the entire county or for the unincorporated area of the county. Other roles include:[7]

• *participating in a joint city-county police agency such as the Nashville-Davidson County (Tenn.) Police Department;*

• *providing intensive police services to particular areas of the county through county service districts as is done in Suffolk County (New York);*

• *providing all police services to municipalities by contract as in the case of Los Angeles (Calif.) and other counties;*

• *providing specialized services (such as dispatching or investigation) by contract to municipalities like St. Louis County (Missouri) and Cook County (Illinois);*

- *intergovernmental cooperation in joint ventures such
  as sharing the costs of communication equipment, law
  enforcement buildings, and
  central dispatching staffs;
  and,*

- *participating in mutual aid
  agreements and cooperative
  efforts to establish road blocks
  to capture fleeing suspects.*

**County Judicial Functions.** County judicial services are an integral part of the criminal justice system in addition to their civil court functions. County officials have an important role in the lower two tiers of the state and local court system pictured in Figure 7-1.

State supreme courts and intermediate appellate courts are state courts and county officials have little or no part. Trial courts are also generally state courts organized on a county or multi-county basis. In Michigan, Circuit Courts have jurisdiction over one to five counties, and the judges' salaries are paid by the state with county boards permitted to supplement these salaries.[8] In Georgia, the general trial court is called the Superior Court with both the state and county contributing to the judges' salaries.[9] Many of the key staff persons serving the major trial courts are either county employees or are paid from county funds. In Michigan, these staff include:[10]

- *the county court clerk or deputy clerk who is responsible
  for attending court sessions,
  collecting fees, accounting
  for court funds, and having
  custody of court records;*

- *the court stenographer, ap-*

*pointed by the Governor on
recommendation of the circuit court judge, but paid
from county funds;*

- *the friend of the court whose
  salary is paid by the county
  and who helps protect children
  particularly with regard to
  divorce decrees, financial
  support, and other matters;
  and,*

- *the county sheriff and his
  deputies who are required to
  attend sessions of the court,
  serve civil process papers and
  execute court orders.*

Below the major trial courts are courts of limited jurisdiction. Some of these are staffed and financed by county government. They include:

- *probate courts which deal with
  the settlement and disposi-
  tion of the estates of deceased
  persons. (In states such as
  Michigan and Georgia, these
  are county-administered
  courts.);*

- *county courts which are county-administered courts with
  jurisdiction over misdemeanors and minor civil cases;*

- *magistrates courts which
  handle minor civil and criminal cases and where suspects
  also may make their initial ap-
  pearance; and,*

- *juvenile courts which are specialized courts operated by
  counties in some metropolitan areas. These courts hold
  hearings in juvenile cases,
  and sometimes have responsibility for juvenile detention,
  probation, and group homes.*

**Corrections.** In nearly all states, jails and correctional institutions which imprison up to one year are the responsibility of local government. County governments usually have responsibility for maintaining county jails for longer term prisoners, while city governments operate small police lock-ups. While many county jails do not have the educational, counseling, and other services needed for a rehabilitation program, the following counties are among those with modern correctional programs.

*Montgomery County (Maryland).*[11] The County has a modern detention center with many types of recreation programs, group counseling, an educational program with college and high school courses, and a drug treatment system. After a prisoner is admitted, he is assigned to an assessment team consisting of a staff psychologist, a corrections officer, a nurse, an education specialist, and a community release coordinator. The team gets the prisoner to talk about his past life and hopes for the future to determine what types of educational training, counseling, and other programs might benefit him.

Prisoners are eligible for work release if they meet certain criteria in conduct and work habits. The prisoner is placed in a job outside the Detention Center and returns after work each evening. Before a prisoner is finally released from the Deten-

Figure 7-1

STATE COURT ORGANIZATION

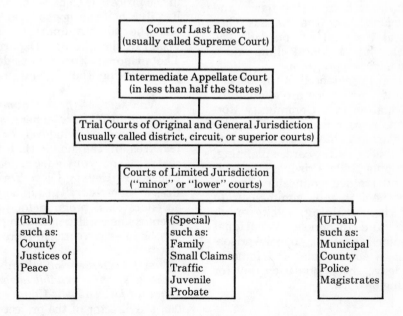

SOURCE: Advisory Commission on Intergovernmental Relations, *State-Local Relations in the Criminal Justice System* (Washington: U.S. Government Printing Office, 1971), p. 88.

tion Center, he sees the community release coordinator who helps prepare him for release and helps him find a job after release.

*Jackson County (Missouri).*[12] The Jackson County correctional program includes screening for pre-trial release and the identification of family, financial, vocational, medical, and other problems which will result from incarceration. The intake interviewer gathers extensive information on each person admitted to jail and identifies individuals such as narcotics addicts, alcoholics, and the mentally ill who need referral to other agencies. Psychiatric and other medical staff provide crisis intervention services during intake.

The Jackson County Jail has a medical unit with x-ray facilities, a pharmacy, a laboratory, and examining rooms. The health unit is staffed by paramedical technicians on a twenty-four hour a day basis, and physicians from the Kansas City General Hospital are on call. The jail also has a dental clinic and a full counseling program.

Prisoners sentenced to the Department of Corrections are eligible for participation in a Community Corrections Center Program. These inmates are provided training in pre-employment skills, career planning, and coping skills. Prisoners are tested, and trained counselors try to place them in jobs commensurate with their training, background, skills, and interests. Vocational education is available to make prisoners more employable, and inmates may leave the prison each day for training or work.

**Alternatives to Institutionalization.** Alternatives to imprisonment have been used by county agencies where they seem likely to promote better rehabilitation of offenders. These alternatives include the following.

*The traditional probation and parole programs.*

*Alcoholic outreach programs.* Here inebriates are treated for health problems rather than drying out in prisons.

*The operation of drug rehabilitation programs.*[13] Newly arrested persons may be placed in the program with the approval of a judge rather than being placed in jail. If the arrestee successfully completes the programs, the charges against him may be dropped.

*The use of halfway houses.* In Boulder County (Colorado), a halfway house is used to bring prisoners step-by-step from living in prison to living in a community.[14] One step in the process is to have the prisoner live in a halfway house located outside the jail but under the supervision of the Sheriff's Department. The prisoner works outside this house during the day but returns at night.

*"Non-secure" group homes for youthful offenders.* There are no fences, bars on windows, or other features of the home that would restrain the youth from leaving. Rensselaer County (New York) utilizes a "non-secure" group home and an educational program for juvenile offenders as an alternative to placing youths in a conventional correctional institution.[15]

*Pre-trial intervention which substitutes a specific rehabilitation program for jail.* In Dade County (Florida), the director of the project meets with the youthful defendant and his family and works out a rehabilitation plan which may involve vocational, educational, and psychological assistance.[16] If the plan is approved by the Assistant State Attorney assigned to the project, the prosecution of the case against the defendant is deferred pending successful completion of the approved rehabilitation plan. When this is completed, the case is dismissed, and the defendant retains an unblemished record.

**Legal Services and Prosecution.** Most states have county prosecuting attorneys whose responsibility is to present the state's case in criminal trials.[17] The prosecuting attorney generally has the additional function of presenting evidence against the accused at the preliminary hearing.[18]

The county prosecuting attorney in most counties also serves as legal counsel to the county board. He defends the county in suits against it and advises county officials on the legality of proposed actions. In some counties, the civil legal advisor is an official appointed by the county executive or county board, while the criminal prosecution functions are performed by an elected prosecuting attorney.

Since the 1963 U.S. Supreme Court decision in Gideon v. Wainwright, there has been a large increase in the use of public defenders as defense counsel for indigent persons.[19] Many of these are paid by county government, and others are financed from private sources. Santa Clara County (California), for example, has had a public defender's office since 1964 with a caseload which has grown within a decade to 17,000 cases a year.[20] The office had a staff of more than 70 employees in 1974 providing services for citizens from the entire county.

**Other Public Safety Services.** County governments provide three public safety services which relate to the criminal justice system. Disaster preparedness first became an important county program when the threat of nuclear attack resulted in the establishment of a national civil defense program. Local agencies were designated as responsible for finding and stocking fallout shelters, and federal grants were provided for this purpose. In most states, county governments were given this responsibility. Since the 1960s, county disaster preparedness agencies have broadened their scope to include preparation for many other types of emergencies such as floods, tornadoes, hurricanes, forest fires, or major industrial explosions. Coordination of local government officials is absolutely essential in responding to large scale disasters, and county disaster preparedness agencies have developed training exercises in which city, county, and non-governmental officials work together to respond to a simulated disaster.

Most counties also provide some form of emergency medical services for the entire county. Los Angeles County serves the unincorporated area directly and also provides emergency ambulance service on a contract basis to cities within the county. Weld County (Colorado) operates four fully equipped ambulances: three located at the County Hospital in Greeley and one in the northern part of the county.[21] To facilitate the reporting of emergency calls, many counties have a well-publicized central emergency telephone number where citizens can reach an operator twenty-four hours a day.

A number of county governments have fire departments which provide fire prevention and fire fighting services, mainly to the unincorporated areas of the county. Some county fire departments, such as the Los Angeles County Department, employ paramedics who respond to emergency calls and who may be asked to help bring a victim from a burning warehouse, rescue an injured man from the face of a cliff, or remove a woman pinned in her car as a result of a traffic accident.

**Criminal Justice Planning.** Recognizing the lack of coordination and planning in criminal justice administration, Congress passed the Law Enforcement Assistance Act of 1965 and the Omnibus Crime Control and Safe Streets Act of 1968.[22] The latter Act required the governor of each state to establish a state law enforcement planning committee to receive block grants from the U.S. Law Enforcement Assistance Administration and disburse sub-grants to other state agencies and local government. Since enactment of this legislation, an entirely new tier of local agencies has been established on a county, city-county, and regional basis to receive the criminal justice sub-grants and prepare comprehensive criminal justice plans.

These criminal justice plans include: defining the major criminal justice problems in the area, establishing goals and priorities, evaluating individual criminal justice projects, and preparing a multi-year financial plan for the future. County governments have three major roles in criminal justice planning:[23]

- *senior partner in a single county planning agency. Orange County, California, for example, is considered a region for criminal justice planning, and the Orange County Criminal Justice Council has both county and city representatives;*

- *partner in a city-county criminal justice planning unit such as the Toledo-Lucas County Regional Planning Unit in Ohio; and,*

- *participant in a multi-county criminal justice commission such as the South-Eastern South Dakota Criminal Justice Commission serving Clay, Lincoln, McCook, Minnehaha, Turner, and Union Counties.*

## HUMAN SERVICES SYSTEMS

County government furnishes a wide variety of services designed to enhance the income, health, job opportunities, education, and welfare of its citizens. These services, sometimes referred to as human services, are among the most costly provided by counties.

In many cases, the individual requests these services. For example, a mother with a crippled child may request that the child be given medical, surgical, and other services to alleviate orthopedic or other crippling conditions. In the same way, a person who is out of work may apply for a public service job, a woman without financial support for her children may apply for Aid to Families with Dependent Children, and a high school youth may request admission to a county community college. After the application is submitted, reviewed, and approved, the human services delivery systems operate in various ways to supply the needs of the applicant for health care, an income, a job, an education, or whatever was requested.

In some situations, however, the human services system operates without a formal application. For example, no application is needed to bring a child to elementary school; and many health services, such as inspecting restaurants and testing the purity of public water supplies, are furnished for all citizens without a specific request.

County human services are usually classified into four major groups: health; public assistance and social services; manpower; and education. Human resource planning programs are a means of coordinating these services.

**Public Health.** County governments have been providing public health services for more than a century, but most of the services furnished by county health departments are either modern or rely on recent medical techniques. County health departments have had the following seven basic functions for the past fifty years, although many of the techniques have changed during this time.

*Collection of vital statistics.* Statistics on births and deaths are particularly important in making population projections and in determining trends in various causes of death.

*Investigation and control of communicable diseases.* The Allegheny County (Pennsylvania) Health Department program, for example, provides: immunization of young children against polio, diphtheria, and other diseases; detection and pre-

vention of tuberculosis; and venereal disease control.[24]

*Maternal and child health care.* Many county health departments have clinics to which mothers bring their children for physical examinations, immunizations, and discussions with a doctor or nurse about their health. The Salt Lake City-County Health Department also provides health services for school-aged children, including class sessions on subjects such as weight reduction, maturation, and venereal disease.[25]

*Home health care.* Public health nurses provide this care when they visit homes to give injections, dress wounds, check blood pressure, and perform other health functions. In Orange County (New York), any county resident is eligible for these services, and the County Health Department is the only agency in the county authorized under the Medicare and Medicaid programs to provide these services.[26] In Orange County, home health care may also include the services of a physical therapist and a home health care aide. Aides may serve as housekeeper and cook for a limited period of time so the ill individual or couple can remain in their home until they are able to provide these services for themselves.

*Environmental sanitation.* For the past fifty years, environmental sanitarians have assured that water, milk, meat, and other foods are disease free. To accomplish these ends, one city-county health department inspects milk plants and dairies; licenses milk haulers; inspects restaurants, bakeries, food warehouses, slaughter houses, and other food handling establishments; tests public water supplies; and reviews plans for subdivisions to make sure septic tanks are adequate. Environmental sanitation also includes taking steps to eliminate mosquitoes, flies, rabid dogs, and other carriers of disease.

*Laboratory.* Larger county health departments have laboratories used to conduct bacteriological tests on water samples taken from public water supplies and other places, to analyze strains of viruses, and to perform other public health functions.

*Public health education.* County health departments prepare pamphlets for free distribution, news releases, slides, and programs for use in schools and community meetings. They inform the general public of health problems, educate them on ways they can improve their own health, and enlist support for community public health programs.

In the past several decades, newer county health programs have been developed or existing programs have greatly changed in the following areas.

*Alcohol control.* In combatting alcoholism, Los Angeles County uses identification services, detoxification, and residential treatment programs at the Antelope Valley and Warm Springs Rehabilitation Centers, and non-residential treatment through self-help groups, day treatment, vocational rehabilitation, and drop-in services.[27] Lake County (Illinois), Broward County (Florida), and Adams County (Colorado) are among a number of other counties with excellent alcoholism programs.[28]

*Drug control.* County drug programs include drug detoxification centers, drug education for school-aged youths and adults, and drug law enforcement through police officials. Contra Costa County (California) has a center which combines drug education with mental health treatment and juvenile delinquency prevention.[29]

*Dental health.* Dentists and dental hygienists in a number of county health departments fill cavities, treat diseased gums, give dental examinations, and encourage patients to take better care of their own teeth. Most dental health programs provide service mainly for low income children and adults.

*Animal control.* County sanitarians have been trying to control rodents for decades, but massive rat control programs are of more recent origin. Allegheny County (Pennsylvania) has won national acclaim for its program of removing debris from vacant lots, poisoning rats, placing tight fitting lids on garbage cans, and other means of greatly reducing the rodent population. Baker County (Oregon) is one of a number of counties which has a program to innoculate all dogs for rabies to control this disease.

*Nutrition programs.* A number of county health departments participate in a new federal supplemental food program entitled the Women, Infants, and Children Program. Under this program, low income women (from pregnancy to a year following delivery) and children (from birth through five years) are eligible for vouchers which can be cashed at stores for additional food.

Many county governments also operate health institutions for the people of the entire county. The following kinds of institutions are operated by various counties.[30]

*General hospitals and outpatient facilities.* Westchester County (New York) administers a large general hospital at Grasslands which provides care for about 6,200 patients a year. The hospital offers numerous specialized services, and maintains sixty outpatient clinics.

*Mental health facilities and outpatient centers.* County governments operate both mental hospitals and community mental health centers. Dallas County (Texas), for example, has two community mental health centers for adults and one for children. These centers provide day treatment, outpatient services at various locations in the county, and a twenty-four hour a day counseling program.

*Institutions and programs for the mentally retarded.* In some counties, such as Duplin County (North Carolina), programs for the mentally retarded are provided as part of the services furnished by a mental health center. In Dallas County (Texas), in contrast, the county has several developmental centers solely for mentally retarded children and two work training centers for vocational training for older adolescents and adult retarded persons.

*Nursing homes and homes for the aged.* Maintaining a home for the aged is a traditional county function. A number of counties have either remodeled these homes into nursing homes or built new, modern nursing homes. The Orange County (New York) nursing home has physical therapists, a recreation department, and a speech therapist, as well as nurses and physicians.

Each of the separate health care services provided by county government can be considered a subsystem of the larger health care system within the county. County health departments cooperate with federal, state, city, and other agencies which operate other health care facilities and programs in the area. The role of county government in health care services is mainly to establish, administer, and finance health departments and health care institutions which serve the entire county. County governments also join in the operation of joint city-county health departments, such as the Salt Lake City-County Health Department, or multi-county agencies, such as the three-county mental health program of Henry, Louisa, and Jefferson Counties in Iowa.[31] County health departments may also provide health services under contract, as Orange County (New York) provides home health care for Medicare patients under contract to the federal government.

**Public Assistance and Social Services.** County governments have been providing poor relief in various forms since the 1600s. The usual form of county assistance in the early 1800s was the almshouse or poor house which cared for the aged poor, children abandoned because of the death or desertion of their parents, the insane, the feeble-minded, inebriates, and other poor persons. One of the major aims of welfare reform in the 1800s was to provide different institutions for the aged, dependent children, the insane, and other groups living in the county almshouse. As a result of the reforms, the almshouses eventually were replaced by public institutions for the mentally ill and mentally retarded, homes for dependent children, and nursing homes for the aged.

During the 1930s, another wave

of reforms occurred, and the financial burdens of welfare were shifted more to the state and federal governments. In 1935, Congress passed the Social Security Act which included a series of public assistance grant programs providing funds to selected categories of indigent persons (i.e. persons 65 and older, the blind, the disabled, and women with dependent children).[32] Some states directly administered the federally aided public assistance programs themselves, leaving county and city welfare programs to furnish assistance to a smaller group of indigent persons who did not qualify for federal programs. In other states, such as New York, California, and Minnesota, state governments delegated the responsibility for providing both federally and non-federally aided public assistance to local government—principally county government.

There have been many changes in county public assistance programs since the 1930s. Direct cash grants to the aged, blind, and permanently and totally disabled (formerly a state or county administered function) are now specifically administered by the U.S. Social Security Administration. The federal government, through this Administration, now operates the Medicare program which provides medical benefits for elderly and disabled persons who formerly would have received medical care from state and county programs. However, county welfare functions have expanded greatly since the 1930s to administer the food stamp programs and furnish many types of social services not provided earlier.

Although welfare is a traditional county function, the services pro-vided have changed so extensively in the past century that, in some ways, it is actually one of the most modern county programs. Currently, federal-state-local public assistance and social services programs can be grouped into three broad categories: (1) income maintenance programs which provide the daily living expenses of indigent persons; (2) medical care programs; and (3) social services. Table 7-1 lists the level (or levels) of government responsible for direct administration and funding of each of these programs.

In the mid-1970s, county governments were responsible for administering the following public assistance and social services programs in various parts of the nation.

*Aid to Families with Dependent Children.*[33] In some states, this program of direct cash assistance to indigent women with dependent children is administered by county government using federal, state, and county funds. In Orange County (New York), as in many other counties, a woman who wishes Aid to Families with Dependent Children (AFDC) is interviewed by an intake worker in the County Department of Social Services to determine what income and assets she owns. If she is divorced and not receiving alimony from her husband, she is assisted in getting court action to try to get the amount due her. If she and her children are eligible for public assistance, the intake worker will first compute their needs, taking into account an allowance for rent, utilities, food, clothing, and incidentals. The intake worker will deduct income from alimony and other sources in computing the grant. Those participating in the program receive a monthly

Table 7-1

**FEDERAL-STATE-LOCAL PUBLIC ASSISTANCE AND
SOCIAL SERVICES PROGRAMS IN 1975**

| Program | Direct Administration | Source of Funding |
|---|---|---|
| Income maintenance programs | | |
| Social Security | Federal | Federal (from contributions of employees and employers) |
| Supplementary security income for the aged, blind and disabled | Federal | Federal |
| Aid to Families with Dependent Children | State, county, cities and other local government units | Federal, state, and local. However, many counties supplement these payments using their own funds. |
| Food stamps | State and local | Federal funds pay the cost of the stamps, and federal, state, and local funds are used for administration |
| Emergency Assistance | State and local | Federal, state, and local |
| Medical care | | |
| Medicare* | Federal | Federal |
| Medicaid | State and local | Federal, state, and local |
| Social services and other services | State and local | Federal, state, and local |

*Fiscal intermediaries (usually private insurance companies) and state and local governments may also have a role in processing claims or providing medical services.

grant, food stamps, Medicaid, and the services of a social worker if they request it.

*Food stamps.* Public assistance recipients are automatically eligible for food stamps, and other people with low income are eligible if their income and assets fall below a certain amount. A person applying for food stamps is asked to list his or her income and assets, and this information is used to determine the amount of stamps he or she is eligible to purchase and the price to be paid. With the proper authorization, a person may purchase food stamps and turn them in for groceries. The store owner, in turn, redeems the stamps and receives a small handling fee as well as reimbursement for the stamps.

*Income maintenance emergency assistance.* There are many low income persons who qualify for food stamps but do not qualify for other forms of income maintenance because they are not 65 or older, blind, disabled, or a mother with dependent children. These individuals may turn to the county for emergency assistance. Warren County (Kentucky), for example, has an emergency program which provides funds for food, clothing, rent, utilities, fuel, and drugs for needy persons.[34] The means of providing food is a grocery order which the person takes to a food store and uses to purchase food up to the amount of the order.

*Medicaid.* The Medicaid program is an expanded program of federal grants for health care costs of needy persons of all age groups and should not be confused with the Medicare program, a federally administered medical program for persons sixty-five years of age and older and some disabled persons. Those eligible for Medicaid include: indigent persons with dependent children, the blind, the disabled, children in foster care, and other low income persons. They receive hospitalization, physicians' services, home health services, nursing home care, prescription drugs, and other types of medical care. In Orange County (New York) and in other counties, administration of Medicaid is integrated with other county social service and health programs such as home nursing, social services, and the nursing home.

*Individual and family social services.* County governments are providing many types of social services to adults to help them achieve self-sufficiency. Mothers receiving aid for dependent children may receive training and employment counseling to help them become employable. During the period of their training,

their children may be cared for in child care centers and their transportation to and from the training institution may be paid. The Pueblo County (Colorado) Department of Social Services has even established an Emergency Crisis Unit which provides suicide prevention and crisis intervention services.[35]

*Child welfare.* Child welfare caseworkers in county social service departments have provided social services to the courts in determining whether to place dependent and delinquent children in foster homes or child caring institutions, or to allow them to remain in their own homes as wards of the court. They may also be asked by the courts to find foster homes for children and provide counseling to children in foster homes or in their own homes. Child welfare workers have also furnished adoptive services for children and investigated cases of child abuse. Individual and group counseling for disturbed youth is sometimes provided by counties, and Wayne County (Michigan), for example, has a referral center for developmentally disabled and retarded youth.[36]

*Day care.* County governments may administer day care programs for particular groups of children such as those whose mothers are receiving aid to families with dependent children and are in training programs to make them employable. To assist day care center personnel, Nassau County (New York) provides classroom instruction for them in child care, nutrition, and other subjects.[37]

*Programs for the aging.* Westchester County (New York) has established a County Office for the

Aging with an information service which refers senior citizens to agencies which provide financial, medical, and other types of assistance.[38] This office also organizes volunteers to provide transportation for shopping trips for the elderly and contributes to the cost of more than fifteen social centers for senior citizens. Hot noon meals are served at these centers, and the county supervises the nutritional aspects of this hot meal program as well as maintaining lists of public and low income housing for use by senior citizens. Nassau County (New York) has a program which recruits retired senior citizens as volunteers to help in nursing homes, school libraries, and Head Start programs. Ventura County (California) provides mobile grocery services which go to the elderly who cannot get out to shop.[39] The combined pressures of an aging American population, continuing early retirement, scarce jobs, and greater amounts of leisure time are all likely to cause increases in county programs for the aging for years to come.

County public assistance and social services programs have changed greatly since the county almshouses of the 1800s, and further change is to be expected in the future. The national-state-local public welfare system has become a center of controversy—particularly in the last decade. Many are concerned about the mounting costs of welfare, the number of ineligible recipients, and the effect of welfare in undermining the ethic of hard work which built the nation. Others are critical because they feel grants are at bare subsistence levels, welfare policies are demeaning to recipients, and

insufficient emphasis is placed on giving recipients the training and social services they need to become self-sufficient. Concern has also been expressed about the lack of uniformity in the welfare system with grants in the wealthiest states averaging several times those in the poorest states. Among the many recommendations for sweeping reform in the welfare system have been proposals for a family assistance program, a children's allowance system, a negative income tax, and reforms which place greater fiscal responsibility on state governments and those which involve greater federal administration and financing.[40]

In 1976, the National Association of Counties developed its own proposal for welfare reform which called for the gradual replacement of Aid to Families with Dependent Children and general assistance with three separate and distinct programs.[41]

*A work security program for employable persons.* This would aid employable persons who are available for work, persons potentially employable, and the working poor whose earnings are below a federally established minimum level. The aim of the program would be to provide employment opportunities at adequate wages. It would provide employment services, job development training and work experience. The stress would be on the creation of jobs in the private sector first, but there would be jobs created in the public sector in times of need.

The program would provide recipients with an income during periods of training and unemployment, but persons receiving work security benefits would be required to accept work or training as a condition of eligibility. Where work security employment is necessary, jobs would be federally financed but responsibility for job development would lie primarily with local government.

*An income security program for persons unable to work.* The objective of this program would be "to assure basic necessities for health and decent living for those who are clearly unemployable, and to minimize the problems of family disruption caused by lack of an adequate income."[42] It would provide uniform standards of eligibility throughout the nation with variations in grants as needed to account for regional differences in the cost of living. The costs of this program would be met by the federal government.

*Social services program.* This would be "designed to achieve the full objectives of encouraging self-support, self-reliance, strengthening of family life and the protection of children and adults."[43] It would be a locally administered program which would receive federal funding.

Recognizing that it may take many years for Congress to take the necessary action to implement the long range plan, the National Association of Counties has proposed a number of interim reform measures such as simplification of welfare and food stamp regulations.

Proposed welfare reforms have been described in some detail in this chapter in order to indicate that substantial changes in county public assistance and social services programs are likely to occur in the next decade. President Carter is an exponent of welfare reform and, as this book goes to press, his proposals are being prepared in final form for presentation to Congress.

**Manpower.** County manpower programs grew out of the needs of the hard-core unemployed for counseling, education, on-the-job training, and placement in private and public service jobs. The Comprehensive Employment and Training Act of 1973 (often called CETA) consolidated many of the earlier manpower programs into a single bill and greatly expanded the small grants available to cities and counties for manpower programs in the early 1970s.[44] The Act also provided state and local government control over programs previously operated by direct contract with federal agencies. The major sections of CETA administered by local governments are:[45]

- *Title I, which provides an unemployed or poor person the opportunity to get the counseling, further education, and on-the-job training he or she needs to find a job in private business or public service.*

- *Title II, which furnishes a public employment program to see that unemployed and underemployed persons are placed in jobs in state government, local government, or private non-profit agencies. The program is intended to provide transitional employment to individuals to learn new skills, develop new careers, and move into public or private jobs within a year or two.*

- *Title VI, which was added a year after the passage of the rest of the Act, and provides for an emergency public works program intended to supply large numbers of short-term jobs for periods when national unemployment is very high.*

The key local administrative agencies for the CETA program (called prime sponsors) operate the manpower programs on their own or subcontract with others to deliver these services. A prime sponsor could be: a state government; a unit of general purpose local government (i.e. county, city, town, or township) which has a population of 100,000 or more persons; or, any combination of local governments (called consortia) where one of the governments has 100,000 or more persons.[46] In fiscal 1977, there were 179 county governments, 66 city governments, and 135 consortia (or combinations) of local governments acting as prime sponsors.[47]

County governments have three basic roles under the CETA manpower programs.

*Prime Sponsor.* In this role county manpower agencies work directly with federal officials and are supported 100% by federal funds. They develop their own counseling, training, and public service placement programs under federal guidelines and can contract with (or pay) other local agencies for part of the work. For example, the Orange County (New York) Manpower Administration has a close working relationship with the County Board of Cooperative Educational Services which runs the vocational school in the county.[48] The vocational school makes periodic studies of the job market to determine what skills employers need and trains unemployed persons in these skills. When the vocational

school finds a need for a particular skill, such as welding, in the county, the County Manpower Administration pays the tuition of the unemployed trainees plus their living expenses while they take the course.

The Orange County Manpower Administration also works with city and township officials in developing public service jobs under Title II of the CETA program. The Orange County Manpower Administration administered the Title VI program entirely on a county basis in the winter of 1974-75. County department directors were asked to list the positions they most needed to fill, job descriptions were prepared by the County Personnel Department, and 110 county public service positions were filled in less than a month.

*Member of a consortium.* This is a second role of county government in manpower programs. King and Snohomish Counties, the city of Seattle, and six smaller cities have formed a consortium in western Washington. In northeastern Florida, the consortium covers Duval, Baker, and Nassau Counties, and the administration of the three-county program is under the Manpower Division of the Jacksonville-Duval County Human Resources Department. The Mayor of the consolidated city-county of Jacksonville-Duval County and the Chairmen of the County Commissions of Baker and Nassau Counties sign the official consortium documents.[49]

*Sub-grantee.* Acting as a program agent, a county government receives an allocation from a prime sponsor to provide certain manpower services. During the spring of 1976, for example, the Kennebec County

(Maine) CETA Office was a program agent for the State Office of Planning and Coordination in Maine.[50] The Kennebec County CETA Office developed jobs for the hard core unemployed and handled the fiscal reimbursement of cities, towns, and other governmental and non-profit agencies which employed CETA workers.

**Education.** Educational services have been provided by county governments for more than a century, but the types of services have changed significantly since World War II as new needs have arisen. The traditional educational functions of counties have been to administer elementary and secondary school systems in certain parts of the nation, to collect property taxes for school districts and other school systems, and to provide a variety of services to local school districts through a county superintendent of schools. These county services continue although the office of county superintendent of schools has been abolished in some states. Since World War II, county governments have undertaken newer responsibilities in establishing community colleges and vocational technical schools.

*Public schools.* In 1971-72, more than five hundred counties operated public school systems which provided education for nearly 3.4 million school children. County school systems were the predominant form of school organization in Alaska, Maryland, North Carolina, Tennessee, and Virginia in 1971-72 and were also found in nine other states.[51] There are a number of outstanding county school systems, including the Montgomery County (Maryland)

system which had an enrollment of 124,000 students in 1974-75.[52] Educational policy in the Montgomery County system is made by an elected, seven-member Board of Education, and the system is administered by a professional staff headed by a board-appointed Superintendent of Schools. The school system is a service of county government: the County Executive makes budget recommendations for the schools, and the County Council decides the amount which will be appropriated for schools in the county.

*The county superintendent of schools.* Although the importance of this office is diminishing in many states, the county superintendent still plays a useful role in states like Nebraska. In Hall County (Nebraska), the Superintendent of Schools is elected on a non-partisan basis and serves as a coordinating officer between the twenty school districts in the county and the State Education Department.[53] Other functions of the Hall County School Superintendent include assisting in curriculum development, visiting schools, handling teacher certification, reviewing budgets and annual financial reports, and holding teachers' institutes. In other states, the county superintendent of schools may help maintain a film library for schools, assist in preparing curriculum guides, and provide remedial reading teachers and other specialists which small school districts cannot otherwise afford. Regional superintendents are elected in some multi-county areas in Illinois.[54]

*Vocational-technical programs.* County vocational school systems are found in states like Maryland, which operate their own school sys-

Table 7-2

## PUBLIC SCHOOL SYSTEMS IN THE UNITED STATES IN 1971-72

| | October 1971 | | |
| --- | --- | --- | --- |
| | Number of Public School Systems | Public School Enrollment | Enrollment Percent |
| Independent school districts | 15,780 | 38,933,329 | 81.1% |
| Municipal school systems | 300 | 4,289,846 | 8.9 |
| County school systems | 508 | 3,384,500 | 7.0 |
| Town or township school systems | 643 | 1,192,809 | 2.5 |
| Pennsylvania "joint schools" | 3 | 7,752 | z |
| State school systems | 3 | 200,838 | 0.4 |
| Total | 17,237 | 48,009,074 | 100.0% |

SOURCE: U.S. Bureau of the Census, *Public School Systems in 1971-72, 1972 Census of Governments* (Washington: U.S. Government Printing Office, December, 1972), p. 8. The Census of Governments is published every five years and the 1972 Census provides the latest comprehensive statistics on school enrollment. The U.S. Bureau of the Census counts Alaskan boroughs as a county government. The symbol "z" used in the table by the Bureau of the Census means less than one-tenth of one percent.

tems, and New Jersey, in which the vocational school system is separate from the elementary and secondary system. Typical of the separate vocational school system is the one administered by the Camden County (New Jersey) Vocational Board of Education.[55] The county operates two vocational high schools with students spending half a day in academic and other classroom work and the other half day enrolled in vocational programs such as auto mechanics, arc welding, tool and die work, brick laying, and food processing. Four mobile vocational units are stationed in trailers and move periodically from school to school to provide instruction in computerized typesetting, laminating press operation, and other skills.

*Community colleges.* More than three hundred county governments either directly administer community colleges or provide financial, legal, or other types of support to them. Most county community colleges have been established since World War II. Montgomery County College, (Md.) for example, was begun in 1946. The founding group of parents and teachers were concerned about the difficulty experienced by returning servicemen in entering four year colleges, and about the problems faced by high school graduates from middle and lower income families in financing college tuition and living expenses away from home.[56]

Montgomery College currently has an enrollment of more than 13,000 students and offers three different curricula. It has a "transfer curriculum" which leads to an associate in arts degree and is considered a stepping stone to the junior and senior years at a four year college or university. The College also has a career curriculum in fields such as computer technology, law enforcement, and medical and dental laboratory technology which enables a student to enter a career after his first two-year associate degree. The third curriculum is a one year program leading to a certificate in a particular employment field such as child care aide, dental assistant, secretary, or instructional aide.

County community colleges provide an education for many low income students who can afford a college education only because they can live at home and work part-time while going to school. As William Harper has pointed out, the community college has particularly benefited hard working individuals from less favored socio-economic groups such as a young, black, legless Vietnam veteran who attended Burlington County College (New Jersey).[57]

Community colleges have also aided county government. A 1975 study conducted by the National Association of Counties showed that 70% of the reporting county community colleges had training programs for county and other local government officials; 70% cooperated with county government in providing services to the public; and 30% performed some research for county government.[58] Examples of the specialized training programs offered by county community colleges to meet county needs include: training sessions for foster parents offered by Westmoreland County Community College (Pennsylvania); the Institute of Local Government at Westchester County Community College (New York); project work in planning of-

fered at the Genesee County (New York) Community College; and managerial courses and workshops developed for county government personnel by the Prince George's County (Maryland) Community College.[59]

County educational systems provide valuable services for other county human needs programs. For example, vocational-technical programs in counties such as Morris County (New Jersey) and Madison County (Illinois) help county manpower agencies provide unemployed persons with the skills they need to find jobs.[60]

**Human Services Planning.** County human services planning involves analyzing existing programs for health, public assistance, social services, manpower, and education within a county area and planning for better coordination. One of the problems encountered by county government in furnishing such services is coordinating programs among agencies providing similar services to the same family at the local level. A family, consisting of a mother with dependent children, may be receiving aid to families with dependent children, food stamps, counseling and vocational education through a county manpower program, day care for her children while in training, and a number of health services including free physical examinations and immunizations for her children in health clinics. Since the various agencies providing services may inadvertently work at cross-purposes, it is very important that social workers, physicians, nurses, and manpower specialists working with the family maintain close contact with one another. This can best be done when all (or almost all) agencies providing service to the same family are administered by the same unit of government. In some areas of the nation, county governments provide all of these services.

A comprehensive study of human services administration in six counties showed that the delivery of human services was improved by a reorganization or fundamental change in the structure of county government.[61] Contra Costa County (California) for example, improved human services delivery by placing all health, social services, and mental health services into a Human Resources Agency. Weld County, the first county in Colorado to adopt a charter, has combined within its Human Services Division, programs on manpower, youth services, day care, head start, supplemental foods, volunteer resources, senior citizen nutrition, and other human resources programs.[62] Counties with home rule charters, like Weld County, have the advantage of greater flexibility in making changes in governmental structure needed to integrate human services.

The coordination of human resources programs has been encouraged by broader federal grants such as those provided by Title XX of the Social Security Act which became law in January, 1976. With the assistance of a federal grant in 1974, the National Association of Counties took an important step in aiding counties to integrate their human resources by locating human resources coordinators in several state associations.[63] They improved the coordination of county-run human resources programs with those of community action agencies and state departments.

## OTHER SERVICE SYSTEMS

Criminal justice and human services are two of five major county service systems. The remaining three are described in the next chapter.

REFERENCES

1. The President's Commission on Law Enforcement and Administration of Justice, *The Challenge of Crime in a Free Society* (Washington: U.S. Government Printing Office, 1967), p. 7.

2. See Table 6-3, Chapter 6.

3. Advisory Commission on Intergovernmental Relations, *State-Local Relations in the Criminal Justice System* (Washington: U.S. Government Printing Office, 1971), p. 14.

4. Ibid., p. 17.

5. Ibid., p. 19. In multi-county and interstate areas, the Commission recommended that regional criminal justice planning agencies, councils of governments, or multi-county

agencies perform these functions. The President's Commission on Law Enforcement and Administration of Justice, *The Challenge of Crime in a Free Society,* p. 123, recommended that each county should take action toward consolidation of police services through the particular technique which would provide the best law enforcement at the least cost.

6.  The survey is described in S. Anthony McCann, "Law Enforcement Agencies in Urban Counties," *The County Year Book, 1975* (Washington: National Association of Counties and International City Management Association, 1975), p. 111. Police forces in 97 counties of 250,000 or more people responded to the survey.

7.  The county examples are mainly from The President's Commission on Law Enforcement and the Administration of Justice, *Task Force Report: The Police* (Washington: U.S. Government Printing Office, 1967), pp. 68-112.

8.  Kenneth VerBurg, *Guide to Michigan County Government* (East Lansing: Michigan State University, 1972), pp. vi-9, vi-11.

9.  Paul M. Hirsch, *Guidebook to Georgia County Government* (Athens: University of Georgia, 1970), pp. 122-125, describes the Georgia Superior Court.

10. Kenneth VerBurg, pp. vi-12 through vi-14.

11. The information was obtained by the writer from a tour of the Detention Center and discussions with prison officials on January 13, 1976.

12. Data obtained from the Jackson County (Missouri) Department of Corrections.

13. The Alameda County (California) Treatment Alternatives to Street Crimes program of the early 1970s was a good example of such a program. For a full description see S. Anthony McCann, *Local Alternatives to Arrest, Incarceration and Adjudication* (Washington: National Association of Counties Research Foundation, 1974), pp. 20, 21. In 1975, this program was changed, and placement in a drug program is no longer used as a basis for dropping charges against an individual. Loren W. Enoch, letter to Sydney Duncombe, November 12, 1976

14. Boulder County, Colorado, *The Development, Design and Programs of the Boulder County Justice Center,* (Washington: National Association of Counties, 1973).

15. Rennselaer County (New York) Department of Youth, "A Brief History of the Rennselaer County Department for Youth and Its Varied Functions and Responsibilities," December, 1975. (Mimeographed.)

16. S. Anthony McCann, *Local Alternatives to Arrest, Incarceration and Adjudication,* pp. 15, 16.

17. State prosecutor systems are used in Alaska, Delaware, and Rhode Island, and state-appointed local prosecutors are used in Connecticut and New Jersey, according to Advisory Commission on Intergovernmental Relations, *State-Local Relations in the Criminal Justice System,* pp. 112-115.

18. After the preliminary hearing, if the judge believes that a crime has been committed and there are reasonable grounds for believing the defendant guilty, he will "bind" over the suspect for action by the prosecutor or grand jury.

19. Gideon v. Wainwright, 372 U.S. 335 (1963). In Argersinger v. Hamlin, 407 U.S. 25 (1972), the U.S. Supreme Court made clear that defendants had the right to government-paid counsel even to defend them against certain misdemeanor charges if they were in danger of going to jail.

20. The Santa Clara County program is described in National Association of Counties, *Special Report on County Criminal Justice Programs* (Washington: National Association of Counties, 1974), pp. 53-69. This information was updated by later information from the county dated October 16, 1976.

21. Information obtained by an interview with Mr. Glenn Billings, Chairman of the Board of County Commissioners of Weld County, January 2, 1976, and by letter dated October 21, 1976.

22. For an excellent description of the federal legislation and its effect, see Advisory Commission on Intergovernmental Relations, *Making the Safe Streets Act Work: An Intergovernmental Challenge* (Washington: Advisory Commission on Intergovernmental Relations, 1970).

23. Duane Baltz, *Organizing and Reorganizing for Local Criminal Justice Planning: Five Examples* (Washington: National Association of Counties, 1975) was used as the source for the three examples.

24. Information about the Allegheny County Health Department program in this section was obtained from interviews in June, 1976; from the 1975 annual report of the Department; and by letter of October 27, 1976, from the Director of the Department, Dr. Frank B. Clack.

25. The writer is indebted to Dr. Harry L. Gibbons, Director of the Salt Lake City-County Health Department, for personal interviews; a letter of September 20, 1976; and reports which are used to describe the program in this section.

26. Information on the Orange County (New York) program was obtained from interviews in January, 1976, with Dr. Samuel Karling and Mrs. Shirley VanZetta of the Orange County Department of Health.

27. Stanley R. Steenbock, letter to Sydney Duncombe, December 30, 1976.

28. National Association of Counties, *Living Library*, 7th ed. (Washington: National Association of Counties, 1976), pp. 17, 18.

29. Ibid., p. 17.

30. The information on the Westchester and Dallas County programs was provided from publications of these counties. The author obtained information about the Orange County nursing home from a tour of the facilities in January, 1976. The Duplin County program is described in National Association of Counties, *Living Library*, 7th ed., p. 17.

31. The three-county mental health program in Iowa is run by a Board of Directors composed of one of the county supervisors from each of the three counties plus five citizens appointed by these three county supervisors. Information on the Salt Lake City-County Health Department and the Iowa mental health program was obtained from interviews with officials of these counties in June, 1976.

32. The Social Security Act also established an unemployment compensation program, and the Social Security Program collected funds from employers and employees during a person's working years and paid benefits to senior citizens.

33. Information on the Orange County (New York) program was provided by Angelie Parker, Orange County Department of Social Services, in an interview June 14, 1976. In some states, an indigent man with dependent children is eligible for aid to families with dependent children.

34. Information obtained by interview with the Director of the Warren County (Kentucky) Welfare Unit, January 7, 1976.

35. The information obtained for this case is from the 1975 County Achievement Award for Pueblo County, filed in the offices of the National Associaton of Counties.

36. Information obtained from the Achievement Award files of the National Association of Counties.

37. Ibid.

38. Information obtained from interview with personnel of the Westchester County Office of the Aging on January 16, 1976.

39. Clinton Tatum, Administrative Analyst, Ventura County (California), letter to Sydney Duncombe, November 22, 1976.

40. For a description of the family assistance program, see Committee for Economic Development, *Improving the Public Welfare System* (New York: Committee for Economic Development, 1970), pp. 57, 58, and Vincent J. and Vee Burke, *Nixon's Good Deed* (New York: Columbia University Press, 1974). For a brief description of the children's allowance system and the negative income tax, see Joel H. Handler, *Reforming the Poor: Welfare Policy, Federalism and Morality* (New York Basic Books, 1972), pp. 76-80. Other recommendations for reform may be found in Committee for Economic Development, *Welfare Reform and Its Financing* (New York: Committee for Economic Development, 1976) and Linda E. Demkovitch "Welfare Report," *National Journal*, 8(February 21, 1976): 234-240.

41. National Association of Counties, *Welfare Reform—A Plan for a Change* (Washington: National Association of Counties, June, 1976). p. 3.

42. Ibid., p. 5.

43. Ibid.

44. The earlier federal laws included the Area Redevelopment Act of 1961, the Manpower Development and Training Act of 1962, and the Economic Opportunity Act of 1964. For a description of the earlier acts and the Cooperative Area Manpower Program of the late 1960s see Thomas H. Patten, *Manpower Planning and the Development of Human Resources* (New York: John Wiley and Sons, 1971), pp. 640-672.

45. Summarized from the Comprehensive Employment and Training Act of 1973. Title III should also be mentioned although it is federally administered. Some counties have received funds from Title III to administer summer work programs for disadvantaged youths.

46. Comprehensive Employment and Training Act of 1973, Section 102. For a full description of "prime sponsor" and other manpower terms, see National Association of Counties, *Everything You Ever Wanted to Know About Manpower* (Washington: National Association of Counties, n.d.). The National Association of Counties publishes an excellent series of reports on manpower as part of its services to county officials.

47. Data from the U.S. Department of Labor in the files of the National Association of Counties.

48. Information obtained from an interview with the Director of the Orange County Manpower Administration, January 14, 1976.

49. Data on the Northeastern Florida Manpower Consortium was obtained from a letter from

Suzann Dutton, Planning Supervisor, Jacksonville-Duval Manpower Division, dated April 30, 1976, and from other unpublished Manpower Division sources.

50. Kennebec County has since become a prime sponsor. The author interviewed personnel of the Kennebec County Manpower Office in April, 1976.

51. U.S. Bureau of the Census, *1972 Census of Governments,* Volume 1, *Governmental Organization* (Washington: U.S. Government Printing Office, 1973), pp. 40-63, lists the number of county and other types of school systems in each state and the number of pupils enrolled.

52. Information on the Montgomery County school system was provided by reports supplied by the Office of Superintendent of Schools of the county. The Advisory Commission on Intergovernmental Relations considered the system one of the best in the nation in *Performance of Urban Functions: Local and Areawide* (Washington: Advisory Commission on Intergovernmental Relations, 1963), pp. 79, 80.

53. Interview with Elizabeth Saunders, Hall County Superintendent of Education, June 25, 1976.

54. Warren and Henderson Counties (Illinois) share a regional Superintendent of Education.

55. Camden County (New Jersey) Vocational and Technical Schools, *1974-75 Annual Report,* (Camden: Camden County, 1975) provides a more extensive description of this program.

56. The founding of Montgomery College is described in William L. Fox, *Montgomery College, Maryland's First Community College* (Rockville: Montgomery College, 1970), pp. 7, 8. The Montgomery College Catalogue and an interview with a college official are the sources of information on the college program.

57. William A. Harper, "The Big News: Community Colleges," *New County Times,* (Washington), May 5, 1975, p. 5.

58. Survey returns from ninety-six county community colleges provide an excellent source of information on the financing, administration, and programs of these colleges. Thomas P. Bruderle, "Aid Vital to Community Colleges," *County News,* (Washington), May 5, 1975, p. 9.

59. Described in National Association of Counties, *Living Library,* 6th ed., p. 9, and Philip H. Hudson, "Tap the Resources at Your Community College," *New County Times,* (Washington), May 31, 1976, p. 13.

60. See Thomas P. Bruderle, "Counties Fight Unemployment with Education," *New County Times,* (Washington), May 31, 1976, p. 13.

61. For further information on human services integration and planning in Contra Costa and five other counties, see Al Templeton, *Human Services Integration at the Community Level: A Six County Report* (Washington: National Association of Counties Research Foundation, 1973). See particularly pp. 79-81.

62. Weld County Division of Human Resources, *Annual Report for 1975-76* (Greeley: Weld County Division of Human Resources, 1976).

63. The work of the eight human resources coordinators is described in National Association of Counties Research Foundation, *The Rural Human Resources Project, A Status Report* (Washington: National Association of Counties, 1974).

# Chapter 8

# Public Works, Parks, and Planning Systems

"Pinellas County, Florida faced a serious water supply problem during the 1950s. The water supply became endangered by salt water intrusion into areas of fresh water wells as rapid urbanization depleted fresh water reserves below the necessary level to balance the underlying salt water. Pinellas County acted in the mid-1950s to acquire water rights in the Eldridge fields in the northeast part of the county.

The county faced an even more severe water problem in the 1970s. Shortages made it necessary to reduce the average daily pumping of water from 36 million to 28 million gallons per day. The Pinellas County Water Department had to advise eighteen affected municipalities in the county that the county, as supplier of water, could not assure that an adequate and safe water supply would be available unless curtailment of building permits was required by the municipalities. The county government took the lead in facing the issue of growth and imposing a temporary building moratorium.

To assure that growth will not exceed water supply in the future, the Pinellas County Water Department now calculates monthly the number of gallons of water available for new growth. An allocation formula is applied to determine the amount of water available to each of the eighteen municipalities in the county and to the unincorporated areas. All building permit applications are being reviewed by the County Water Department to determine projected water consumption. Water connection permits are being issued by the County Water Department for municipal customers as well as those in unincorporated areas. When the specific allocation of water is reached, no further water connection permits are issued that month. The water shortage has forced a policy of managed growth in Pinellas County, and it is the county government which has taken the lead in setting the policies and the administration of the water allocation process.[1]

The water shortage faced by Pinellas County illustrates the exceedingly close relationships among water consumption, population growth, and the issuance of building permits. The shortage was caused by the failure of the underground water system to replenish itself faster than water was drawn from underground storage by wells. The result was the lack of underground reserves of fresh water necessary to balance the underlying salt water off the coast, creating a danger of salt water intrusion into the county's wells. The county first acted to acquire water rights to new underground fields, to bring new water supplies into the system and reduce dependence on existing wells. When this proved insufficient, a systems approach suggested consideration of alternative ways of reducing the use of underground water supplies. Rather than considering water supply, growth management, and the issuance of water connection permits as separate functions, county officials considered them together and calculated the number of gallons of water available for new growth. They then allocated this water to the eighteen municipalities and the unincorporated area of the county and controlled new use of the water supply by the issuance of water connection permits.

This chapter describes about half of the services listed in the survey of county functions in Table 6-3 of Chapter 6. The functions are grouped into three major service systems—some of which can be further divided into component sub-systems. The Pinellas County case study illustrates the degree to which county functions, such as water supply and growth management, are interconnected.

# TRANSPORTATION, UTILITY, NATURAL RESOURCES, AND ENVIRONMENTAL MANAGEMENT

County governments are involved in four related groups of functions which frequently require the services of an engineer. Transportation, utility, natural resources, and environmental management services all have an impact on air, water, land, and energy and thus affect our key environmental systems. For example, the type of transportation systems built within our counties affects the extent of air pollution from transportation, the use of scarce energy resources, and the location and extent of the use of land for roads, parking, airports, and other transportation facilities. The types of sewage treatment and solid waste disposal facilities used affect the purity of our water, the quality of our air, and the uses of land. In rural areas, county programs, such as flood control and soil conservation, have an impact on the quality of the soil and the amount of silt in water draining from agricultural lands.

**Transportation.** Construction and maintenance of roads and bridges is a traditional county function dating back to colonial times while airports, mass transit, and other forms of transportation services are modern county functions. County governments today furnish an increasingly important part of a transportation system which includes highway, rail, air, water, and mass transit elements.

*Road construction and maintenance.* County governments are responsible for maintenance of all or some roads and bridges in forty states. State governments maintain all rural roads in Alaska, Delaware, North Carolina, Rhode Island, and West Virginia, and a combination of state and town governments maintain roads in five New England states. Some of the differing roles counties play in highway administration are listed here.

- *In Nashville-Davidson County (Tennessee), the Department of Public Works is responsible for a single consolidated system of county highways and city streets. This practice is common in other city-county governments.*

- *In Milwaukee County (Wisconsin), Westchester County (New York), and other counties, the county government maintains an expressway or parkway system serving the entire county.*

- *In Michigan, the county and township road system has been merged and placed under the control of county road commissions.² These commissions are responsible for roads in the unincorporated areas of the county and also about 900 miles of roads inside cities and villages. The three members of the board of road commissioners are appointed by the county commissioners in most counties but are elected in a dozen counties. A professional county engineer is responsible for the day-to-day administration of the road system.*

- *In Mississippi, county government is responsible for a rural road system of more than 50,000 miles.³ The county board of supervisors may*

*choose to maintain roads on a county-wide basis, or each supervisor may be responsible for the improvement of roads in his or her own district.*

- *In Idaho, county government is responsible for the rural road system in nearly half the counties in the state.⁴ In some counties, county road departments and highway districts maintain highways in different sections of the county. In a few counties, all rural roads are highway district responsibilities with some elements of control in the hands of the county commissioners.*

- *In New York, Ohio and other states, there is a division of responsibility between county and township governments for rural roads. In Ohio, this division is largely determined by county commissioners who use reports from township boards of trustees.⁵*

*Traffic safety.⁶* County traffic safety programs include the collection of accident statistics to identify high accident locations and a system of taking traffic counts to determine where the volume of traffic requires new highways or traffic signal devices. Counties such as Sussex (New Jersey) also survey highways to determine appropriate speed limits. A system of traffic lights and other traffic signals is part of many county highway safety programs. Los Angeles County (California) uses computerized traffic control systems and has encouraged greater uniformity in traffic control systems in municipalities in the county. A system of traffic signs, route markers, and street signs which adequately identify county highways and streets is also important for traffic safety since motorists unsure of directions are often the cause of accidents. Fairfax County (Virginia) has an automated street directory system and maintains a current file of all streets in the county.

County traffic safety programs also include marked crosswalks used to improve pedestrian safety on county streets; county traffic codes; programs of reducing traffic accidents due to alcohol; and emergency medical services at the scene of accidents. County governments are even involved in driver education programs in counties operating school systems. For example, the Ventura County (California) Superintendent of Schools has developed a safety training program using color film strips for school children in the county's twenty-one school districts.

Traffic safety is frequently a responsibility of the County Engineer's Office, as in Shelby County (Alabama), but some counties such as Washington County (Oregon) coordinate safety programs through a Traffic Safety Office.

*Airports.* County governments have become involved in the provision of airport services in a number of ways. In Oakland County (Michigan), the county assumed ownership of the Oakland-Pontiac Airport in 1967 when a survey showed that only 5% of the persons, businesses, and corporations basing aircraft at the airport came from the City of Pontiac.[7] In the case of San Bernardino County (California), five airports built by the federal government suddenly reverted to county ownership after World War II.[8] The

county was faced with operating a coordinated airport system to insure that the flight patterns at the five county airports did not interfere with each other and with the other airports in the Los Angeles area. In the case of the Rock County Airport in Wisconsin, the decision to build a county airport came in 1943 after years of discussion and the realization that neither of the two main cities in the county could finance an airport by itself.[9]

A recent listing of county supported airports shows that there are ninety-two county governments, forty-seven city-county agencies, and seventeen county airport authorities with commercial service.[10] In addition, there are many more counties which operate smaller airports suitable for private and business planes. County governments have three major roles in airport administration:

- *to operate an airport system directly as Milwaukee County (Wisconsin) administers the major commercial airport in the area and a smaller private field;*

- *to participate in city-county operation of an airport as do Laramie County (Wyoming) and the city of Laramie; and,*

- *to administer an airport system through an authority such as the Indianapolis Airport Authority, an agency of the Metropolitan Government of Indianapolis and Marion County (Indiana).*

*Mass Transit.* Mass transit includes bus transportation, commuter railroads, subways, and other forms of transportation for large numbers of people. With a few exceptions, county governments have not provided railroad or other forms of non-highway mass transit. However, counties have a number of important roles in providing bus transportation as the following examples show:[11]

- *Operation of a city-county bus system. The Metropolitan Government of Nashville-Davidson County (Tennessee) has acquired a bus system and operates it through a Metropolitan Transit Authority.*

- *Subsidization of a city bus service. Los Angeles County (California) has used revenue sharing funds to subsidize seven municipal bus lines in the Los Angeles area. This has made possible a reduced bus fare to senior citizens.*

- *County operation of a bus system after a city system failed. Two years after the Muskegon City transit system was financially unable to continue bus services, Muskegon County (Michigan) established its own bus system serving the City of Muskegon and the surrounding area.*

- *County rural transportation system. The Dutchess County (New York) rural transportation system links the more rural central and eastern parts of the county with the more urbanized area around Poughkeepsie. The system began as a service for the disadvantaged and has expanded to provide bus service to the general public.*

- *County bus service for veterans. Ingham County (Michigan) owns and operates vans used to transport veterans to hospitals and other places.*

- *County bus system using volunteer drivers. Douglas County (Minnesota) has a bus system for the elderly which covers the entire county using volunteer drivers.*

- *County assistance to a multi-county bus system. Five Minnesota counties (Koochiching, Itasca, St. Louis, Cook, and Lake) contribute funds to a system of bus transportation operated by the Arrowhead Community Action Program for the five county area.*

*Parking, Bikeways, and Ferries.*[12] Montgomery County (Maryland) is one of a number of counties which have constructed parking facilities. The Division of Parking in the Montgomery County Department of Transportation is responsible for the planning, development, and operation of four parking lot districts within the county which employ nearly one hundred persons. The Division manages more than ten parking garages and thirty-five parking lots with a total capacity of more than ten thousand cars.

Recognizing that the bicycle has become an important mode of transportation in Dane County (Wisconsin), the City of Madison and Dane County have cooperated on a program of designated bicycle routes. The city has developed a network of bicycle trails within the city which connect with bicycle routes developed by the county. The County Highway Department has paved the shoulders of many county highways so that bicyclists do not have to ride on heavily traveled auto lanes.

A few counties operate ferries. Lack of a highway bridge across the Coosa River in Alabama prevented a direct highway connection between the county seat of Shelby County and the industrial center of neighboring Talladega County. The Shelby County Department of Public Works has acquired and is operating a ferry system to provide sixteen-hour-a-day ferry service.

**Water Supply, Sewage Treatment, and Power Generation.** County government historically has had a very limited role in the operation of utilities. Traditionally, private corporations or federal agencies (such as the Tennessee Valley Authority) have supplied most of the electric power in the nation. Cities, villages, towns, and water and sewer districts have usually provided most of the water to urban homes and carried away most of the sewage. Private and city utilities have financed their operations mainly from the sale of services, charges paid by home and business owners, and the issuance of revenue bonds. Generally, there has been little need for county utilities because rural residents could buy electricity from a private company, get water from their well, and run household sewage into a septic tank.

One of the reasons for the establishment of county utilities has been the difficulty experienced by existing utilities in expanding service. For example, the City of Decatur in De-Kalb County (Georgia) was unable to rely on Peachtree Creek for sufficient water in the 1930s, and the city could not pass a bond issue to cover the cost of the much larger water system needed to obtain water from the Chattahoochee River.[13] The Decatur Water System was leased to DeKalb County, and the county developed an entire system including water storage lakes, a pumping station, a filtration plant, and a water distribution system. The Decatur water system, which served 20,000 people, was sold to the county in 1975. The county now has the responsibility of serving 425,000 people—about 85% of the county population.

The economy of large scale operation of water supply and sewage disposal is another reason for county responsibility for these facilities. Authorities on water supply systems estimate that the cost per acre-foot of treated water may be more than 2½ times greater in a small water system than in a large one.[14] Counties are able to operate huge water systems at less cost per person than small special districts. Westchester County (New York), for example, is able to provide water to a large area of the county (including three cities of more than 50,000 people) at a lower cost than the water could be supplied by smaller cities.[15]

Environmental regulations might result in county operation of a sewer system because new types of treatment or new facilities are required but smaller units of government are unable to finance them. In Muskegon County (Michigan), for example, environmental requirements prevented reliance on primary sewage treatment with direct effluent discharge into Lake Michigan.[16] The county has developed an entirely different sewage treatment system in which the effluent is given secondary treatment, disinfected, and spray irrigated on crops. The effluent is filtered through the soil, collected in an underdrain system, and discharged into a river. The land treatment is equivalent to tertiary treatment and will meet Environmental Protection Agency standards through 1983.

In providing water and sewage disposal, county governments have assumed a variety of roles including the following:[17]

- *provider of the service to all or part of the county;*

- *creator of county subordinate districts as in the Westchester County (New York) water district;*

- *partner in a joint city-county or multi-county system (Cobb and Fulton Counties in Georgia, for example, have jointly funded a large sewage treatment plant); and,*

- *cooperator with city government in the extension of city services to unincorporated areas of the county as Guilford County (North Carolina) helped finance the extension of the sewer lines of Greensboro and High Point into the unincorporated areas of the county.*

Counties have only a minor role in electric power generation. County revenue from power amounted to only $11 million nationally in 1974-75.[18] County government may have an important future role in the development of solar heating systems for county buildings, such as the one used by Los Angeles County (California) to heat an enclosed swimming pool and the one used by Butler County (Ohio) to heat a county home for the aged.[19]

**Natural Resources Management.** The traditional types of natural resources management programs administered by counties involve drainage, flood control, and soil erosion prevention. In Michigan, an elected county drain commissioner plays an important role in reducing damage from excess water on agricultural and urban lands.[20] After a serious flood, Salt Lake County (Utah) was made responsible for building a storm drainage system in the unincorporated area of the county and extending this system through city areas.[21] While the largest national program to prevent soil erosion is administered by the U.S. Soil Conservation Service, counties have contributed funds to soil conservation districts. Moreover, some counties, such as Fairfax County (Virginia), have helped control sedimentation in residential areas through the adoption of sediment control ordinances which require preliminary plats of new subdivisions to show plans to prevent sediment runoff.[22]

The Arab oil boycott of October, 1973 and the resulting oil shortages have brought county governments yet another responsibility—conservation and management of energy. County governments have acted to manage their own energy consumption more wisely.[23] Orange County (California), for example, has reduced electricity 26% and fuel oil 56% through conservation measures such as installing time clocks in heating systems to reduce heating at night and time clocks in parking lot lighting systems to turn the lights off when not needed. County governments have also acted to encourage energy conservation by the general public. Ocean County (New Jersey), for example, created a citizens council which studied means of reducing energy consumption and made specific recommendations such as a car pooling plan to save gasoline. Nassau County (New York) created a Bureau of Energy Resources in 1973 which has been conducting an extensive public education program through the distribution of booklets and the use of radio programs, weekly newspaper columns, and public meetings. The Nassau County Bureau has had an "Econo-Van" parked at convenient locations in the county, and has invited citizens to test their cars for gasoline economy.

**Environmental Control and Management—Air, Water, and Solid Waste.**[24] County governments are responsible for two types of air pollution control. In those areas of the nation in which state government has the primary responsibility for enforcing air pollution emission standards against such large polluters as factories, county and city governments enforce air pollution control standards against small, localized sources.

In some metropolitan areas, counties have the main responsibility for enforcing air pollution standards. Allegheny County (Pennsylvania), for example, has the main air pollution control responsibility within the county.[25] The County Health Department uses more than one hundred air quality monitors to measure particulates, sulfur dioxide, and other pollutants, and analyses of air samples are made hourly so that Department officials can quickly discover and avert an air pollution buildup. The Allegheny County Health Department also makes emission tests of pollutants

from factory smokestacks. A system of emergency restrictions goes into effect when air pollution exceeds certain levels. Erie County (New York) has an air pollution program which has been very successful in securing voluntary compliance with the air pollution control code.

Federal and state, rather than county, agencies provide the main enforcement of water pollution controls. However, county health departments are frequently called upon to take water samples, check municipal water supplies, test the effluents of sewage treatment plants, and inspect the sanitation in public facilities. County sanitarians make sure that where septic tanks are used, there is a sufficiently large drain field so that lakes, streams, and ground water will not become polluted. In some cases, poor soil conditions make it hazardous to approve further septic tanks, and a county health department (such as the Allegheny County Health Department which serves Pittsburgh, Pennsylvania) will approve very few new septic tanks.[26] A few counties, such as Chester County (Pennsylvania) and Lee County (Florida), have systems of monitoring the purity of streams or lakes on a regular basis.[27]

The passage of the national Solid Waste Disposal Act of 1965 and subsequent state legislation have encouraged counties to establish their own solid waste collection and disposal systems.[28] These systems include many components: collection of refuse; transfer to disposal sites; disposal mainly through landfills and incineration; and, in some counties, recycling or recovery of materials from solid waste.[29] Refuse placed in garbage containers by home owners is collected by city, county, town, or private collectors and is usually taken directly to the disposal site. In some areas, however, it is taken to a transfer station where it is compacted and loaded mechanically into much larger trucks for transfer to a disposal site. In many rural areas, oversized containers have been placed at the junctions of rural roads and the main highway for the use of residents, and county-operated or franchised refuse collection trucks empty these containers.

Where sufficient land is available, the sanitary landfill is generally the most economical means of solid waste disposal. The refuse is usually placed in a large trench, compacted, and covered each night with about six inches of dirt. Covered sites have been used for county parks, golf courses (such as the one under construction in Mecklenburg County, North Carolina), a 250-foot-high winter sports hill (in DuPage County, Illinois), and cemented into dikes to prevent flash floods (in San Bernardino County, California).[30] Methane gas from landfill sites may also be used as a fuel, and Los Angeles County sanitation districts have contracted for its extraction.[31] Incineration is a method of reducing the volume of solid waste by burning the waste and placing the residue in a sanitary landfill. It is used in more populous areas where land is very expensive for landfills. The government of Nashville-Davidson County contracts with a public service corporation to operate an incinerator which produces heat for metropolitan buildings.

Some counties have used recycling to reclaim usable materials from solid waste.[32] Hennepin County (Minnesota) has dumped leaves in windrows, treated them with bacteria to expedite the decomposing process, shredded them, and then sold the product to the public as compost. Washington County (Arkansas) and Dade County (Florida) are among the counties which have sold abandoned cars to private firms for shredding and recycling. Ingham County (Michigan) has operated a pyrolysis plant for recycling and conversion of refuse.

Most county governments are not involved in resource recovery at this time, but are involved in the following ways in solid waste collection and disposal systems:[33]

- *Provider for the entire county. Carroll County (Missouri) is an example of a small county which operates a solid waste system for the entire county. Six garbage dumps have been replaced by a single sanitary landfill.*

- *Provider for the unincorporated area of the county. San Bernardino County (California), for example, has a solid waste system for the less densely populated areas of the county.*

- *Provider of the landfill. Hopkins County (Kentucky), for example, has constructed a sanitary landfill in an abandoned strip mine and is allowing cities in the county to use it for their refuse.*

- *Participant in multi-county agencies. County governments in Appanoose, Lucas, Monroe, and Wayne Counties in south-central Iowa have cooperated to manage a four-county solid waste system.*

## PARKS, RECREATION, AND CULTURE

Although the first county park was established in Essex County (New Jersey) in the 1890s, parks and recreation are not traditional functions of county government.[34] In 1932, only $8 million was being spent on parks and recreation by all counties in the nation. More than half the counties which now have parks and recreation programs did not begin them until after World War II. The involvement of most counties in cultural programs has also occurred in the past three decades. Parks, recreation, and cultural programs are optional functions; counties are not required by law to provide them.

The objectives of a parks system and a recreation program are basically similar. They are to "provide for all citizens, to the extent practicable, a variety of adequate year-round leisure opportunities which are accessible, safe, physically attractive, and provide enjoyable experiences."[35] They may also contribute to mental and physical health, thus decreasing crime and delinquency. Cultural activities provide enjoyment and experiences in art, music, and other intellectual and artistic pursuits.

**Parks.** County governments own more than 8.1 million acres of recreation land including: 1.3 million acres in parks and recreation areas, 4.0 million acres in forests, and 1.4 million acres in fish and game areas. County governments own less recreation land than the federal and state governments, but own more land than the combined recreation land holdings of city, township, and park district governments.

The park system developed by each American county varies greatly depending upon the needs of the county and the availability of federal, state, and county parks in the area. The following short case studies illustrate differing park systems which were developed to meet the needs of different size counties.

*Baker County, Oregon (14,919).*[36] The county is well endowed with mountain ranges, lakes, and national forest campgrounds. Its only city of more than 1,000 people has a city park with playground facilities. With many park and recreation needs supplied by other means, the county does not need to provide an entire park system. It has built the only park on the western side of a thirty mile long reservoir for fishing and boating. It is developing a larger park in a historic area previously dredge-mined for gold. A narrow gauge railway is being rebuilt for recreation purposes.

*Warren County, Kentucky (57,432).*[37] Warren County needs a larger park system than Baker County because it does not have the mountains, lakes, and forest campgrounds of Baker County. The largest city in Warren County, Bowling Green (36,253), has some small parks and an organized recreation program for city residents. The role of Warren County is to provide the largest park in the county with lighted ball fields, tennis courts, basketball courts, picnic areas, shelters, and other facilities. The county also owns a community center and eleven smaller parks scattered throughout the county.

*Shawnee County, Kansas (155,322).*[38] Shawnee County is the center of

TABLE 8-1

PUBLIC RECREATION ACREAGE BY TYPE OF AREA
AND ADMINISTERING JURISDICTION, 1972

(in thousands of acres)

| Administering Jurisdiction | Total | Regional, Community, and Neighborhood Parks and Recreation Areas | Forest Areas | Fish and Game Areas | Historic and Cultural Areas | Wilderness, Primitive, and Natural Areas | Other |
|---|---|---|---|---|---|---|---|
| Federal | 266,720 | 19,107 | 160,165 | 32,790 | 1,311 | 28,095 | 25,253 |
| State | 41,795 | 4,412 | 19,058 | 15,771 | 49 | 1,432 | 1,071 |
| County | 8,132 | 1,299 | 4,048 | 1,407 | 11 | 1,338 | 29 |
| City | 1,629 | 697 | 383 | 210 | 8 | 232 | 99 |
| Township | 631 | 74 | 496 | 38 | 1 | 22 | 1 |
| Park and Recreation Districts and Regional Councils | 336 | 167 | 10 | 45 | 2 | 94 | 18 |
| Total | 319,243 | 25,756 | 184,160 | 50,261 | 1,382 | 31,213 | 26,471 |

SOURCE: U.S. Bureau of Outdoor Recreation, *Outdoor Recreation, A Legacy for America* (Washington: Bureau of Outdoor Recreation, 1973), p. 24. Details may not exactly add to totals due to rounding.

a small metropolitan area, and its largest city, Topeka, has its own parks system. The role of the Shawnee County park system is to provide large regional parks with recreational facilities not found in city parks. The county currently operates a 616-acre park with a golf course, picnic areas, and a lake which provides boating, water skiing, fishing, and swimming. The county has a second park in the southern part of the county on an abandoned Air Force base and is developing a third park (with a community center and two fishing lakes) in the northern part of the county.

*Bucks County, Pennsylvania* (296,382).[39] Bucks County lies along the Delaware River within the Philadelphia metropolitan area. There are some state parks within the county

and a few city parks. The role of the county park system is to provide a balanced system of large and small parks which complement other parks within the county. The Bucks County Department of Parks and Recreation maintains twenty parks (having a total of 5,500 acres) with a staff of more than forty employees. Parks vary in size from parks of 500 acres with hiking trails, play fields, picnic groves, swimming pools, and lakes, to smaller parks with more limited facilities.

*Hennepin County, Minnesota (960,080).*[40] Hennepin County is a densely populated county which contains the City of Minneapolis with its well developed system of city parks. The role of Hennepin County is the preservation of 19,000 acres of land within the county for wildlife habitat and regional parks. The Hennepin County Park Reserve district maintains seven major park reserves of 1,000 to 5,000 acres in size which provide swimming areas with sandy beaches, picnic areas, trails for hiking and horseback riding, a golf course, boat launching areas, and other facilities. The parks also provide quiet woods, meadows, and marshes which support deer, heron, and other wildlife within a short drive from Minneapolis.

County governments have even used expressways, ocean liners, and old tires to develop parks and recreation facilities. Westchester County (New York) has turned a four lane, limited access highway into a beautiful parkway and fourteen-mile-long park along the Bronx River. Ventura County (California) turned an ocean liner which ran aground into a recreation facility, and Pinellas County (Florida) used tires to develop eight offshore reefs which have become important fishing areas.[41]

**Recreation Programs.** The traditional recreation programs of county, city, and other local park and recreation departments include:

• *for preschool children—organized playground games, story telling, and arts and crafts;*

• *for school-aged children—team sports such as baseball, softball, flag football and basketball; swimming, tennis, and golf instruction may be included;*

• *for young adults and some middle aged persons—evening softball, basketball, and other team sports as well as individual sports such as swimming, tennis, and golf; and,*

• *for senior citizens—horseshoe and shuffleboard tournaments and a variety of arts and crafts.*

County parks and recreation programs are generally administered by a single department, and there are many ways in which counties take advantage of the unique features of their parks to provide many types of recreation. Orange County (New York) provides a skiing program during the winter by turning the county golf course into a ski slope.[42] County recreational programs have also used films and summer theatre. Films from the Whatcom County (Washington) Library have been shown at Silver Lake Park every Saturday evening during the summer months.[43] Montgomery County (Maryland) brings a company of professional teacher-performers to county recreation programs to provide instruction in radio theater workshops, musical productions, and summer theater.[44]

As in the case of parks, the type of recreational program which a county provides depends upon the needs of its residents and the types of recreational programs provided by other agencies. Four different types of county recreation programs can be seen in these examples.

*Scotland County, North Carolina (26,929).*[45] Scotland County provides a countywide park and recreation program for the entire county. Laurinburg, the largest city in the county, had the only recreation program and the only parks in the county in 1970. After a 1971 survey showed that 54% of the participants in the city recreation program and many of its park users were not city residents, the city requested financial assistance from the county. A Recreation Study Commission recommended instead the establishment of a countywide parks and recreation program.

This program, under the direction of the Scotland County Parks and Recreation Commission, provides: an athletic program; swimming and swimming instruction; a mobile trailer on wheels with a stage used for puppet shows, musical programs, and talent shows; an art program; a community band; and a number of senior citizen programs.

*Warren County, Kentucky (57,432).* [46] The City of Bowling Green (Kentucky) has its own recreation program. The Warren County Parks and Recreation Department has the only organized recreation programs for the nineteen thousand people in the county living outside Bowling Green. This recreation program includes baseball, softball, soccer, small fry football, basketball, and tennis. The county community center is used for arts and crafts, musical activities, motion pictures, and special events.

*Montgomery County, Ohio (606,148).* [47] Montgomery County is a densely populated metropolitan county with one large city (Dayton) nine smaller cities, and ten villages. The City of Dayton has a large recreation program, and five of the smaller cities have less extensive recreation facilities. The Montgomery County recreation program is open to all residents of the county but is aimed mainly at county residents outside the six cities with their own facilities.

The Montgomery County program includes supervised summer playground activities at many different locations within the county, a summer athletic program for adults, and a winter athletic program held mainly in schools for youth and adults. It also includes two summer day camps for children, a concert band which performs at different locations throughout the county during the summer, and a show wagon which travels the county holding talent shows for children.

*Westchester County, New York (894,406).* [48] Westchester County borders New York City and contains several cities of more than 50,000 people, smaller villages, and suburban residential areas. The larger cities and villages in the county have recreation programs. The role of the County Department of Parks, Recreation, and Conservation is to establish and maintain large regional parks with recreation facilities not found in municipal parks, such as camping areas, bathing beaches, and golf courses. The county's recreation staff provides assistance to local recreation departments and special facilities and activities not found in municipal programs. For example, the county recreation program provides countywide clinics and tournaments in swimming, golf, tennis, and other sports.

The County Department operates a summer camp for children, five swimming pools, five beaches, a Sportsman's Center with rifle and pistol target areas, and senior citizen recreation programs. The County Department sponsors a Music and Arts Camp for artistically gifted teenagers offering instruction in music, drama, dance, and art. It also operates the Westchester Art Workshop, housed in the Westchester County Center, which provides more than eighty classes a year in fine

202 • *Modern County Government*

arts and handicrafts. Westchester County sponsors many other types of cultural activities, including an arts festival and a youth symphony orchestra.

**Other County Recreational and Cultural Facilities.**[49] County parks and recreational facilities meet only part of the needs of county citizens for publicly supported leisure time programs. Other leisure needs are met by the following types of facilities, owned and operated by county governments in some parts of the nation.

*Zoos.* Salt Lake County (Utah) and Milwaukee County (Wisconsin) are among the many counties with county zoos. The Milwaukee County Zoo covers more than 170 acres, and many of the animals are housed in natural settings outdoors and are separated from spectators only by deep moats. The zoo grounds are beautifully landscaped, and a zoo train gives spectators a ride around the grounds.

*Stadiums.* Erie County (New York) and Milwaukee County (Wisconsin) operate large stadiums used for professional football and/or baseball teams. Rich Stadium in Erie County is the home of the professional football team, the Buffalo Bills, and produces up to a half million dollars a year in additional revenue. The Milwaukee County stadium, with a seating capacity of over 56,000, is operated by the Milwaukee County Parks Commission. The stadium is used for professional baseball, music festivals, rock concerts, and civic and religious gatherings. The County built the stadium rather than the City of Milwaukee because it was intended for use on a countywide basis.

*Convention Centers.* Salt Lake County is one of a number of counties which operate a large convention center. The Salt Palace was constructed in 1969 at a cost of nearly $20 million. The Salt Palace has an auditorium which seats 12,000 people and has been used for professional basketball and hockey, ice shows, rodeos, rock concerts, and conventions. Its concert hall is used for symphonies, concerts, and plays, while the convention center is popular because it has a large auditorium and many smaller meeting rooms. Since the Salt Palace was constructed, a number of hotels, motels, and restaurants have been built close to it. The Salt Palace has stimulated a dramatic increase in tourist income in Salt Lake City.

*County fairs and fairgrounds.* The county fair serves two purposes. By providing prizes to the best livestock, vegetables and other produce, it serves to promote good agricultural practices. Farm machinery dealers sometimes display their products, and farmers have an opportunity to gain useful information on newer types of equipment, fertilizers, insecticides, and seeds. However, there is a leisure value in the socializing and amusement park activities which usually accompany a county fair. Some counties make use of the county fair on a year-round basis. Shawnee County (Kansas), for example, uses the fairgrounds for football, baseball, track, and other sports and uses one of the fair buildings for ice skating during the winter.

*Museums.* Hall County (Nebraska), Nassau County (New York), and Monmouth County (New Jersey) are among the counties which provide their citizens with museums. The Monmouth County Museum is on the Brookdale College campus and is visited by more than 50,000 school children and many adults each year. The Museum has been able to borrow art, artifacts, and exhibit materials at minimal cost from art galleries and private collections and conducts classes and lectures for adults and children.

*Other county facilities.* Milwaukee County provides as part of its park program a conservatory, a botanical garden, a boat marina, and two musical amphitheaters. The conservatory consists of three large domes, 85 feet high, which display plants grown in tropical regions, desert plants, and seasonal flowers. The musical amphitheater seats 15,000 people and is used for outdoor concerts and musicals in the summer.

Nassau County (New York) has established an Office of Cultural Development and operates a County Center for the Fine Arts in Roslyn, New York. The Cultural Center offers indoor chamber music and art exhibits, outdoor symphonic concerts, and a variety of art, theater, and craft programs.

## PLANNING AND DEVELOPMENT

Land use planning has traditionally been used to manage and control the location and development of land for industry, commercial uses, housing, recreation, and other activities. Comprehensive plans tend to be particularly thorough physical plans used to guide decisions about the physical development of the community.[50] They include land use plans and also plans for community facilities, transportation patterns, and other social, economic, and administrative matters. County planning agencies are involved in land

use and comprehensive planning and are increasingly concerned with the control and management of population density. County planning agencies and other county departments are also involved in many types of program planning such as criminal justice, human resources, and wastewater treatment planning.

The comprehensive planning process, described in this section, begins with the existing pattern of land use, physical facilities (such as streets, parks, etc.), and social and economic factors. Through a process of research, citizen participation, and decisions by the county planning agency, a comprehensive plan is developed. This plan is implemented through zoning, subdivision regulations, capital improvements, budgeting, and other means. Community development, industrial and economic development, and growth management are additional means of implementing county plans.

**Comprehensive Planning and Planning Organization.** The county comprehensive plan is a document (accompanied by maps) which is generally prepared by a professional planning staff and adopted by a county planning commission and the county governing body. The introductory section of the plan usually contains sections on the history, geography, population, and economic base of the county. Following this are the elements of the plan, typically describing proposed land use, county and community facilities, transportation, utilities, and other factors. The final sections of the plan generally discuss the implementation of the plan.

Comprehensive plans address serious land use issues within the county. The Weld County (Colorado) comprehensive plan, for example, faces the fact that suburbanization was taking some of the best irrigated farm land in the county and undermining the agricultural base of the county.[51] The Weld County Plan takes the following position on the agricultural issue:

- *prime agricultural land should be retained for agricultural use, while suburbanization of this land is to be discouraged through strict agricultural zoning;*

- *normal residential, business and industrial growth is to be encouraged in the county's twenty-seven incorporated towns, but only to the extent that the towns wish that growth, channeling population growth largely into already urbanized areas rather than into farm lands; and,*

- *agricultural green belts will be created around and between communities.*

The Weld County Comprehensive Plan serves as an overall master plan for the entire county. The City of Greeley and some other cities have their own comprehensive plans, and the Weld County Planning Commission has provided technical assistance in the preparation of a number of these plans.

Warren County (Kentucky) has used a second approach to county planning. Rather than using a county planning commission as does Weld County, the county has a joint city-county planning commission. The City-County Planning Commission of Warren County has eleven members; five representing Bowling Green (the largest city in the county), three representing Warren County, and one each from three smaller cities in the county.[52] The cost of the Planning Commission is shared by the county and participating cities, and the Commission has prepared a number of excellent planning documents encompassing the entire county.

A third approach is the multi-county planning district. The Mount Rogers Planning District, for example, encompasses Bland, Carroll, Grayson, Smyth, Washington, and Wythe Counties in southwestern Virginia, with a combined 1970 population of nearly 140,000.[53] The governing commission of the district consists of thirty-six persons: three commissioners from each of the six counties, three representatives from the two largest cities in the area, and a representative each from twelve smaller cities. The full thirty-six-member commission meets twice a year, and a smaller executive committee, which includes a county commissioner from each county, meets monthly. The planning district staff provides planning assistance to counties (like Bland) which have no planning staff and technical assistance to counties (like Smyth) which do have a county planner. The staff is also responsible for water, recreation, and law enforcement planning in the area.

**Zoning.** Zoning is a means used to control the use of land in accordance with the comprehensive plan. County zoning is established by an ordinance passed by the county governing body. This ordinance establishes the zones permitted in the county, and a map showing the boundaries of the zones is commonly made a part of the ordinance. The zones established vary from county to county but usually include agricultural, residential, commercial, industrial, and various types of recreational and public zones. The following land use zones established for Warren County (Kentucky) are typical:[54]

A   *Agricultural District*

R-1  *Low Density Residential District*

R-2  *Medium Density Residential District*

R-3  *Medium High Density Residential District*

R-4  *High Density Residential District*

P   *Public District*

B-1  *Neighborhood Business District*

B-2  *General Business District*

B-3  *Central Business District*

B-4  *Highway Service District*

FP  *Fountain Square Park District*

OP  *Office and Professional District*

I-1  *Light Industrial District*

I-2  *Heavy Industrial District*

MR  *Mobile Home Residential District*

MP  *Mobile Home Park District*

The zoning ordinance describes the uses of land permitted in each zone and the regulations for the zone. For example, the description of the B-1, neighborhood business district would list the types of stores permitted in the zone; and the section on the R-1, residential district would list the minimum number of square feet in the lot, the minimum width of the lot, and the minimum side and back yards.

A zoning ordinance is commonly enforced by the use of building permits. Individuals or businesses who wish to construct a building must apply for a building permit and bring a sketch or scale plat which indicates the shape, size, height, and location of buildings to be erected and the intended use of the building. The building inspector checks the building permit against the zoning map and ordinance and approves the building permit if the building meets requirements. In the Bowling Green-Warren County Zoning Ordinance, if the building does not meet standards, the Building Inspector or neighborhood property owners may institute legal action which will prevent the occupancy of the building, and the owner of the building in violation may be guilty of a misdemeanor.

A zoning ordinance, like any county governing ordinance, may be amended by action of the county governing body. The usual practice is for the planning commission to study the requested change in the ordinance and make its recommendations to the county governing board. Then this board takes action on the amendment. Often zoning ordinances also establish a board of adjustment to hear appeals on the administration of the ordinance.

Zoning ordinances can be adapted to the special needs of coastal and lakefront areas which are particularly vulnerable to ecological damage from homes and businesses built too close to the shore. After the passage of the U.S. Coastal Zoning Act of 1976 and legislation in states like California and Oregon, a number of counties have engaged in coastal zoning. The Minnesota Legislature applied the concept of coastal zoning to lakefronts, and Minnesota counties are now developing lakefront plans.[55] Within several hundred feet of shore, lot size is controlled, and sewage systems and septic tanks are rigorously inspected.

At the time a zoning ordinance is adopted, there are almost always some uses of land and buildings which do not conform to the new zoning ordinance. These are called "non-conforming uses" and are generally allowed to continue as long as the use is not extended, enlarged, or discontinued for some period of time and then resumed. If a building is burned more than a certain percent (often 50%), the owner generally loses his ability to rebuild the same type of non-conforming use.

Zoning implements land use plans because it is a means of bringing, over a period of time, existing land uses in a community into conformance with the land uses specified in the comprehensive plan. As new buildings are constructed, the process of making sure the uses and characteristics of the buildings meet the zoning ordinance should insure that they also conform with the comprehensive plan. A comprehensive plan is often required by state law before a zoning ordinance can be adopted because the ordinance needs to be based on a rational long-range plan for the entire area of a county.

County governments provide zoning in unincorporated areas of the county because they are generally the only unit of local government which has the staff and legal authority to zone in unincorporated areas. Counties may also provide zoning for small incorporated cities, towns, or villages in the county under contract or agreement with these municipalities, and may join together with cities to administer a zoning ordinance for the entire county area under the direction of a city-county planning commission.

**Subdivision Regulations.** A subdivision is commonly defined by state law as a group of a certain number of homes or lots developed or built as a unit.[56] County governing boards often adopt regulations requiring the subdivider to do the following.

- *Submit a sketch of his proposed subdivision to the county planning staff along with a map of the location and topographical features of the area. The planning staff can advise the subdivider on whether the subdivision will meet zoning and other county requirements before the subdivider has incurred great expense in making more detailed plans.*

- *Submit a preliminary plat which shows lot lines, proposed streets, the location of water, sewer, utility lines and facilities, and many other features of the subdivision. The preliminary plat is reviewed by a number of county officials to make sure it meets county specifications. For example, the county health officer may review the plans to be sure septic tank drain fields meet sanitary requirements, and the county engineer will make sure the streets in the subdivision are sufficiently wide and intersect at safe angles. After the preliminary plat is approved, the subdivider may begin developing his land.*

- *Guarantee in some way that construction will follow the specifications in the preliminary plat. In some cases, the subdivider may post a performance bond guaranteeing that construction will meet specifications.*

- *File a final plat after construction is completed.*

Subdivision regulations implement the county comprehensive plan by insuring that new subdivisions meet county land use, health, utility, and street requirements. Some counties have used the concept of planned unit development to give the developer the latitude of building on smaller sized lots and making other exceptions to the usual zoning and subdivision requirements, as long as overall standards on population density and other provisions are met.[57]

Enforcement of building, housing, electrical, plumbing, and other codes helps implement the county comprehensive plan by helping to insure that buildings are safe and will not quickly deteriorate into slums. Some of the commonly enforced codes are:

- *housing and building codes designed to make sure existing housing is structurally safe and does not deteriorate into slums;*

- *plumbing codes designed to be sure that plumbing in new buildings and existing buildings meets county standards;*

- *electrical codes developed to make sure electrical wiring meets safety standards;*

- *fire codes used with regular fire safety inspections to reduce losses by fire; and,*

- *gas codes used with inspection of gas lines and fittings to reduce the number of gas related explosions.*

**Urban Renewal, Public Housing, and Capital Improvements Budgeting.** Zoning, subdivision regulations, and code enforcement are regulatory activities which indirectly implement the county comprehensive plan by deterring subdivisions and housing inconsistent with the plan. Urban renewal, public housing, and capital improvements budgeting, in contrast, are more direct actions which have been taken to implement parts of the comprehensive plan.

Urban renewal is used to completely change the land use in a slum section of a city or to deter the spread of slum areas. The term "urban renewal" includes slum clearance, rehabilitation of blighted areas, and conservation of areas which might become blighted. The Housing Act of 1954 authorized federal funds for all three types of urban renewal and required that each community develop a workable program which met federal standards before receiving these funds. The workable program encouraged good planning practice because one of the requirements was that the local government must have a comprehensive land use and capital development plan. The Housing and Community Development Act, passed in 1974, continued to make federal funds available for the acquisition of property which is blighted, deteriorated, or in need of rehabilitation.[58]

A 1975 study, made by the National Association of Counties, showed that most urban counties possessed the legal authority to perform key urban development and redevelopment functions. The Metropolitan Government of Nashville-Davidson County (Tennessee) is a notable example of a city-county government which has made extensive use of urban renewal.[60]

One of the criticism of urban renewal projects was that not enough public housing was built for persons whose dwellings were torn down. Provision of low-income housing involves the creation of housing authorities which purchase and clear land, build new housing units, and rent them to persons with incomes below a certain level. Dane County (Wisconsin), for example, used its housing authority to purchase, rehabilitate, and transform a military housing reservation into much needed family dwellings for low and moderate income people.[61]

Capital improvements programming and budgeting is another means used by county and other local governments to implement their comprehensive plans. A capital improvements program is "a long range schedule of projects with their estimated costs over a period of five to 10 years."[62] This program is commonly linked with a capital improvements budget which lists the project together with the amounts and sources of funds for the coming fiscal year. The county board is thus able to see both the amount requested for the coming year as well as future costs of the projects.

A capital improvements program is also a means of presenting, for county board review, all proposed projects during a five to ten year period and thus enabling the board to indicate its priorities for future development. Montgomery County (Maryland) has a six-year capital improvements program which is amended each year as existing projects are completed and new projects are added. The two-volume plan contains nearly a thousand projects.[63]

**Growth Management.** According to John DeGrove and Carolyn Lawrence, "growth management has evolved primarily out of concern for the degradation of the environment which has characterized much of urban development in the United States."[64] The techniques of growth management are the application of planning, zoning, capital improvements budgeting, and similar techniques to accomplish specific objectives such as keeping land in agricultural uses, preserving open spaces, and channeling growth into those areas of the county most suitable for growth.

One means of preserving the best farm land for agricultural use is to zone the land for agriculture and prohibit the building of residential subdivisions, factories, and commercial establishments on this land. For example, Rio Blanco County (Coloado) uses agricultural zoning to protect the river bottom areas which are essential to ranchers in the county for the raising of winter feed for their cattle. Another means of preserving prime agricultural land is for the county to purchase the development rights. These are all the rights of an owner of real property except the right of ownership, right of exclusive possession, and the right of agricultural use. Suffolk County, New York, originally solicited bids on the development rights to 56,000 acres of farmland.[65] Bids were submitted on nearly 18,000 acres.

Open spaces also may be protected by zoning or purchase. Sonoma County (California) has used zoning to prevent uncontrolled development in the remote hill lands surrounding the Lake Sonoma-Warm Springs dam project.[66] Jefferson County (Colorado) has levied a one-half cent sales tax to purchase open space, and park lands.[67] The county government purchases land under this program, develops trails, maintains the area, and provides grants to cities for similar purposes.

Channeling urban growth into the areas best suited for growth is accomplished by planning, zoning, and other means. For example, Rio Blanco County (Colorado) officials are using planning and agricultural zoning to channel population growth in the county into the two existing cities of the county which have good supplies of water rather than having growth spill over into prime agricultural land.[68] Pinellas County (Florida) has used the issuance of building permits to keep growth within manageable limits. Broward County (Florida) has used computer systems to help the county wisely manage its valuable land and its rapid growth. The computer system determines the impact of each potential development on public utilities, services required by local government, and on the environment. Collier County (Florida) has developed a blueprint for planned growth and bought development rights as a means of protecting environmentally sensitive areas from uncontrolled growth. To be successful, the various means of managing urban growth must be based on a county comprehensive land use plan.

In areas of rapid growth, such as new energy sites, management of urban growth requires planning for new hospitals, schools, housing, water and sewer facilities, and expanded county and city services. Sweetwater County (Wyoming) doubled in population between 1970 and 1974 after construction began on a large coal-fueled electric generating plant.[69] The Sweetwater Board of County Commissioners took an active role in planning for growth by appointing a Priorities Board to recommend solutions to problems of growth. The county also built needed facilities such as a new hospital.

**Industrial, Commercial, and Agricultural Development.** Counties in a number of states have the power to actively seek new industry and expand the economic base of the county. In North Carolina, any municipality, county, or group of cities and counties may create an economic development commission and furnish it with a full-time staff.[70] The commission may conduct industrial surveys, advertise in periodicals to try to attract new industries, and encourage the formation of private business development corporations. The activities of the economic development commission may be financed from surplus county funds or a special tax levied for this purpose.

In Mississippi, counties may appropriate funds to advertise the resources of the county and may establish economic development districts.[71] A Mississippi county has the authority to sell bonds and purchase land, buildings, and equipment for rental to a new industry willing to settle in the county. For example, Lauderdale County used a five-million-dollar bond issue to encourage a northern industrial plant to move into the county.[72]

Some counties actively encourage tourism and conventions. Salt Lake County (Utah) has a Convention and Visitors' Bureau, financed by a 3% tax on motel and hotel rooms.[73] The Bureau has a staff which assists groups holding conventions in the area, helps develop ski plans for tourists, and prepares brochures to attract tourists to the area.

County governments have traditionally aided agricultural development by providing offices and some of the funds for the salaries of cooperative extension agents. These extension agents advise farmers on the best way to grow, store, and market crops; provide information to ranchers on research on animal diseases and other subjects; give guidance to 4-H clubs; and perform many other functions. County governments also aid agriculture through controlling predatory animals, encouraging agricultural exhibits at the county fair, and eradicating weeds. Latah County (Idaho) has a county program of spraying weeds which has prevented millions of dollars of damage to the wheat crop in the county.

**Comprehensive Planning, Program Planning, and County Growth and Development.** The comprehensive planning process and its means of implementation, described in this section, have an important impact on the administration of county programs described in this and previous chapters. For example, the policy of a county board (expressed in the county comprehensive plan) to preserve open spaces, keep the best farm land in agricultural use, and channel residential and industrial growth into existing urban areas will have far reaching effects on the county's park, highway, agricultural, environmental, utility, and other programs. Criminal justice, human services, and taxes will also

be affected by county capital improvement programs and policies on growth.

Program planning also has an important impact on the county comprehensive plan. For example, wastewater treatment program planning (done in accordance with Section 208 of the Water Pollution Control Act Amendments of 1972) affects the county comprehensive plan by identifying sewage treatment plants which will be needed to treat municipal and industrial wastes over a twenty-year period.[74] The wastewater treatment planning process also provides for the establishment of regulatory programs, and the development of a process to identify agricultural, mining, and other sources of waste. In New Castle County (Delaware), one of the first counties in the nation to be designated an areawide wastewater treatment management planning area, planning will include identification of current water quality problems and the suitability of public land in the county for future development based on the adequacy of water supplies, sewer services, highways, and other public facilities.[75]

The wastewater treatment planning process evaluates the need for future public works projects such as wastewater treatment facilities. It may also result in decisions (such as not to extend sewage treatment to certain areas of the county) which have widespread impact on county growth. Because program planning and comprehensive planning are so extensively interrelated, it is important that there be some agency within a county area with the power to require coordination of these plans. The logical coordinating agency in most counties is the county governing board and the county executive or administrator.

## FINANCING COUNTY SERVICE SYSTEMS

Some county services are financed mainly through the revenues which they generate and through revenue bonds. For example, water systems, sewer systems, and refuse collection and disposal are operated mainly from these two sources. Some county services have the benefit of taxes earmarked for their use alone. Parks and recreation departments in states like Ohio receive an earmarked portion of the property tax. Federal and state funds provide most of the financial support of many county health and welfare departments. For many county services, however, the main source of funds is general county taxes—particularly the property tax. The adequacy of county revenues to support the level of services which county citizens demand will be discussed in the next chapter.

## REFERENCES

1. The Pinellas County water policy is described more fully in National Association of Counties, *Pinellas, Florida, Resource Needs and Managed Growth Plan* (Washington: National Association of Counties, 1974).

2. Kenneth VerBurg, *Guide to Michigan County Government* (East Lansing: Michigan State University, 1972), pp. IV-34, IV-35.

3. Dana B. Brammer, *A Manual for Mississippi County Supervisors* (University: University of Mississippi, 1973), pp. 97-103.

4. Michael S. Vollmer, Herbert Sydney Duncombe and Katherine D. Pell, *Handbook for County Officials in Idaho* (Moscow: Bureau of Public Affairs Research, University of Idaho, 1974), pp. 84, 85.

5. *Page's Ohio Code Annotated*, Sections 5541,01 and 5541,02.

6. For more information on highway safety programs see Mel D. Powell, Michael K. Gemmell, Donald Murray, and Warren P. Howe, *Community Action Program for Traffic Safety* (Washington: National Association of Counties Research Foundation, 1970). References to the highway safety programs of specific counties are further described in case studies from the files of the National Association of Counties.

7. J. David VanderVeen, Director of Aviation, Oakland County, letter to Sydney Duncombe, April 6, 1977. Mr. VanderVeen states that the county with its larger financial base was in a better position than the city to develop and improve the airport.

8. *County News* (Washington), July 8, 1974, p. 7.

9. Theodore Florey, Member of the Rock County Board of Supervisors, letter dated August 5, 1976.

10. Tabulated from National Association of Counties, "County and City-County Sponsors of Airports with Commercial Service," 1976. (Typed.)

11. The Minnesota examples are from Association of Minnesota Counties, *County Progress in Rural Transportation Programs* (St. Paul: Association of Minnesota Counties, 1976). The remaining examples are based on interviews or case studies in the files of the National Association of Counties.

12. For more information on the Montgomery County parking program see Montgomery County, Maryland, *Plan for Progress, Public Services Program 1973-78*, (Rockville: Montgomery County Executive, 1972), pp. 334, 335. The Dane and Shelby county programs are described further in case studies in the files of the National Association of Counties.

13. D.D. Brown, Director of the DeKalb County, Water and Sewer Department, letter to Sydney Duncombe, May 24, 1976.

14. Advisory Commission on Intergovernmental Relations, *Performance of Urban Functions: Local and Areawide* (Washington: Advisory Commission on Intergovernmental Relations, 1963), pp. 200-203 provides a number of illustrations of economies of scale in water supply and sewage treatment systems.

15. Westchester County, New York, "Report of the Department of Environmental Facilities, 1974." (Multilithed.)

16. For more information on the Muskegon County treatment plan see Muskegon County, Michigan, "Wastewater Management System No. 1," an undated Muskegon County publication. After being sprayed on the land, the liquid seeps into the earth and the nutrients are taken up by the soil and by plants. The water which filters through the soil has been tested and found to be pollution free.

17. Information provided by county officials or reports in the files of the National Association of Counties.

18. In contrast, revenues of county water systems were $168 million in 1974-75. U.S. Bureau of the Census, *County Government Finances in 1974-75* (Washington: U.S. Government Printing Office, 1976), p. 7.

19. The Los Angeles and Butler County solar heating systems are described in case studies in the files of the National Association of Counties. For further information on county solar heating systems see *County News*, (Washington), September 8, 1975, p. 3.

20. Kenneth VerBurg, *Guide to Michigan County Government*, pp. iv-46 through iv-54 gives an excellent description of this office which is found in most Michigan counties.

21. Information obtained from interviews with Salt Lake County Commissioners on December 31, 1975.

22. For further information on the Fairfax County soil erosion problems and ordinances, see U.S. Department of the Interior, *Urban Soil Erosion and Sediment Control* (Washington: U.S. Government Printing Office, 1970), p. G-3.

23. The National Association of Counties received a federal grant to study the impact of energy shortages on county government. *County News* (Washington), June 10, 1974, p. 2. The county energy programs cited are from case studies in the files of the National Association of Counties.

24. For an excellent description of federal legislation, state and local administration, and intergovernmental relations in environmental programs see J. Clarence Davies III and

Barbara S. Davies, *The Politics of Pollution,* 2nd ed. (Indianapolis: The Bobbs-Merrill Company, Inc., 1975).

25. Bureau of Air Pollution Control, Allegheny County Health Department, "Air Quality in Allegheny County, 1976" is the source of information for this case study. For more information on county air pollution control programs see National Association of Counties Research Foundation, *Air Pollution Control* (Washington: National Association of Counties Research Foundation, 1971).

26. Allegheny County Health Department, *Annual Report, 1975* (Pittsburgh: Allegheny County Health Department, 1976), p. 12 states that only 33 septic tanks were approved. The county had a 1970 population of 1,605,016.

27. For more information see case studies in the files of the National of Counties.

28. According to a 1975 estimate, there were more than 14,000 unauthorized dump sites in the nation. Part of the problem was lack of rural solid waste collection services and reliance on open dumps rather than sanitary landfills. The Solid Waste Disposal Act of 1965 encouraged national research and development programs for improved methods of solid waste disposal and provided technical and financial assistance to state and local governments in the conduct of solid waste disposal programs. States such as Missouri then passed laws requiring counties to submit master plans for solid waste management including plans for cities within their borders. For more information see Rodney R. Fleming, "County Solid Waste Management Programs," *The County Year Book, 1975* (Washington: National Association of Counties and International City Management Association, 1975), pp. 113-115.

29. An excellent description of solid waste collection, transportation and disposal systems may be found in National Association of Counties Research Foundation, *Solid Waste Management* (Washington: National Association of Counties Research Foundation, n.d.), part v.

30. Ibid. and case studies in the files of the National Association of Counties.

31. James A. Hayes, "County Creates Energy From Buried Garbage," *Palisadian Post* (Pacific Pallisades) February 6, 1975.

32. Award winning case studies in the files of the National Association of Counties are the source of information on Hennepin, Washington, Dade, and Ingham Counties. For information on other solid waste management projects see Robert A. Colonna and Cynthia McLaren, *Decision Makers Guide in Solid Waste Management* (Washington: U.S. Environmental Protection Agency, 1974), p. 8.

33. See Kay Stouffer, "Garbage No Longer Local Worry," *County News* (Washington), June 23, 1975, p. 6 and case studies in the files of the National Association of Counties.

34. For a history of local parks and recreation programs see Virginia Frye, "Development of Municipal Parks and Recreation" in Sidney G. Lutzin and Edward H. Storey, ed., *Managing Municipal Leisure Services* (Washington: International City Management Association, 1973), pp. 13-40. For an excellent current description of federal, state, and local parks and recreation programs, see Clayne R. Jensen, *Outdoor Recreation in America* (Minneapolis: Burgess Publishing Company, 1970), pp. 59-106.

35. Harry P. Hatry and Diana R. Dunn, *Measuring the Effectiveness of Local Government Services—Recreation* (Washington: The Urban Institute, 1971), p. 13.

36. Interview with Judge Dennis Fuller, in Baker (Oregon), December 29, 1975.

37. Interview with Director of Parks and Recreation of Warren County, in Bowling Green (Kentucky), January 7, 1976.

38. Interview with Commissioner Mary Bogart, Shawnee County, in Topeka (Kansas), January 5, 1976.

39. The Bucks County, Pennsylvania, Department of Parks and Recreation, "The Bucks County Park System," n.d. (Printed Brochure.)

40. Hennepin County, Minnesota, "Official Highway Map," 1975. The Hennepin County Park Reserve District is a quasi-county agency. Its budget is submitted to the Board of County Commissioners, and three of the eleven members of the Park Reserve District Board are appointed by the Board of County Commissioners.

41. The information on Ventura and Pinellas Counties was from the 1975 Achievement Award Files of the National Association of Counties.

42. National Association of Counties, *Living Library*, 6th ed., (Washington: National Association of Counties, n.d.), p. 18.

43. "Saturday Night at the Watcom Movies," *County News* (Washington), May 19, 1975, p. 6.

44. Scott Franklin, "Street 70 Paved through Joint City-County Effort," *County News* (Washington), September 9, 1974, p. 3.

45. Case study on the Scotland County (North Carolina) parks and recreation program in the Achievement Award Files of the National Association of Counties.

46. Interview with the Director of Parks and Recreation of Warren County, in Bowling Green (Kentucky), January 7, 1976.

47. Interview with officials of the Montgomery County Parks Department, in Dayton (Ohio), June 22, 1976, and brochures supplied by these officials.

48. Information provided by the Westchester County Department of Parks, Recreation, and Conservation was used for this case study, including a letter dated June 29, 1976, from Paul E. Lohner, Director of Programs and Services.

49. The information on county programs is based primarily on interviews with county officials, tours of the facilities described, or case studies in the files of the National Association of Counties.

50. The distinction between land use and comprehensive planning used in this book was made by John Baker, *Urban Politics in America* (New York: Charles Scribners' Sons, 1971), p. 287. An excellent description of the elements of a comprehensive plan may be found in Alan Black, "The Comprehensive Plan," *Principles and Practices of Urban Planning*, William I. Goodman and Eric C. Freund, ed., (Washington: International City Management Association, 1968), pp. 376, 378.

51. Information on this county plan comes from Weld County Planning Commission, *Weld County Comprehensive Plan* (Greeley: Weld County Planning Commission, 1973) and from an interview with Mr. Glenn K. Billings, Chairman of the Board of County Commissioners of Weld County, in Greeley, Colorado, January 2, 1976.

52. Information on this program comes from City-County Planning Commission of Warren County, *Overall Program Design and Annual Report* (Bowling Green: City-County Planning Commission of Warren County, 1975) and from an interview with John B. Matheney, Director of the City-County Planning Commission, in Bowling Green on January 7, 1976.

53. *Mount Rogers Planning District News,* Winter, 1975.

54. City-County Planning Commission of Warren County, *Zoning Ordinance—Resolution* (Bowling Green: City-County Planning Commission of Warren County, 1973), p. 13, as amended by letter of November 12, 1976 from John B. Matheny, Director of the City-County Planning Commission.

55. Interview with Ralph Keyes, Executive Director, Association of Minnesota Counties, in Boston, September 17, 1976.

56. In Idaho, a tract of land divided into five or more lots, parcels, or sites for the purpose of sale or building development constitutes a subdivision.

57. For an excellent short description of planned unit development see Phillip P. Green, "Land Subdivision," *Principles and Practices of Urban Planning,* William I. Goodman and Eric C. Freund, ed., pp. 480, 481.

58. The Community Development Act also provides funds for code enforcement in deteriorated areas, development of parking facilities, solid waste disposal, fire protection, and other services. The funds may also be used for clearance, demolition, removal and rehabilitation of buildings, and relocation payments for individuals and businesses displaced by urban renewal. For a good summary of this Act see Mary K. Nenno, "The Housing and Community Development Act of 1974," *Journal of Housing,* 8 (1975), pp. 350, 351.

59. These functions include urban renewal, public housing, water and sewage, and solid waste disposal. For more information see Bruce B. Talley, Constance W. Maffin, and Jayne S. Seeley, *Community Development Capabilities Study—An Urban County Report* (Washington: National Association of Counties Research Foundation, 1975), pp. 3-7.

60. One project cleared ninety-six acres of slums near the State Capitol in Nashville. The land was resold for construction of apartments and was used for a municipal auditorium, attractive walks, and parking areas for state employees. Described in Herbert Sydney Duncombe, *County Government in America* (Washington: National Association of Counties Research Foundation, 1966), p. 208.

61. Case study in the files of the National Association of Counties.

62. Lachlan F. Blair, "Programming Community Development," *Principles and Practices of Urban Planning,* William I. Goodman and Eric C. Freund, ed., p. 389.

63. The page or two on each project includes: a map showing the site; an estimate of acquisition, site improvement, construction, equipment, and other costs; and the effect of the project on the relocation of individuals and businesses. Department of Community and Economic Development of Montgomery County, *Recommended Capital Improvements Program for Fiscal Year 1977-1982* (Rockville: Department of Community and Economic Development of Montgomery County, 1976).

64. John DeGrove and Carolyn B. Lawrence, "Changing Patterns in County Government Service Delivery" in National Association of Counties, *A Symposium on the Future of County Government* (Washington: National Association of Counties, 1976), p. 15.

65. More information on the Suffolk County program and a definition of development rights may be found in Suffolk County Select Committee on the Acquisition of Farmlands, "Report to the Suffolk County Legislature," November 7, 1974. Later information was supplied by Arthur Bergmann, Chief Deputy Suffolk County Executive, letter to Sydney Duncombe, April 26, 1977.

66. National Association of Counties, *Living Library,* 7th ed. (Washington: National Association of Counties, 1976), p. 21.

67. Case study in the files of the National Association of Counties.

68. The information on Rio Blanco County is based on an interview with William Brennan, Rio Blanco County Commissioner, September 14, 1976. The programs of other counties described in the paragraph are from National Association of Counties, *Living Library*, 7th ed., p. 22.

69. Information on the Sweetwater County, Wyoming, program of managing urban growth is from National Association of Counties, *Controlling Boomtown Development, Sweetwater and Unita Counties, Wyoming* (Washington: National Association of Counties, 1976). ·

70. Philip P. Green, "Planning for Physical and Economic Development," in Joseph S. Ferrell, ed., *County Government in North Carolina* (Chapel Hill: University of North Carolina, 1975), pp. 388, 389.

71. Information on industrial development in Mississippi in this section is from Dana B. Brammer, *A Manual for Mississippi County Supervisors* (University: Bureau of Governmental Research, University of Mississippi, 1973), pp. 175-180.

72. Interview with William F. Ready, Attorney for the Lauderdale, Mississippi, County Board, September 17, 1976.

73. Information on the Salt Lake County Convention and Visitors' Bureau was obtained from an interview with the Director of the Bureau, Bruce McDaniel, in Salt Lake City on June 29, 1976.

74. Section 208, P.L. 92-500 may be found in *U.S. Code and Administrative News, 92nd Congress, Second Session, 1972*, (St. Paul: West Publishing Co., 1972), pp. 981, 982.

75. Information on the New Castle County wastewater treatment planning process is from Merna Hurd, "208 Planning in an Urban Region: New Castle County, Delaware," *Environmental Comment*, January, 1976, pp. 3, 4.

# Chapter 9

# Financial County Services

"It took over a century and three-quarters, from the nation's birth until 1953, for the annual aggregate general revenue of county governments in the United States to reach $4 billion. In the next 20 years, general revenues of county governments increased sixfold to $28.4 billion in fiscal 1972-73. The dynamic growth of county government fiscal activity has been especially pronounced in the past decade."[1]

"...Counties everywhere have been squeezed between their rapidly rising costs and revenues which are increasingly difficult to raise. The public demand for services seems nearly insatiable at a time when there is grave resistance to increased taxes..."[2]

The first quotation describes the rapid growth of county revenues and leaves the impression that county government is blessed with ever expanding revenue sources and a dynamic growth pattern. The second quotation gives a more pessimistic impression. County government is pictured as being squeezed between rapidly rising costs and citizen resistance to increased taxes. The observations raise several important questions about the continued financial growth of counties, such as:

*Why have county revenues and expenditures grown so rapidly, particularly in the past twenty years?*

*Is it caused by population growth with greater numbers of people receiving service? Is it the effect of inflation on tax collections and costs, or is it the growth of county services?*

*Is the county and revenue structure adequate to meet future demands for service, or is it inflexible and over-dependent on one or two tax sources which cannot be depended on to increase in proportion to the increased demand for county services? If so, what changes need to be made in the county tax structure?*

This chapter attempts to provide an answer to these questions, by first exploring county expenditure trends and then the sources of county revenue. A third section of the chapter will describe county cash balances and debt.

## EXPENDITURE TRENDS`

County government expenditures have increased more than eighty-five times from 1913 to 1974-75, as Table 9-1 shows. During this same period, the population of the United States has more than doubled, and prices have increased more than four times. Assuming that increases in county expenditures would parallel price and population increases, the combined effect of these two factors would account for about an elevenfold increase in county expenditures, not the eighty-five-fold increase which actually occurred.

Index X in Table 9-1 represents the degree to which population and price level increases do not account for the increase in county general expenditures. It is computed by dividing the index of county general expenditures by the product of the price level and population indexes.

TABLE 9-1

COUNTY GENERAL EXPENDITURES AND INDICES OF POPULATION, PRICE
LEVELS, AND COUNTY SERVICE LEVELS, 1913 to 1974

| Year | County General Expenditures (in millions) | Index of County General Expenditures | Price Level Index | Population Index | Index X |
|---|---|---|---|---|---|
| 1913 | $ 385 | 1.00 | 1.00 | 1.00 | 1.00 |
| 1932 | 1,412 | 3.67 | 1.55 | 1.28 | 1.85 |
| 1952 | 3,802 | 9.88 | 2.68 | 1.61 | 2.29 |
| 1957 | 5,900 | 15.32 | 2.90 | 1.76 | 3.00 |
| 1962 | 8,690 | 22.57 | 3.12 | 1.91 | 3.78 |
| 1966-67 | 12,629 | 32.80 | 3.37 | 2.02 | 4.81 |
| 1971-72 | 23,932 | 62.16 | 4.24 | 2.13 | 6.88 |
| 1974-75 | 32,744 | 85.04 | 5.30 | 2.18 | 7.36 |

SOURCES: County government expenditures are from the following U.S. Bureau of the Census sources published by the U.S. Government Printing Office: *Wealth, Debt, and Taxation, 1913*, pp. 210 and 211; *Financial Statistics of State and Local Governments, 1932*, p. 28; *Finances of County Governments, 1962*, p. 9; *Finances of County Governments, 1972*, p. 9; *Historical Statistics on Governmental Finances and Employment*, p. 47; and *County Government Finances in 1974-75*, p. 5. The price index was computed by linking indexes found in the U.S. Bureau of the Census, *Historical Statistics of the United Staes, Colonial Times to 1957* (Washington: Bureau of the Census, 1961) and from later price statistics found in various Statistical Abstracts published by the U.S. Bureau of the Census. Population figures were also from U.S. Bureau of the Census sources. The indexes were built on a 1913 base for county expenditures, population and price levels. Adjustments were made in the price and population indexes to correspond to the reporting of county expenditures on a fiscal year basis in 1966-67, 1971-72, and 1974-75.

Index X mainly reflects the establishment of new county programs or program expansions. The 1974-75 index figure of 7.36 is an indication that county government provided greater than seven times more services to its citizens in 1974-75 than it did six decades earlier.

A closer look at expenditures in the most recent two census reporting periods shows that county expenditures have increased much more rapidly in the last five years of the decade than in the first four and a half years. The expenditures in newer county functions, such as sewage, parks and recreation, and fire protection, were among those expenditures which increased the most in the last half of the decade.

Figure 9-1, illustrating direct county expenditures for the four most costly functions of county government, shows that the cost of three of these programs has more than doubled in less than a decade. The decline in public welfare expenditures since the 1972-73 fiscal year is due primarily to the transfer of administration of public assistance income maintenance programs for old age, blind, and disabled recipients to the U.S. Social Security Administration in January, 1974.

The latest available census data, comparing per capita county expenditures by state, shows significant variations among states.[3] The highest annual expenditure per capita was in Alaska ($807), Maryland ($478), Hawaii ($355), Virginia ($330), California ($277), North Carolina ($273), and Nevada ($272). The annual average expenditure per capita for all counties in the United States during the same period (1971-72) was $133.17. It is significant that nearly

all of these states are southern and western states in which counties provide extensive services in one or more functions. Alaskan boroughs and county governments in Maryland, North Carolina, and Virginia operate many of the school systems in the state. Hawaiian counties have extensive police protection and park functions; California counties have costly public welfare responsibilities; and Nevada counties have a large hospital system. The lowest county expenditures per capita were in Vermont ($.89), Maine ($8), Massachusetts ($19), and New Hampshire ($23).[4] Counties in New England tend to have low per capita costs because towns provide many of the services in New England which counties furnish in other states.

As Table 9-2 shows, the most costly county functions are public assistance, education, highways, and hospitals. The figures shown are for the fiscal year beginning July 1, 1974 and ending June 30, 1975.

Variation between expenditure patterns of individual counties is even more striking. The 1974-1975 census data on individual counties of 100,000 or more people shows that counties having a higher than average per capita expenditure rate are likely to operate their own school system, administer income maintenance programs such as Aid to Families with Dependent Children, or have an extensive highway or hospital program.

One of the problems faced by county governments is that they do not have complete control over their expenditures. Counties in which welfare is an important function have found

**Figure 9-1**

**TRENDS IN COUNTY DIRECT GENERAL EXPENDITURE
FOR SELECTED MAJOR FUNCTIONS
1965-66 TO 1974-75
(billions of dollars)**

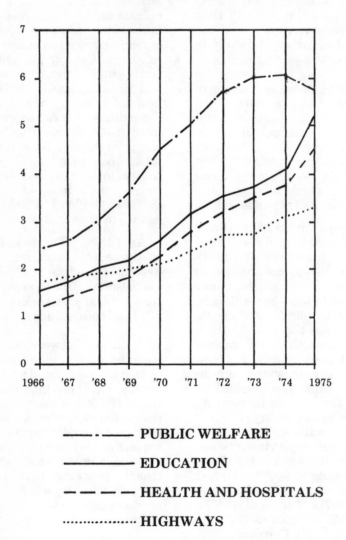

————·———— PUBLIC WELFARE

———————— EDUCATION

— — — — HEALTH AND HOSPITALS

················ HIGHWAYS

SOURCE: U.S. Bureau of the Census, *County Government Finances in 1974-75* (Washington:
U.S. Government Printing Office, 1976), p. 3.

that federal and state regulations, unemployment, and inflation are greatly adding to county welfare costs. Fourteen county executives from New York State testified that their counties faced deficits totaling $70 million due to increased welfare costs in 1975.[5] Moreover, county governments have little control over costs of many state-mandated functions such as assessing, recording, and automobile licensing and titling.

## SOURCES OF REVENUES

Faced with rising expenditures, county governments should be concerned about whether their revenue sources will be adequate in the decades ahead. The revenues of county governments have increased 39% from the 1971-72 fiscal year to 1974-75.[6] Since this has been slightly more than the 37% increase in general expenditures during the same period, there seems to be no cause for alarm. However, the problem faced by county government is that it depends very extensively on two sources of revenue: the property tax and revenue from state government. Counties also receive funds from nonproperty taxes, federal aid, revenue sharing, charges for services, and other sources. Although these revenues are growing in amount, they still constitute less than a third of the funds received by counties.

The pattern of county government revenues differs from state to state. As Table 9-5 shows, counties in states like Vermont, Montana,

Table 9-2

**COUNTY GENERAL EXPENDITURE BY FUNCTION FOR THE 1974-75 FISCAL YEAR**

| Expenditure Function | Amount of Expenditure (in millions) | Percent of Total Expenditures |
|---|---|---|
| Public welfare | $ 6,169 | 18.8% |
| Education | 5,643 | 17.2 |
| Highways | 3,458 | 10.6 |
| Hospitals | 3,337 | 10.2 |
| General control | 1,986 | 6.1 |
| Police protection | 1,450 | 4.4 |
| Health | 1,428 | 4.4 |
| Correction | 980 | 3.0 |
| Financial administration | 883 | 2.7 |
| General public buildings | 824 | 2.5 |
| Interest on public debt | 795 | 2.4 |
| Sewage | 742 | 2.3 |
| Parks and recreation | 741 | 2.3 |
| Natural resources | 510 | 1.5 |
| Libraries | 270 | .8 |
| Fire protection | 252 | .7 |
| Other and unallocable | 3,277 | 10.0 |
| Total general expenditure by function | 32,744 | 100.0% |

SOURCE: Prepared from U.S. Bureau of the Census, *County Government Finances in 1974-75* (Washington: U.S. Government Printing Office, 1976), pp. 5, 6. Details may not add to totals due to rounding.

Table 9-3

**PER CAPITA EXPENDITURES OF SELECTED COUNTIES, 1974-75**

| County and State | Total | Welfare | Education | Highways | Hospitals | Other |
|---|---|---|---|---|---|---|
| Counties with school systems | | | | | | |
| Montgomery, Maryland | $856 | 14 | 504 | 23 | 0 | 315 |
| Greater Anchorage, Alaska | 811 | 1 | 539 | 20 | 0 | 251 |
| Arlington, Virginia | 746 | 41 | 285 | 36 | 0 | 384 |
| Counties with large welfare programs | | | | | | |
| Rockland, New York | 391 | 140 | 51 | 15 | 10 | 175 |
| San Joaquin, California | 368 | 132 | 26 | 26 | 54 | 130 |
| Ramsey, Minnesota | 270 | 149 | 0 | 11 | 53 | 57 |
| Counties with extensive highway and/or hospital systems | | | | | | |
| Clark, Nevada | 423 | 19 | 0 | 38 | 59 | 307 |
| Hamilton, Tennessee | 325 | 11 | 134 | 10 | 90 | 80 |
| Milwaukee, Wisconsin | 276 | 119 | 2 | 6 | 92 | 57 |
| Lane, Oregon | 159 | 6 | 13 | 52 | 0 | 88 |

SOURCE: U.S. Bureau of the Census, *County Government Finances in 1974-75* (Washington: U.S. Government Printing Office, 1976), pp. 31-51.

and Massachusetts are very heavily dependent on the property tax. Boroughs in Alaska and counties in North Carolina, Minnesota, and Colorado receive over half their general funds from state government. Counties in Alabama, Indiana, Nevada, New York, and Tennessee have a more balanced tax base with substantial income from non-property taxes and charges. There is no single revenue source in the latter five states which provides more than half of county general revenues.

Figure 9-2 depicts county revenue trends for the past decade. Intergovernmental revenue has increased the greatest amount. Non-property taxes, charges, and miscellaneous revenues have more than tripled, although the amounts of these revenues still total less than $8 billion. The increase in the property tax

failed to keep up with increases in other forms of revenue during the period shown by Figure 9-2.

As county government continues to meet the needs of its citizens, it will require additional funds. Where will these funds come from? An examination of current and alternative revenue sources shows some of the weaknesses and strengths of the county fiscal position.

**Property Taxes.** One of the two most important sources of county revenues, property taxes, has been falling behind as a revenue source. From 1966-67 to 1971-72, general county revenues increased 90% and property tax revenues only 64%.[7] From 1971-72 to 1974-75, general county revenues increased 39% and property tax revenues only 20%.[8]

There are three basic types of taxable property: (1) state assessed property such as railroad and utility property; (2) locally assessed personal property; and, (3) locally assessed real property such as land, buildings, and other improvements of a permanent nature. Personal property includes both tangible property such as household furnishings, livestock, farm machinery, and automobiles and intangible property such as stocks and bonds. The total assessed valuation available for local general property taxation was $845 billion in 1973, of which 7.0% was state assessed property, 12.6% personal property, and 80.4% real property.[9] The time lag between the assessment of the property and the collection of the property tax is from one to two years.

If county governments need additional funds, it does not appear that either state assessed or personal property taxes can provide much of the increase. State assessed railroad, utility, and other property declined from 7.9% to 7.0% of all assessed value in the twelve-year period ending in 1973.[10] Railroad property led the decline as many miles of railroad tracks have been abandoned, and some railroad land and buildings have been sold. Personal property also declined as a percent of all taxable property from 16.0% to 12.6% in the 1961 to 1973 period.

Property taxes on personal property have traditionally been difficult to administer. Assessors find it hard to discover the amount of intangible personal property (such as stocks and bonds) a taxpayer has unless it is voluntarily listed. Evasion of taxes on jewelry, household furnishings, and certain other types of personal property has been so widespread

Table 9-4

COUNTY GENERAL REVENUE FOR
THE 1974-75 FISCAL YEAR

| | | | | |
|---|---|---|---|---|
| Taxes | | | | |
| Property | $10,316 | | 31.4 | |
| Other | 2,345 | $12,660 | 7.1 | 38.5 |
| | | | | |
| Intergovernmental general revenue | | | | |
| From state government | 11,842 | | 36.0 | |
| From federal government and other sources | 2,913 | 14,755 | 8.9 | 44.9 |
| | | | | |
| Charges and miscellaneous revenue | | | | |
| Current charges | 3,704 | | 11.2 | |
| Interest earnings | 913 | | 2.8 | |
| Special assessments | 122 | | .4 | |
| Sale of property | 53 | | .1 | |
| Other and unallocable | 685 | 5,478 | 2.1 | 16.6 |
| | | | | |
| Total general revenues | | $32,893 | | 100.0% |

SOURCE: Adapted from U.S. Bureau of the Census, *County Government Finances in 1974-75* (Washington: U.S. Government Printing Office, 1976), p. 5. Detail may not add to totals due to rounding.

Table 9-5

PERCENT DISTRIBUTION OF GENERAL REVENUES OF COUNTY GOVERNMENT
BY SOURCE, IN SELECTED STATES IN THE 1971-72 FISCAL YEAR

| | Property Taxes | Non-Property Taxes | Revenue from State | Current Charges | Other | Total |
|---|---|---|---|---|---|---|
| Pattern 1—Heavy dependence on the property tax | | | | | | |
| Vermont | 86 | 0 | 8 | 3 | 3 | 100 |
| Montana | 78 | 5 | 5 | 9 | 3 | 100 |
| Massachusetts | 72 | 1 | 5 | 12 | 10 | 100 |
| South Dakota | 65 | 12 | 9 | 8 | 6 | 100 |
| Utah | 61 | 5 | 10 | 13 | 11 | 100 |
| | | | | | | |
| Pattern 2—Heavy dependence on state sources | | | | | | |
| Alaska | 20 | 4 | 64 | 5 | 7 | 100 |
| North Carolina | 23 | 3 | 62 | 8 | 4 | 100 |
| Minnesota | 31 | z | 54 | 10 | 5 | 100 |
| Colorado | 32 | 1 | 53 | 10 | 4 | 100 |
| Wisconsin | 33 | z | 51 | 10 | 6 | 100 |
| | | | | | | |
| Pattern 3—Balanced pattern with dependence on several sources | | | | | | |
| Alabama | 25 | 26 | 31 | 11 | 7 | 100 |
| Indiana | 33 | 4 | 31 | 29 | 3 | 100 |
| Nevada | 28 | 25 | 9 | 36 | 2 | 100 |
| New York | 29 | 16 | 44 | 7 | 4 | 100 |
| Washington | 37 | 14 | 26 | 12 | 11 | 100 |

SOURCE: U.S. Bureau of the Census, *Census of Governments, 1972,* Vol. 4. No. 3, *Finances of County Governments* (Washington: U.S. Government Printing Office, 1974), p. 12. The character "z" designates a percentage between .1% and .5%. Similar state-by-state figures are not available in annual census publications since 1971-72. Details may not add to totals due to rounding.

that these items are no longer taxed in many states. As a result, the personal property tax base has been largely reduced to several difficult-to-hide items such as business equipment, store inventories, farm machinery, and livestock.[11] it seems likely that this base will be further nibbled away as certain groups such as merchants and farmers convince state legislatures that it is inequitable to tax just a few items of personal property.

The burden of the property tax is falling more and more on real prop-erty. This is a regressive tax. It weighs heavily on low income, older residents who own their own homes and farms, although property tax circuit breakers do somewhat reduce the regressive effect of the property tax.[13] Increased political pressures at both the state and local levels have reduced real property tax yields. At the local level, pressures exerted on local assessors and other factors have tended to reduce residential assessment levels in many counties. In Delaware, the ratio of assessed value of residential property to the sales price declined from 57% in 1961 to 36½% in 1971.[14] In New York, the decline was from 35% of sales price to 26% in ten years. In the last five years for which statistics are available (1966 to 1971), thirty-eight states had declines in their ratios of assessed value to sales value and only twelve states had increases. As a result, the increases in the sales prices of property during this period were not being fully reflected in real property tax collections. At the state level, state financed property tax relief is beginning to reduce property tax collections.[15]

The real property tax cannot be depended upon to provide the funds needed to meet anticipated increases in county government expenditures. County officials have mixed views about the property tax. On one hand, the National Association of Counties has recognized that "the property tax is a regressive and inequitable tax which has become burdensome to all property owners and those on fixed incomes."[16] On the other hand, NACo recognizes that the property tax raises a substantial amount of money and ". . .must be regarded as a necessary part of an overall tax system."[17] The National Association of Counties platform recommends reforms in the assessing process and concludes:

*"The property tax base is not adequate to support local government. The demands of education and public assistance have been the most rapidly expanding elements in recent years, and removal of one or both would have an immediate beneficial effect. However, from the long-range standpoint, it is doubtful, even then, that the property tax base is elastic enough to meet local financial needs."[18]*

**Non-Property Taxes.** Non-property taxes increased 522% from $449 million to $2,345 million from 1966-67 to 1974-75, but still constituted only 7% of total county revenues.[19] More than 20% of all county general revenue in Alabama and Nevada came from non-property taxes in 1971-72, and 10-20% of county general revenues in nine other states came from this source. The principal non-property taxes are the county sales taxes used in Alabama, California, Illinois, and other states and selective sales taxes on cigarettes, gasoline, and other commodities.

County sales taxes are most effective when they are imposed by all counties in an area; otherwise consumers on the borders of the taxing county may shop in neighboring counties. While most counties administer their own sales tax, counties in California and Illinois have the tax collected for them by the state. Selective sales taxes, such as gasoline taxes, cigarette taxes, and taxes on beer, are also levied by some counties. Nevada counties receive funds from a county tax on gambling establishments, and other counties have various forms of business taxes and licenses.

Non-property taxes are an important, and largely untapped, source of revenue. The income tax, in particular, is largely unused by county government. In 1973, the Indiana Legislature authorized a county income tax, and as of July, 1974, thirty-six counties had imposed this tax.[20] Recognizing that the income tax was used by relatively few counties because of state restrictions, the Na-

Figure 9-2

**TRENDS IN COUNTY GENERAL REVENUE FROM SELECTED MAJOR SOURCES:
1965-66 TO 1974-75**

**(billions of dollars)**

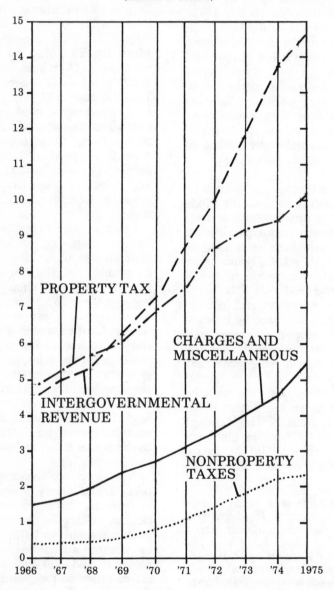

SOURCE: U.S. Bureau of the Census, *County Government Finances in 1974-75* (Washington:
U.S. Government Printing Office, 1976), p. 1.

tional Association of Counties urged states with income taxes to give local government the authority to "piggyback" on the state income tax. This would give local governments the benefit of a state collection system which will collect the county tax at the same time it collects state taxes.[21]

NACo has also suggested that states authorize counties to adopt real estate transfer taxes. Congress repealed the federal documentary stamp tax on real estate transfers, opening this tax field up for the exclusive use of state and local governments. *The American County Platform* states that: ". . .Since the transfer of property titles is recorded primarily by county officials, a real estate transfer tax is particularly well suited to enforcement at the county level."[22]

**Current Charges and Other County Sources.** Current charges amounted to $3.7 billion in 1974-75 and were a major source of county revenues in Indiana, Nevada, Mississippi, Texas, and other states.[23] Approximately half of the amount counties receive in current charges is paid by patients in county hospitals. User charges such as the charges to property owners for road and street improvements in local improvement districts are another source of funds. Most of the remaining revenue is from user fees from golf courses, swimming pools, airport rentals, and miscellaneous other sources. While fees are a large revenue source, revenue increases generally require a nearly compensating increase in expenditures. Other general revenue sources, such as interest income, special assessments and sale of property, are minor.

There are two potentially important sources of county revenue outside the county general fund. Counties in Maryland and North Carolina received $128 million in liquor store sales in 1972-73 and expended $110 million in liquor store operations.[24] Expansion of county liquor stores in other states could provide an additional source of county funds. County governments in sixteen states had county utility systems and collected $200 million in 1974-75 from their water, electric, gas, and transit utilities.[25] While counties are less likely to operate utilities than cities, some county utilities are large. Dade County (Florida), for example, operates a major transit system. The residents of a county gain an advantage in revenue sharing funds if a county operates the area transit system or collects the taxes which pay for the system rather than having a special district handle all the financing.[26]

**Revenue from State Sources.** State government is the single largest source of county revenue. In the 1972 calendar year, state intergovernmental aid to county governments amounted to $9.7 billion. Of that $1.1 billion was general local government support, $1.8 billion was for education, $1.5 billion for highways, $4.4 billion for public welfare, $100 million for hospitals and $800 million for other purposes.[27] Most of the funds for public welfare and part of the funds for education, highways, and hospitals are federal funds which have been passed through the states to county government. In contrast, funds for general local government support are almost always state funds. Table 9-6 shows the varieties of state aid and state shared revenue in a small state, Idaho.

In larger states (like California, New York, Michigan, and Maryland), counties receive more types of state intergovernmental assistance. Table 9-7 shows that in 1972 California and New York counties received most of their state aid payment for public welfare, Michigan counties received extensive state payments for highways, and Maryland counties received large amounts of state payments for education.

Most types of state general government support are particularly useful to county government since they can be used for a wide variety of functions. Some examples of this type of aid are described below.[28]

*Per capita grants.* New York State distributed $.65 to each county government for each person residing in the county in 1972.

*Local government funds.* Ohio places a portion of the proceeds of individual income taxes and the intangible tax on financial institutions into a local government fund. A budget commission in each county redistributes its share of the local government fund to county government and to municipalities, park districts, and townships in the county on the basis of need for current operating expenses. In counties of less than 100,000 people, not less than 10% must be distributed to

Table 9-6

STATE INTERGOVERNMENTAL REVENUES IN IDAHO IN 1972

| | Primary Source of Funds | |
|---|---|---|
| | State | Federal |
| 1. General local support (the use of most of these funds is unrestricted). | | |
| a. General sales tax (20% of the sales tax is distributed to local governments). | x | |
| b. Alcoholic beverage monopoly profits. | x | |
| 2. Highways | | |
| a. Highway user revenues. | x | |
| b. Federal forest reserve funds returned to counties in which forest land is located. | | x |
| 3. Other revenues | | |
| a. Hospital construction. | | x |
| b. Federal grazing revenue—A portion of federal grazing fees returned to the state and redistributed to the county of origin. | | x |

SOURCE: U.S. Bureau of the Census, *Census of Governments, 1972,* Vol. 6, *Topical Studies,* No. 3, *State Payments to Local Governments* (Washington: U.S. Government Printing Office, 1974), p. 37.

**Table 9-7**

**NUMBERS OF TYPES OF STATE INTERGOVERNMENTAL PAYMENTS AND AMOUNTS RECEIVED BY COUNTY GOVERNMENT IN SELECTED STATES IN 1972**

**(in millions of dollars)**

| | California | | New York | | Michigan | | Maryland | | Idaho | |
|---|---|---|---|---|---|---|---|---|---|---|
| | No. | Amount | No. | Amount | No. | Amount | No. | Amount | No. | Amount |
| General local support | 8 | $487.0 | 2 | $22.1 | 6 | $41.9 | 9 | $35.1 | 2 | $7.1 |
| Education | 2 | 54.2 | 4 | 60.1 | 0 | 0 | 21 | 339.0 | 0 | 0 |
| Highways | 5 | 198.1 | 4 | 71.6 | 2 | 159.4 | 3 | 58.2 | 2 | 12.5 |
| Public Welfare | 12 | 1,848.1 | 8 | 780.8 | 5 | 66.3 | 12 | 63.6 | 0 | 0 |
| Hospitals | 2 | 2.3 | 1 | 1.8 | 3 | 12.0 | 1 | .2 | 1 | .6 |
| Miscellaneous and combined | 24 | 189.0 | 20 | 152.4 | 8 | 47.0 | 10 | 57.3 | 1 | z |
| Total | 53 | $2,778.8 | 39 | $1,088.9 | 24 | $326.7 | 56 | $553.3 | 6 | $20.3 |

SOURCE: U.S. Bureau of the Census, *Census of Governments, 1972*, Vol. 6, *Topical Studies*, No. 3, *State Payments to Local Governments* (Washington: U.S. Government Printing Office, 1974), pp. 14, 15, and 24-81. The character "z" indicates less than one million dollars. Details may not add to totals due to rounding.

townships.

*Sales tax allocations.* In Idaho, 20% of the sales tax is distributed to counties, cities and other units of local government on the basis of the personal property taxes collected on business inventory in the years 1965 to 1967.

*Income tax allocations.* In Michigan, nearly 6% of the state income tax was distributed to county governments in 1972 in accordance with population.

*Motor vehicle funds in lieu of property taxes.* Motor vehicle license fees, collected in lieu of property taxes in California, are distributed, after deductions, half to county governments in proportion to population and half to city governments on the same basis.

*Selective sales tax distributions.* In Maryland in 1972, half of the proceeds of a six-cent cigarette tax (after a deduction for administration) was distributed to the City of Baltimore and Maryland counties on the basis of population. Part of the alcoholic beverage sales tax was also distributed to counties.

State grants-in-aid differ from shared taxes and general grants. They are earmarked for specific purposes and generally require county matching expenditures. For example, in 1972 Ohio counties received a number of public assistance grants which were specifically earmarked. The state general relief grants were made as partial reimbursement of county expenditures for general relief. The grants for child welfare services were funds from federal and state sources which were distributed as partial reimbursement for child welfare administration costs. In each of these Ohio examples, the funds were received from state government for specific purposes, and the counties which accepted the grants were committed to programs which required county contributions.

From the county government point of view, it is important that at least a third of all state funds come in the form of shared taxes or general revenue sharing grants which are relatively unrestricted in use. Counties need these funds to provide the fiscal flexibility to fund new and existing programs in functional areas which do not benefit from specific grants-in-aid. State governments seem likely to continue to provide increases in intergovernmental revenue, but it is doubtful that all the increased county needs can be met with state sources.

**Federal Intergovernmental Revenues.** In 1971-72, intergovernmental revenues from non-state sources to counties amounted to $704 million dollars and consisted largely of federal grants.[29] Census statistics show that intergovernmental revenues largely from federal sources, reached $2.9 billion in 1974-75.[30] Part of this increase can be attributed to increases in federal grants going directly to county government. A more important reason for the increase is that a few months after the close of the 1971-72 fiscal year, the first federal revenue sharing payments reached county government. One writer estimated that $1.58 billion in revenue sharing funds were distributed to counties during the October, 1974-July, 1975 period—about 5% of what counties collected from all sources in 1974-75.[31] General revenue sharing funds were of even greater importance when compared against county tax collections in some southern states. Arkansas, Kentucky, Mississippi, and South Carolina counties received revenue sharing funds which were equal to more than half the amount of taxes collected by the county.[32]

Federal revenue sharing was extended by Congress in October, 1976, through September 30, 1980. The amount will increase from $6.65 billion in the 1977 federal fiscal year to $6.85 billion in the following two years, with one-third of the amount going to state governments and two-thirds distributed among counties, cities, and other general purpose units of local government.[33] Federal revenue sharing is particularly valuable to county government because it has very few requirements and may be used for any type of county expenditure.[34] Individual county officials, the National Association of Counties, and other local government officials and groups worked hard to influence Congress to extend revenue sharing, but they will face a problem in 1979 and 1980 when revenue sharing legislation must again be extended. If they spend most of their funds for current operations, they will be building operating expenses to the point where they cannot sustain them with tax funds if Congress does not renew revenue sharing in 1980. If they spend most of their revenue sharing funds for capital expenses (as many counties do), they will avoid building the base of current operations but may expend some of their money on second priority capital items. What counties and other local units most need, and what NACo and other groups have advocated, is a federal commitment to make revenue sharing a permanent part of the federal budget.

Payment-in-lieu of taxes is another important type of federal aid. Since the federal government does not pay property taxes on federal lands, the in-lieu-payments are meant to partially compensate counties and other units of local government for loss of tax revenues. The payments are based on the amount of federal acreage within the county and limited by a per capita population factor.[35] In-lieu-payments are not set high enough to compensate counties for all the revenue they lose because of their inability to tax federal lands.[36] However, the passage of the new law (HR 9719) in October, 1976, considerably eased the pressure on counties (such as Pope County, Illinois) which were nearing bankruptcy because of large amounts of tax exempt federal lands.

Federal grants-in-aid are another growing source of county revenue. Although grants from federal agencies which by-pass state government and go directly to counties probably amounted to less than $1.5 billion in 1974-75, much more federal aid is routed to counties through state government. Federal funds are particularly crucial to the support of county welfare, health, manpower, parks and recreation, sewage treatment plant construction, mass transit, highway planning, and air pollution control programs.

## COUNTY CASH, SECURITY HOLDINGS, AND DEBT

At the end of the 1974-75 fiscal year, county governments in the United States had cash and deposits of $9.1 billion, held securities of $1.6 billion, and held $3.8 billion in retirement funds.[37] The $14.5 billion in cash and security holdings were more than five times the county holdings of $2.6 billion eighteen years earlier. One reason for the increase was the growth of employee retirement system holdings which increased six times in less than two decades. The Los Angeles County employees' retirement system had holdings of nearly $1.5 billion in 1974-75.

More than offsetting the $14.5 billion county cash and security holdings was an $18.9 billion county debt in 1974-75. Long term debt was $17.6 billion in 1974-75, of which $2.3 billion was for schools and the remainder for other purposes. Short term county debt in 1974-75 amounted to $1.3 billion. County debt rose sharply from $14.0 billion in 1971-72 to $18.9 billion in 1974-75, and one writer predicted a further sharp rise in the future due to extensive issuance of pollution control bonds.[38]

The two main types of long term county bond issues are revenue bonds and general obligation bonds. Revenue bonds are issued to finance revenue producing county projects and are repaid from the revenues of these projects. The county is not obligated to repay these bonds from general revenue sources if the project revenues should fall short of expectations. In contrast, general obligation bonds are repaid from the general revenue of the county. Investors prefer general obligation bonds, and a county can receive lower interest rates on these bonds.

As a result of the New York City and other fiscal crises of 1975, state and local governments had increasing difficulty in raising money through bonds.[39] Municipal bond interest rates increased from 5.22% in 1973 to 7.06% in 1975.[40] County governments, as well as cities, had to pay more to borrow funds, and the increased interest rates mean higher costs in repaying those bonds over the lifetime of the issues. A Changing bond market can decrease rates as evidenced in 1976-77. The issuance of county bonds is a complex procedure in which the bonds are normally sold through bond houses or security dealers who resell them to investors.

Standard and Poor's, and Moody's are the two institutions which have developed a system to examine the fiscal and political affairs of a governmental unit in order to determine the various degrees of risk a purchase carries. These ratings and the national economic climate are two factors which affect the interest level a jurisdiction will pay on a bond issue.

## THE FISCAL BASE

County government depends on two sources (revenue from state government and the property tax) for slightly more than 67% of its general revenues.

Some promising sources of county revenues are non-property taxes and federal assistance. County government could much more extensively utilize the income tax, sales tax, and selective sales taxes on cigarettes, liquor, gasoline, and other products. Particularly promising are "piggybacking" arrangements by which counties levy an income or sales tax and have the tax collected by state tax agencies at the same time they collect their own taxes.

Counties are subject to a variety of restrictions in state constitutions and laws on amount and manner of incurring debt. Frequently there is a debt limit which a county cannot exceed. For example, the Michigan Constitution states that county debt may not exceed 10% of the equalized value of the county.[41] Some types of debt, such as revenue bonds and drainage bonds which do not pledge the county's full faith and credit, are excluded from the constitutional debt limit. Constitutional and statutory debt limits for local governments were severely criticized by the Advisory Commission on Intergovernmental Relations. The Commission recommended repeal of these limitations on the grounds that they cause problems in budgeting.[42] County government debt limits have also encouraged the establishment of special districts, because districts are not bound by these debt limits and may be established to finance needed improvements which counties are not able to finance.

The splintering of local governments into many separate units diminishes the fiscal capability of local tax systems. The smaller the area of a city or village, for example, the easier it is for a taxpayer to escape sales and selective sales taxes by driving beyond its borders to make his purchases. From the standpoint of fiscal capability, the county provides a broader and better tax base than a small city or village.

County government has greater fiscal potential than any other unit of local government because of its greater area and fiscal capability. To achieve this potential, county governments need a third major source of revenue or a combination of revenue sources which would provide more than a third of all county income.

## REFERENCES

1. John R. Coleman, "Trends in County Finances," *The County Year Book, 1975* (Washington: National Association of Counties and International City Management Association, 1975), p. 19.

2. Susan Walker Torrence, *Grass Roots Government* (Washington: Robert B. Luce, Inc., 1974), p. 33.

3. U.S. Bureau of the Census, *Census of Governments, 1972,* Vol. 4, No. 3, *Finances of County Governments* (Washington: U.S. Government Printing Office, 1974), pp. 21-69 was used as the source of information on per capita county costs. The Census of Governments is published every five years.

4. Ibid.

5. *County News* (Washington), May 12, 1975, p. 6.

6. Computed from U.S. Bureau of the Census, *Census of Governments, 1972,* Vol. 4, No. 3, *Finances of County Governments,* p. 9 and U.S. Bureau of the Census, *County Government Finances in 1974-75* (Washington: U.S. Government Printing Office, 1976), p. 5.

7. U.S. Bureau of the Census, *Census of Governments, 1972,* Vol. 4, No. 3, *Finances of County Governments,* p. 9.

8. U.S. Bureau of the Census, *County Government Finances in 1974-75,* p. 5. and U.S. Bureau of the Census, *Census of Governments, 1972,* Vol. 4, No. 3, *Finances of County Governments,* p. 9.

9. U.S. Bureau of the Census, *Property Values Subject to Local General Property Taxation in the United States: 1973* (Washington: U.S. Government Printing Office, 1974), p. 10.

10. For the 1961 assessment, see *Census of Governments, 1972,* Vol. 2, *Taxable Property Values and Assessment—Sales Price Ratios,* Part 1, *Taxable and Other Property Tax Values* (Washington: U.S. Government Printing Office, 1973), p. 4.

11. Household personal property was taxed in only 24 states in 1971, and motor vehicles were taxed in only 22 states. In contrast, commercial and industrial personal property was taxed in 47 states, and agricultural personal property was taxed in 42 states. Ibid., p. 9.

12. For example, Idaho merchants convinced the State Legislature that personal property taxes on store inventories were inequitable in 1967. Idaho farmers joined forces with the store owners to gain additional personal property tax exemptions for themselves.

13. The circuit breaker generally is part of the state income tax process. When the property tax bill of an elderly or low income person reaches a certain amount, the circuit breaker goes into effect and relief is granted. In some states, the applicant files a supplemental

statement with his income tax return, and the state income tax staff computes the amount of relief due the property tax owner from the property tax paid and the amount of the person's income. A check is sent by the state to the individual for the amount due in property tax relief. For further information on the use of circuit breakers, see Advisory Commission on Intergovernmental Relations, *Property Tax Circuit Breakers: Current Status and Policy Issues* (Washington: Advisory Commission on Intergovernmental Relations, 1975).

14. For further information on the ratios of assessed value to sales value in residential assessment levels, see Advisory Commission on Intergovernmental Relations, *The Property Tax in a Changing Environment* (Washington: U.S. Government Printing Office, 1974), p. 9.

15. John R. Coleman, p. 19.

16. National Association of Counties, *The American County Platform* (Washington: National Association of Counties, 1976), p. 87.

17. Ibid.

18. Ibid.

19. U.S. Bureau of the Census, *Census of Governments, 1972*, Vol. 4, No. 3, *Finances of County Governments*, pp. 9, 12. Statistical data quoted on non-property tax collections in individual states may be found on page 12 of the same source. See also U.S. Bureau of the Census, *Finances of County Governments, 1974-75*, p. 5.

20. John R. Coleman, p. 19.

21. National Association of Counties, *The American County Platform*, p. 83, 84. L.L. Ecker-Racz, *The Politics and Economics of State-Local Finance* (Englewood Cliffs, N.J.: Prentice-Hall, Inc., 1970), p. 111, points out that Maryland authorizes counties to levy personal income taxes with the requirement that the local tax be based on state tax liability (up to 50%) and collected by the state when it collects its own tax.

22. National Association of Counties, *The American County Platform*, p. 83.

23. U.S. Bureau of the Census, *Finances of County Governments, 1974-75*, p. 5.

24. John R. Coleman, p. 21.

25. U.S. Bureau of the Census, *Finances of County Governments, 1974-75*, p. 7.

26. John R. Coleman, p. 21 makes this point. If a county collects taxes for the transit system, the amount collected will count as additional tax effort by the county and add to the amount of the county's general revenue funds.

27. U.S. Bureau of the Census, *Census of Governments, 1972*, Vol. 6, *Topical Studies*, No. 3, *State Payments to Local Governments* (Washington: U.S. Government Printing Office, 1974), p. 14.

28. The examples are for the year 1972 and are contained in U.S. Bureau of the Census, *Census of Governments, 1972*, Vol. 6, *Topical Studies*, No. 3, *State Payments to Local Governments*, pp. 24-85.

29. U.S. Bureau of the Census, *Census of Governments, 1972*, Vol. 4, No. 3, *Finances of County Governments*, p. 9.

30. U.S. Bureau of the Census, *County Government Finances in 1974-75*, p. 5.

31. John R. Coleman, p. 19.

32. Ibid.

33. *County News* (Washington), October 4, 1976, p. 14 provides a comparison of the current revenue sharing provisions with the former Act.

34. Governments receiving funds must hold public hearings on the proposed use of the funds seven days before submitting the budget to the legislative body; they must report planned and actual expenditures of the funds; and they must not discriminate or pay less than prevailing wages on construction projects using 25% or more of revenue sharing funds. Other requirements for local governments include auditing and accounting requirements and a prohibition against using revenue sharing funds for lobbying. The provision of the 1972 Act, which limited local government use of the funds to only eight categories of operating and maintenance expense, was eliminated from the 1976 Act.

35. *County News* (Washington), October 25, 1976, p. 1, reports: "Counties will receive the greater amount of either (A) 75 cents per acre of entitlement lands less current timber, mineral or grazing payments, or (b) 10 cents per acre in addition to current payments. These payments will be limited to $50 per capita for counties under 5,000 population with a sliding scale to $20 per capita at 500,000 population."

36. Ibid. It was estimated "that Los Angeles County, California, alone would derive more than $150 million annually in property taxes if its federal lands were taxed as though privately owned."

37. The statistical information in this section is from U.S. Bureau of the Census, *Census of Governments, 1972*, Vol. 4, No. 3, *Finances of County Governments*, pp. 18, 19, U.S. Bureau of the Census, *Finances of County Governments, 1974-75*, p. 6., and John R. Coleman, pp. 21, 22.

38. John R. Coleman, p. 22.

39. For further information on the effect of New York City's financial problems see Joel Haveman, "Cities, States Aren't Buying Proposals to Shore Up Bond Market," *National Journal*, March 27, 1976, pp. 394-399.

40. Ibid., p. 395.

41. Kenneth VerBurg, *Guide to Michigan County Government* (East Lansing: Michigan State University, 1972), p. VIII-45.

42. Advisory Commission on Intergovernmental Relations, *State Constitutional and Statutory Restrictions on Local Government Debt* (Washington: Advisory Commission on Intergovernmental Relations, 1961), p. 75.

# Chapter 10

# The Future of American County Government

"In all but the largest metropolitan areas, the county appears to be the most appropriate jurisdiction for carrying out those functions that are tied directly to individuals or are territorially regional. Indeed, in many areas of the country, the county may have to supplant the municipality as a prime purveyor of public services.

This is because the metropolitanization of our population in urban areas and the thinning out of population in many of our rural areas has resulted in a wider total area to be served than encompassed within municipal jurisdictions. The inevitable result is that more and more functions will gravitate up from the municipal to the county level. The county is likely to emerge as a kingpin of local government during the next two decades. As its responsibilities and functions increase under the pressure of more diffused and mobile development, the traditional concept of the county as simply a sub-state jurisdiction will weaken and grow obsolete. We can expect increasing public pressure to broaden the county into a truly accountable local instrumentality of government with its own legislative powers. This will be resisted in many areas because the status quo is more comfortable for many states and counties. But reality will catch up and public opinion will bring change despite the initial disruption. By the year 2000, the county is likely to be quite different in structure and function from that we know today."[1]

These views, expressed by Ralph Widner, were among a number of predictions of the future of county government in papers presented at the Symposium on the Future of County Government in Boston, September 15-17, 1976. Ralph Widner is President of the Academy for Contemporary Problems and has based his assessment on the trends he sees developing in the political system for the next two decades.

The conference on the future of county government brought together county officials, academicians, businessmen, and state and national officials. Each participant was asked to react to the papers presented and discuss the future role of county government. This chapter will present views on the future of county government by participants in the conference, writers in various fields, county officials, and the author.

## THE IMPACT OF POPULATION AND ECONOMIC TRENDS ON COUNTY SERVICES

Population change, inflation, the energy crunch, and other national trends will have an important impact on county government in the next decade. One of the most predictable trends is the changing composition of our population by age group. The dramatic reduction in the nation's birth rate since 1960 has increased the average age of the population from 27.9 years in 1971 to 28.6 in 1974. The average age is projected by the Bureau of the Census to increase to 31.1 years in 1985 and 34.8 by the year 2000.[2] The decline in birth rates has already affected public school enrollment. County officials, such as Alastair McArthur, have commented that the lowering birth rate and a slowing of immigration into his county (Montgomery County, Maryland) has caused a decline in elementary school population.[3] The decline in the birth rate will affect college enrollments in the 1980s and the number of adults in the 25-34 age bracket in the 1990s.

The changing age composition of our nation will affect a number of county programs. Alastair McArthur expects that more emphasis will be placed on programs for the elderly in his county; Joseph Torrence anticipates that the Nashville-Davidson County Health Department will move toward community clinics to relieve the pressures on the general hospital.[4] Ralph Widner suggests that "as the number of Americans in working years begins to decrease relative to the number of older persons in retirement, the financial integrity of retirement pension systems, including Social Security, will be in jeopardy unless the approach to funding these systems is changed."[5] If his prediction is correct, county governments may need to put additional funds into their own retirement systems, and county welfare programs may face the additional costs of providing stopgap aid to retired persons unable to draw funds from bankrupt retirement systems.

**Regional Migration, The Energy Crunch, and Boom Counties.** The shift in migration patterns in the United States, noted by Ralph Widner, Alan Campbell, and others, will probably continue to cause growth in the South and certain areas of the West during the next few decades.[6] County governments in states like Florida, Texas, and Arizona can continue to expect problems of managing substantial population growth, while some counties in the Northeast and Midwest will face problems of revenue loss through declines in population and loss of industry. Alan Campbell has commented that the people who are moving from the northeastern and north central sections of the country to the South and Southwest generally have higher incomes, more education, and are younger than those remaining.[7] If this movement continues to weaken the northeastern and north central states, as Campbell expects, we may see national government programs to reverse these trends.

The energy crunch will affect counties in energy short areas of the nation (particularly New England) and in energy producing areas. Ralph Widner believes that our nation must pass through a critical transition of about a quarter of a century as it shifts from a reliance on fossil fuels to newer energy sources.[8] He sees the need for local policies aimed at the conservation of energy and federal programs which minimize the social and economic dislocation in energy resource importing areas of the nation. County energy conservation programs may become increasingly important in the future, not only to reduce consumption of energy in county buildings, but also to stimulate reductions in energy use by homeowners and businesses within the county. Los Angeles County Supervisor James Hayes has developed a program for counties to help conserve energy by making an inventory of every energy using activity in the county (public and private), calculating future energy needs, and developing plans to reduce energy consumption in the county by 20%.[9]

Energy shortages will cause dramatic growth in some energy producing counties, and Widner believes that "states in the West will have to devise ways to enable energy and resource development to occur in sparsely populated jurisdictions with minimal social and environmental disruption."[10] County officials in energy producing counties anticipate that growth will require new and expanded county services and are trying to control the direction of this growth in ways which will minimize environmental and agricultural disruption. The future of Rio Blanco County in western Colorado, for example, will be greatly affected by whether two oil shale leases are developed. Development of the leases near Rangely and Meeker would require about four thousand people in a county that had a 1970 population of 4,840. County Commissioner William Brennan commented:

"I expect that the growing energy shortage will require the nation to develop its oil shale resources in the next decade, and this will result in the two oil shale leases being developed. In ten years the population of our county will be double—perhaps triple—what it is now.

Our problem in county government is to control population growth so it does not destroy our ranching and the scenic eastern part of our county used for summer homes and camping. I am particularly concerned about the use of the agricultural lands along the White River for industry and residences. This is where our cattle ranchers raise the hay and alfalfa they need to feed their cattle through the winter.

We have our own three-person planning staff now and a good countywide comprehensive plan and zoning ordinance. In the decade ahead, I expect us to use planning and zoning to keep our county growth within the cities of Rangely and Meeker. Both cities now have good sources of water and would benefit in economies of scale from a population growth to double or triple their current size. I expect to see our agricultural zoning policy strictly enforced in the next ten years to keep the growth from spilling over into ranching, farming, and tourist areas."[11]

Sparsely settled counties undergoing growth will face problems in providing needed services. In Sweetwater County (Wyoming) the construction of a large, coal-fired electric generating plant required growth in medical facilities, schools, sewer and water lines, housing, social services, recreation, planning, and other services.[12] The Chairman of the Sweetwater Board of County Commissioners became a prime mover in an effort to resolve county growth problems. In Rio Blanco County, Commissioner William Brennan anticipates the following effects of growth on county services, staffing, and finance:

"If our county does double in population in the next decade, county government will need to expand to furnish more services. I see a considerable expansion of the County Sheriff's Office, and we will need a full-time rather than a part-time prosecuting attorney. Our public health department of two part-time health nurses will need to expand, and we will certainly need a full-time sanitarian to check septic tanks. Our current welfare staff of three persons will expand unless the federal government or State of Colorado administers aid to families with dependent children. With the large influx of new people, there may be a need for new types of social services such as day care, counseling, and perhaps some program for the aged. Our mental health caseload will expand, but I expect to see our three-county mental health department continue to provide services.

The population expansion in the next decade will probably not affect our county road department as much as you would think. If most of the growth occurs within city limits, as we hope, the cities and subdividers will have most of the new construction. I anticipate also that the county will be constructing a small airport suitable for a commercial feeder

airline in the next decade and may need to develop a parks program. I expect Rangley and Meeker (located fifty miles apart) to continue to be responsible for solid waste disposal and no attempt made to develop a single county landfill between them. If we grow as I expect in the next decade, perhaps the greatest pressure will be on the Planning Department. We will need to have a larger department and will need to continue coordinating with the planning staffs of Meeker and Rangely.

The growth of county government in Rio Blanco County will also affect county finance and county organization. If the county triples in population and the number of county employees also increases, I anticipate we will need an administrative assistant to work with the county commissioners. We will also need some new means of finance. If the property tax bears the entire burden of the cost of increased services, many farmers and ranchers in our county will go bankrupt. I look for counties to be able to use a small sales tax or severance tax collected by state tax officials."[13]

**Slow Growth in the Typical Non-Metropolitan County.** During the 1960s, non-metropolitan counties lost nearly three million people with the losses being particularly great in predominantly farm counties. From 1970-73, non-metropolitan counties gained 4.2% in population compared to a population gain of 2.9% in metropolitan counties.[14] The slow growth of most non-metropolitan counties seems likely to continue throughout the 1970s as manufacturing is "more and more able to locate in non-metropolitan areas and draw its labor force via commutation from a large surrounding area."[15] The growth of recreational activities, the in-migration of retired people, and the growing worldwide demand for farm products will also contribute to a revival in many rural counties which had been losing population and economic strength during the 1960s.[16]

Growth in county services and continued experimentation with intergovernmental cooperation seem likely in most non-metropolitan counties. Bernard Smith, County Supervisor of Sioux County (Iowa), has seen his county grow from 27,996 in 1970 to 29,300 in 1975 and expects population and county services to continue to grow slowly during the next decade.

"I do not expect us to grow rapidly, but we should remain a relatively prosperous farm county. We have been hurt by the loss of railroad lines needed to transport our grain to the market. This will greatly increase the use of our roads by cattle and grain trucks and necessitate greater road repair.

There are some shifts in functions which may occur during the next decade. Road construction and maintenance equipment is becoming increasingly more expensive with some equipment costing nearly $100,000. Our smaller cities cannot afford the equipment they need, and I expect the county to provide some construction and maintenance of city streets on a contract basis. Law enforcement is becoming more expensive for our smaller cities also, and I expect the county to provide law enforcement on a contract basis to smaller communities so they can have 24-hour police protection.

There may be growth in other new county functions. For example, we have established a county-wide ambulance service which can reach anyone in the county within ten minutes. There may be a movement to decentralize the provision of care for the mentally retarded to county government."[17]

**Trends Affecting the Core County of a Metropolitan Area.** Significant population changes have occurred since 1960 in the counties which form the core of our metropolitan areas. Most of the larger central cities in the nation are losing population. As Table 10-1 shows, only six of the twenty-one cities having a population of 500,000 or more people in 1960 gained population between 1960 and 1970, and only three (Houston, San Antonio, and San Diego) gained population between 1970 and 1973. In the next two decades, many of our largest cities will undoubtedly continue to lose population.

The impact of a substantial population decline in many large cities will undoubtedly be the continued decline in the political power base of big city mayors. Moreover, as our largest cities lose population and tax base, they will face increasing financial pressures and may be ready to transfer more areawide functions to county government. Loss of population by large cities may also result in the abandonment of housing in many areas around the core of these cities. Ralph Widner predicts large scale abandonment of neighborhoods in older industrial centers, which will be given impetus by "rampant crime, bad schools, mismatch between the location of jobs and the location of housing, and the rapid deterioration of public services in these areas."[18]

The plight of the larger cities will undoubtedly bring a continuing effort by big city mayors to get increased federal and state aid. It may also bring renewed interest in city-county consolidation as a means of gaining greater efficiency and providing a broader tax base for urban

Table 10-1

POPULATION OF SELECTED CENTRAL CITIES IN 1960, 1970, AND 1973
(in thousands of people)

| | 1960 | 1970 | 1973 Est. | Change from 1970 to 1973 |
|---|---|---|---|---|
| Baltimore, Maryland | 939 | 906 | 878 | -28 |
| Boston, Massachusetts | 697 | 641 | 618 | -23 |
| Buffalo, New York | 533 | 463 | 425 | -38 |
| Chicago, Illinois | 3,550 | 3,367 | 3,173 | -194 |
| Cincinnati, Ohio | 503 | 453 | 426 | -27 |
| Cleveland, Ohio | 876 | 751 | 679 | -72 |
| Dallas, Texas | 680 | 844* | 816 | -28 |
| Detroit, Michigan | 1,670 | 1,511 | 1,387 | -124 |
| Houston, Texas | 938 | 1,233* | 1,320* | +87 |
| Los Angeles, California | 2,479 | 2,816* | 2,747 | -69 |
| Milwaukee, Wisconsin | 741 | 717 | 691 | -26 |
| New Orleans, Louisiana | 628 | 593 | 573 | -20 |
| New York, New York | 7,782 | 7,895* | 7,647 | -248 |
| Philadelphia, Pennsylvania | 2,003 | 1,949 | 1,862 | -87 |
| Pittsburgh, Pennsylvania | 604 | 520 | 479 | -41 |
| St. Louis, Missouri | 750 | 622 | 558 | -64 |
| San Antonio, Texas | 588 | 654* | 756* | +102 |
| San Diego, California | 573 | 697* | 757* | +60 |
| San Francisco, California | 740 | 716 | 687 | -29 |
| Seattle, Washington | 557 | 531 | 503 | -28 |
| Washington, D.C. | 764 | 757 | 734 | -23 |

SOURCE: U.S. Bureau of the Census, *Statistical Abstract of the United States, 1976* (Washington: U.S. Government Printing Office, 1976), pp. 22-24. An "*" denotes an increase in population since the previous reporting period.

services. The consolidation of Nashville and Davidson County has been particularly successful in its fifteen years of existence. The city-county government provides services throughout the entire county, and residents outside the urban services district pay a general services tax rate. The residents of the urban services district are taxed at a higher rate for city-type services. Reviewing the future of the Metropolitan Government of Nashville and Davidson County, Finance Director Joseph Torrence stressed shifts in the urban services district and changes in programs, but not the desperate need for funds faced by some large city mayors.

"In the next ten years, I expect that the current urban services district will expand. Water and sewer lines will be extended further into the county and the urban services district will expand at the same time. I anticipate that fire protection will be provided countywide within a decade rather than being just provided in the urban services district. Extension of water lines of appropriate size is the major problem to extending class "3" fire service.

There will be increased costs during the next ten years. We will need to expand our sewage treatment plant because of EPA regulations and population increases. We now subsidize bus rates and pay part of the cost from a Urban Mass Transit Administration grant. I expect this to continue. Fortunately we have ample water and pumping capacity for the next decade, and I do not anticipate much cost increase in this area.

There will be some significant shifts in emphasis in the next ten years. Our Health Department will move more towards community clinics to relieve the pressures on our general hospital. There will be more emphasis on preventive medicine. We anticipate better coordination between health, social services, and criminal justice programs in the future and an increased public interest in the reform of the court system. The urban renewal program will change from the large projects of the past to smaller projects for street improvement, parks, and the development of commercial and industrial sites. I do not anticipate large scale demolition of slum housing but restoration of older housing. In our school system, increased financial pressures may bring us from a five-period day for teachers to a six-period day.

I do not anticipate much, if any, tax increase for seven or eight years, although we may be forced to increase property tax rates. We have a local option sales tax currently, and the proportion of our income from the sales tax is increasing and the percent from the property tax is declining. I anticipate that this trend will continue. However, we have about reached the point where further increases in the sales tax would pose difficulties. Tennessee does not have an income tax, and therefore we have no local option on this as a revenue source."[19]

In other core counties of the nation, the financial problems of the largest cities may be mitigated by transferring functions to the metropolitan county. The process by which this occurs has been previously described in Chapter 6. The result is what is termed an "urban county"— a county government which provides many types of urban services for the entire county area. Dade County (Florida), Los Angeles County (California), and Milwaukee County (Wisconsin) are three core counties which provide many urban services. The fiscal strength of the urban county depends to some extent on whether the core county is itself losing population. From 1970 to 1973, some of the larger core counties—such as Cook County (Illinois), Cuyahoga County (Ohio), and Allegheny County (Pennsylvania)— have been losing population.

**Growth Problems in Fringe Counties of Metropolitan Areas.** Almost all of the fringe counties which surround the core county in existing multi-county metropolitan areas have gained population between 1950 and 1970. Since 1970, two trends are apparent. Counties on the fringes of smaller metropolitan areas and counties in the outer fringes of large metropolitan areas continue to gain population. Population growth has slowed or stopped in some of the more populous counties in the inner fringe of our largest metropolitan areas. These trends are likely to continue.

For the rapidly growing fringe county, the problem is growth management and provision of adequate services particularly in new communities built outside incorporated areas. Shelby County (Alabama) is a growing county on the southern fringe of the Birmingham metropolitan area, and former Judge Conrad Fowler described the future growth of this county and its county government as follows:

"In the next decade, our county, now 50,000, should reach 100,000 people. There are two planned communities on the drawing boards— Inverness, with a potential population of 15,000, and Riverchase, with 25,000. Both communities are being built outside municipalities, and coun-

Table 10-2

GAIN OR LOSS OF POPULATION BETWEEN 1970 AND 1973 OF CENTRAL CITIES,
CORE COUNTIES, AND FRINGE COUNTIES IN SELECTED METROPOLITAN AREAS
(in thousands of people)

| Name of Central City | Central City | Core County Outside the Central City | Core County | Fringe Counties | Metropolitan Area as a Whole |
|---|---|---|---|---|---|
| Cleveland (Cuyahoga County) | -72 | -4 | -76 | +16 | -60 |
| Chicago (Cook County) | -194 | +127 | -67 | +45 | -22 |
| Detroit (Wayne County) | -124 | +50 | -74 | +85 | +11 |
| Milwaukee (Milwaukee County) | -26 | +19 | -7 | +25 | +18 |
| Pittsburgh (Allegheny County) | -41 | -10 | -50 | +8 | -43 |

SOURCE: U.S. Bureau of the Census, *Statistical Abstract of the United States, 1976* (Washington: U.S. Government Printing Office, 1976), pp. 22-39, and U.S. Bureau of the Census, *Current Population Reports* (Washington: U.S. Government Printing Office, 1975). The reports of Ohio, Illinois, Michigan, Pennsylvania, and Wisconsin were used. Actual population estimates rather than provisional estimates were used.

ty government will be called on to provide municipal-type services.

In the near future we will have zoning. Currently, we have comprehensive plan and subdivision regulations but not zoning. We will also need to expand our park program to provide more recreation facilities on the river on our eastern boundary. Within ten years, our county government may be responsible for water supply and sewage collection and disposal. We have many small community water systems that depend on wells. With population expansion, surface water will be needed, and the county may become involved in building a dam and providing the water mains which will connect the source of water and the distribution systems. The county has no sewage treatment plant now, but the first plant has been planned and is likely to be constructed following completion of an EPA study of the Cahaba River.

There are other county services that will inevitably increase in the next ten years. Our public health department will need to expand. We are building a new jail and are planning a new judicial building. More Sheriff's deputies have been added to patrol the unincorporated area. The county library system will expand. When the population reaches 100,000, we will apply to become a prime sponsor under the CETA program."[20]

The counties immediately surrounding a large metropolitan area face the question of whether they should restrict or encourage growth. In some cases, continued population growth hinges upon the availability of additional water, sewage disposal facilities, or moderate priced housing. In Montgomery County (Maryland), the lack of sewage treatment plant capacity has caused a restriction in sewer hook-ups. This has curtailed commercial and industrial development and affected the population growth patterns, assessed valuation, and tax rate in the county.[21] The escalation of housing costs which has made it difficult for young married couples to live in the county has also affected county growth. Alastair McArthur, Coordinator of

Intergovernmental Programs for Montgomery County, described the effect of these and other trends on county services as follows:

"Lower birth rates and a slowing of immigration has caused a decline in elementary school population in the county. As a result, we have closed some schools. In contrast, community college enrollment remains high and work has begun on a third community college campus in Germantown.

During the next ten years, I expect to see more municipalities follow the City of Rockville by establishing their own police departments. Due to their size, some of these municipalities will find it more economical to contract with Montgomery County for these services.

More emphasis will be placed on programs for the elderly during the next decade; however, most health and social services programs should level off. Probably additional smaller parks will be built in the densely populated areas. If growth slows, as I anticipate, then present water sources should be sufficient, but we are continuing to plan for unanticipated water needs through diversion and storage of peak flows from the Potomac River."[22]

## THE IMPACT OF FISCAL AND INTERGOVERNMENTAL TRENDS ON COUNTY FUNCTIONS

One of the surest predictions for the future of county government is that counties will provide more services ten years from now than they do currently and that the percentage of counties furnishing newer, urban services will increase. County governments have added more than a dozen new responsibilities in the past decade including consumer protection, energy conservation, and manpower training. The percentage of counties performing newer functions has increased from 1971 to 1975, and the county officials quoted in the previous section of the chapter predicted more, not fewer, services provided by their counties. The extent to which county services will increase in the next decade depends on a number of fiscal and intergovernmental trends.

**Inflation and Fiscal Retrenchment.** Inflation tends to raise state and local government expenditures more than it raises revenues.[23] Alan Campbell estimates that counties, municipalities, and townships lost, through inflationary increases in costs, an amount equal to almost half the funds they gained through revenue sharing.[24] Inflation will be a major national problem in the decade ahead, and local electorates will be increasingly reluctant to pass bond issues for capital projects and to approve higher property tax levies for operating purposes.

The effects of inflation and a concern about higher property taxes will cause some fiscal retrenchment in counties in the decade ahead, but these effects will be particularly severe in the central cities which are losing population. These central cities may face three options: (1) no-growth budgets, (2) large increases in federal or state financing, or (3) a shift of city functions to the county, regional, or state level.[25] If federal and state aid to central cities does not increase greatly, county governments may face pressure to assume new urban functions at a time when they are facing their own (not as severe) revenue squeeze.

The fiscal crunch in the coming decade may produce innovations in regional financing. Ralph Widner states that we are likely to see "regionalization of the property tax base in metropolitan areas to encompass both growing and nongrowing jurisdictions and eliminate some disparities."[26] One system of regionalization would be for the county government to collect all (or part) of the property, sales, and income taxes on a countywide basis and distribute it to county, city, and other general purpose units of government in the same manner as revenue sharing funds are now distributed.[27]

**Attempts to Correct the Mismatch Between Services and Revenues in the Spread Metropolis.** Ralph Widner contends that there is little correlation between the functions of local government in many areas and the finances available.[28] An individual living in a metropolitan area may live in one community, work in another, shop in a third, and use a park or airport in still another. There is often a mismatch between revenues received from a citizen (which mainly go to the community in which the individual owns his home) and the communities providing services to the individual where he (or she) works, shops, and uses other community facilities. As fiscal conditions deteriorate in our older industrial metropolitan areas, Widner sees no alternative but to correct the mismatch.[29] Transfers of services to urban county governments tend to correct the mismatch, because many people are likely to live, work, shop, and use parking, airport, and other facilities within the same county. If Widner is correct in his assumption that there will be a great need to correct the mismatch, the result may be additional transfers of functions to urban county governments.

A further impetus for the transfer of functions to county governments will stem from the service problems in what John DeGrove and Carolyn Lawrence call the "spread metropolis."[30] In a "peanut butter" style of urban development, with cities interspersed like peanuts among unincorporated residential areas, functional problems such as water, sewage, solid waste, and transportation cannot be easily handled by individual cities. DeGrove and Lawrence feel that these functional problems and the problems of growth management can best be resolved on a county or multi-county basis.[31]

**Attempts to Achieve Greater Rationality in the Assignment of Local Functions.** Attempts will undoubtedly continue in the coming decade to review the assignment of functions to state and local government, with the aim of achieving greater uniformity and rationality in this assignment. The Advisory Commission on Intergovernmental Relations criticized the current service allocation patterns and discussed four characteristics which an ideal system of assigning functions should reflect.[32]

*Economic efficiency.* An efficient unit of government is one which is large enough to realize economies of scale and small enough not to incur diseconomies of scale. It should also provide alternative service offerings to citizens within a price range and level of effectiveness acceptable to local citizens.

*Fiscal equity.* An equitable unit would be large enough to encompass the costs and benefits of a function or willing to compensate other jurisdictions for the costs imposed on them for benefits received from them. It should also have adequate fiscal capacity to finance its public service responsibilities.

*Political accountability.* A politically accountable unit of government would be one that is controllable by, accessible to, and accountable to its residents and one that maximizes citizen participation in the performance of functions.

*Administrative effectiveness.* To be administratively effective a unit of government should be responsible for a wide variety of functions, encompass a geographic area adequate for the function, and have adequate legal authority to perform the function.

Who should do the assigning of functions in the future? The Advisory Commission on Intergovernmental Relations recommends a lengthy process beginning with state legislatures establishing state advisory commissions on intergovernmental relations which would then formulate general criteria for assigning new public services or reassigning established services.[33] After a process of developing functional classification standards, review of individual functions, and preparation of intergovernmental impact statements, recommendations would be made to appropriate state and local bodies. A process somewhat similar to that recommended by the Advisory Commission on Intergovernmental Relations will undoubtedly be established by some state legislatures during the next decade, and the two local units most likely to be the greatest recipients of additional functions are counties and regional councils.

County officials need to take an active role in the process of determining what services counties are best able to provide, and other local government officials and party leaders need to participate in the process. Daniel Lynch, Douglas County (Nebraska) County Commissioner and President of the National Association of Counties in 1976-77, stated:

"One of the most important tasks we have as county officials in the next decade is to determine which services counties are best able to perform. Conferences such as the Symposium on the Future of County Government can help us do that. We need also to involve the citizens of our counties in the process of change in county government. There needs to be more reliance on our two-party system and more reliance on our elective county officials."[34]

**Realignment of Power and Functions Within the Federal System.** County and other local governments will also be greatly affected by shifts of power and realignment of functions within the federal system. Ralph Widner contends that we are unlikely to see fundamental changes in the federal system in the next two decades, but are likely to see attempts to simplify this system.[35] Widner believes that "we will return to general government as the primary instrument of public policy and administration and turn away from special purpose mechanisms except in the category of public finance."[36] If Widner is correct, the shift will be to general purpose units of local government, such as counties, cities, and towns, and away from special districts and authorities.

Ralph Widner and others have predicted a fairly radical realignment of functions within the federal system.[37] Two substantial transfers of functions have already occurred during the 1970s. In the 1960s, state and county governments were the main units administering the aid to the aged, aid to the blind, and aid to the permanently and totally disabled programs. In January, 1974, the administration of these income maintenance programs was shifted to the U.S. Social Security Administration and called supplemental security income.[38]

During the 1960s, counties and other units of local government had little responsibility for manpower training and placement. Passage of the Comprehensive Employment and Training Act of 1973 shifted part of this function from the state level to the counties and cities which became prime-sponsors, members of consortia, and sub-grantees under the CETA progam.[39] As Philip Rutledge has pointed out, other federal legislation, such as Title XX of the Social Security Act of 1974, also brought transfers of functions.[40]

County officials expect some shifting of the financing or administration of county functions to the state or federal level in the next decade. They also anticipate some transfers of city functions to counties. Daniel Lynch, President of the National Association of Counties in 1976-77, states:

"During the next decade, the financing (or administration) of some current county functions could shift to the state or national level. Medicaid is currently a probable, since the county pays 20% of the costs in Nebraska and eligibility determination is done at the state level. The entire cost of Medicaid might be better paid from state or federal funds. There are some city functions which may

shift in my area to county responsibility in the next decade. These include countywide law enforcement, planning and zoning, solid waste disposal, and countywide transportation systems for smaller communities."[41]

County officials are concerned about federal interference in what they feel should be locally determined issues. The sewage disposal situation in Montgomery County (Maryland) is a good illustration of these concerns. The Blue Plains sewage treatment plant, on which Montgomery County chiefly depends, cannot expand its capacity beyond 309 million gallons a day. According to Montgomery County Councilman Neal Potter, the plant temporarily reached this level in 1973 due to heavy rainfall, and Montgomery County had to limit its sewer hookups.[42] An application for a federal grant for building a sixty million gallon treatment plant in Montgomery County was submitted to the Environmental Protection Agency. After supporting the proposal in 1973, the EPA reversed itself in 1976 and wanted Montgomery County to either reduce the size of its proposed plant, locate it elsewhere, build multiple smaller plants, or use a spray irrigation system which would be impractical for a densely populated residential area. Neal Potter expresses his concern about federal intervention in his county's sewage treatment problems as follows:

"I am very concerned about the federal government's role in sewage treatment in Montgomery County. I do not think the federal government should be deciding where the treatment plant is to be located. It has an appropriate role in setting the dollar amount of the grant and determining water quality standards, but not the location of the treatment plant. I am also deeply troubled by the EPA's erratic behavior in requiring a plant of one type and location in 1976, after $10 million had been spent on planning and design."[43]

County officials are also concerned about the federal government creating its own regional agencies and by-passing local government. Francis Francois, Prince George's County (Maryland) Councilman and a Vice-President of the National Association of Counties, writes:

"Yet another possible course for Congress is to directly create its own regional agencies, and give to them the decision-making power, with little or no involvement by either our states or our local governmental units. There are those who favor this concept, and indeed this is the essence of the recent legislation designed to establish federally-created health service agencies across the nation. I believe this approach spells disaster for both state and local governments, and that over the long run it would lead to a centrist national government along the lines of those in Europe. I doubt very much that the American people are prepared to accept this course of events."[44]

**Regional Councils—Partner or Rival of County Government.** The future of county government in the next decade is dependent, to some extent, on the future development of regional councils. In the mid-1960s, regional councils were seen in supporting roles, such as providing a forum for discussion, a staff for area-wide studies, and a lever in prying loose additional federal grants. One of the arguments against the councils of governments during the mid-1960s was that they were "toothless tigers" lacking the legislative power or executive authority to implement their own decisions.

Since 1965, regional councils have been granted power to review and comment upon many types of local government applications for federal aid. Moreover, the regional council itself is an important applicant for federal assistance, and federal grants (rather than local contributions) have become its most important source of revenue. As the regional council has taken on important planning and review functions, county officials have had some concerns about these councils. Daniel Lynch, County Commissioner of Douglas County (Nebraska), is particularly concerned about the danger of the non-elective staffs of councils of governments gaining too much power.

"I am concerned that we may give too much power to non-elective officials. Although the governing boards of councils of governments include elective officials, I am concerned that the appointive staff of COGs may gain too much power in the next decade and act too independently of their boards."[45]

Joseph Torrence, Finance Director of the Metropolitan Government of Nashville and Davidson County (Tennessee), recognizes the increasing power which regional councils have received from new functions, such as wastewater treatment planning. He is particularly concerned about regional councils gaining operating responsibilities.

"We are currently in the Mid-Cumberland Council of Governments. I hope our COG does not go beyond its review and planning functions in the next decade. I cannot imagine anything that would produce more change in local intergovernmental relations than for COGs to begin to assume operating functions. COGs have a lot of power through the A-95 review process now and can often have the leverage from their review powers to influence local government action. Currently staff personnel have a strong influence in the operation of the COGs, and this staff speaks the same language as federal administrators. County government needs to better develop its relationship with state government as a counterbalance for this."[46]

In some states, regional councils have run into determined opposition from city and county officials because of federally financed planning functions which undercut similar functions of city and county planning agencies. The Director of the Oregon Association of Counties, Jerry Orrick, reports strong opposition by city and county officials to increasing the regional planning functions of councils of governments in his state.[47] Any federal attempt to place operating responsibilities in regional councils in the next decade will run into determined opposition from city and county officials throughout the nation.

## LEGAL AND FISCAL LIMITATIONS ON THE FUTURE OF COUNTY GOVERNMENT

County governments have the potential of providing more services than they do currently, either directly or through intergovernmental cooperation, city-county agencies, and multi-county agencies. City-county consolidation, the urban county, and county service contracts offer good means of resolving metropolitan problems. To achieve their potential, however, county governments need to be freed from restrictive provisions of state constitutions and outmoded provisions and concepts of state law. The county home rule movement has provided one means of removing many of these limitations.

**Limitations in Constitution or Law.** Some of the most important limitations faced by county governments are the following.

*Limitations on organization.* County governments in some states are not free to adopt the same forms of government which cities in the same states may adopt. The council-administrator and council-elected executive forms have proved successful in many counties, and there is no valid reason why counties in all states should not have the option of adopting these forms of government. However, there are still eight states which permit only the commission form of county government.

*Limitations on city-county consolidation.* Consolidation of a county government with a city may be the best solution to metropolitan problems in some areas of the nation. It has proved very successful in Davidson County (Tennessee), Marion County (Indiana), Duval County (Florida), and other places in which it has been used. In Tennessee, the state constitution had to be amended to allow consolidation of Nashville and Davidson County. A similar amendment would be needed in other states (such as Idaho) to permit city-county consolidation. The constitutions of all states should permit consolidation by a majority vote of the people of the city and county to be combined.

*Limitations on county consolidation.* Consolidation of two or more counties may be a good solution to county problems in rural (and possibly metropolitan) areas. State constitutional provisions often make it extremely difficult for counties to consolidate. The Idaho Constitution, for example, requires a two-thirds or greater vote in each county to be consolidated and no county consolidation is likely to occur. The people of each county considering consolidation should be able to approve this consolidation by a simple majority vote.

*Limitations on intergovernmental cooperation.* County officials in all states should be able to cooperate in establishing city-county and multi-county agencies. They should have full powers to furnish services through service contracts, mutual aid agreements, and other intergovernmental means.

*Limitations on taxation and debt.* There are some reasonable limitations on local taxation and debt. Since local taxation may pre-empt state sources, the state legislature has a legitimate role in allocating certain tax sources to local gov-

ernment. Moreover, the state constitution (or law) has a legitimate role in establishing a process by which a majority vote is required to incur certain types of debt and raise property taxes beyond a certain limit. However, provisions of state constitutions and laws which go beyond this are unduly restrictive. For example, there is no need for provisions which set a specific dollar limitation on debt and require a two-thirds or greater majority vote to incur debt. State legislatures should not establish an arbitrary limit to the increase in county property taxes as has been done in Iowa.[48]

**Outmoded Legal Concepts.** Three legal concepts underlie many of the problems of county government. The first is the concept of the county as a quasi-municipal corporation which serves merely as an arm of the state. This concept was most strongly expressed by the Ohio Supreme Court in 1857 when it stated that "counties are created by the sovereign power of the state, of its own sovereign will" and that "with scarcely an exception, all the powers and functions of county organization have a direct and exclusive reference to the general policy of the state, and are in fact but a branch of the general administration of that policy."[49] The concept of the county as an arm of the state was more accepted in the mid-1800s than today, but the legal fiction lingers on. As late as 1938, an Alabama Court termed the county "an arm of the state, through which the state operates for convenience in the performance of its governmental function."[50] To the extent counties are regarded as an arm of the state, county agencies are subject to restrictive regulations of state agencies as well as restrictive provisions of state law.

County government is also hampered by the Dillon rule which has been quoted at length in Chapter 5. This rule strictly construes the powers of municipal corporations, limiting them to powers expressly provided, implied, or indispensable to the performance of a municipal function. The same rule has been applied to counties, as quasi-municipal corporations and has required counties to secure a specific provision of the law for each extension of functions.

The final outmoded concept pertains to county uniformity. The Idaho Constitution states, for example, that "the legislature shall establish, subject to the provisions of this article, a system of county government which shall be uniform throughout the state."[51] These and similar constitutional provisions in other states imply that there is some advantage for all counties to have the same organization, functions, and fiscal structure.[52]

But why should all counties be required to conform to the same mold? A Wisconsin report states: "The Constitution requires a uniform system of county government in Wisconsin. The idea of uniformity implies that the units in the uniform system be alike, or at least very largely alike, yet it is a familiar fact that the counties are not alike and have not been alike for a long time, whether they have ever been."[53] One of the strengths of local government is that it allows some flexibility for local officials to shape programs to meet the needs of their citizens. The concept of uniformity undermines this flexibility.

**The Home Rule Movement.** The county home rule movement, described in more detail in Chapter 5, is directed at freeing county government from the excessive restrictions and outmoded legal concepts previously described. One major objective of the county home rule movement is the passage of a constitutional amendment and enabling legislation permitting counties to draft their own county charters. After a county charter is drafted and approved by the voters, it generally serves as the constitution of the county (rather than state law), and county government is freed from excessive restrictions of state law. A second objective of county home rule is the passage of state laws which give counties greater flexibility in organization, finance, and functions. The future strength of county government is dependent, to some extent, on the degree to which the county home rule movement can achieve the following objectives.

*Reversal of outmoded legal concepts.* If counties are to expand their services and powers to meet the needs of their constituents, particularly in metropolitan areas, they need a broader interpretation of powers than those granted under the Dillon Rule.[54] County governments need to be able to exercise all powers not prohibited by state law or the county charter, as the Alaskan home rule constitutional amendment provides.

State constitutional provisions and laws should not try to force uniformity in the services provided by counties with very different populations and needs. Finally, the courts need to recognize that county governments are far different in function than a century ago, and they are just as much municipal corporations as are city governments.

*Optional forms of county government.*[55] The citizens of a county need to be able to choose the form of government which best fits the county's needs. It is particularly important for urban and metropolitan counties to be able to select (if they wish) a form of county government which provides for an elected chief executive or an appointive administrator who can coordinate county services.

The right to choose one of a number of optional forms of government can be provided by constitutional amendment (as in Utah) or by state law (as in New Jersey). There are advantages in having the people of a county periodically review their form of governmental structure, as is done under a Montana constitutional amendment.

*Greater freedom in intergovernmental arrangements.* During the next decade, there will need to be more experimentation in intergovernmental arrangements to determine the best area and organization pattern for each function. It is important for county government to have the authority to cooperate with other units of local government in joint administration of functions, service contracts, and other arrangements. It is also important that the people of all counties be given the option to combine county governments with cities and with other counties where this would provide the best solution to their needs.

*Greater flexibility in finance.* If county governments are to finance an expanded system of services,

it is essential that they be given greater flexibility in the next decade to seek additional forms of revenue. It is particularly important that county governments be permitted to use sales, income, or other non-property forms of taxation so they are not as dependent on the property tax and state shared revenues. Provisions are needed in all states to enable county governments to establish county service districts and to levy taxes just for the services furnished to the residents of the district.

County governments also need to be protected against state legislatures which add to the mandated functions of counties without furnishing additional sources of revenue.[56] This practice drains county resources making it more difficult for county officials to furnish the non-mandated services which county residents may feel are more important.

Underlying the home rule movement is the very important principle of local self-determination. If counties are to be successful in better serving their constituents in the next few decades, they must have greater power to choose the form of government which best fits their needs, to decide the services which their county will provide, and to determine how these services are to be financed.

## COUNTY MODERNIZATION

Unshackling county government from unduly restrictive provisions of state constitutions and laws will give counties needed authority, but will not assure that county government will be able to meet the demands of the next decades. Change needs to occur in county government and in popular attitudes towards county government.

**Factors in County Modernization.** The term "county modernization" has been used in Chapter 2 to describe the trend in county government away from the traditional mold. This includes:

* *the trend toward the performance of modern, optional functions and away from state-mandated functions which were major county responsibilities fifty years ago;*

* *the trend toward some version of the council-elected executive and council-administrator forms of county government and away from the older commission form;*

* *the trend toward county charters and away from over-reliance on state law as a source of legal authority and a trend away from considering county government as an arm of state government; and,*

* *the trend toward more extensive cooperation with other units of local government.*

There are other factors which should be taken into consideration in county modernization. They include: the use of the latest techniques in data processing, budgeting, purchasing, personnel, and other staff and service functions; the reorganization of county agencies to group similar functions together; and innovations in county program administration. The trend toward sales and income taxes and away from over-reliance on property taxes might

also be considered a sign of modernization. In addition, there are harder to define, intangible factors, such as the extent to which county officials have modern, innovative attitudes towards county administration and the role of county government in resolving areawide problems.

**An Index of County Modernization.** As a first step in measuring county modernization, the author has developed a county modernization index. This index provides a measure of three factors in modernization for which information is available: (1) the performance of twenty modern functions of county government;[57] (2) the use of the council elected-executive or council-administrator forms of county government; and, (3) the adoption by the county of a county charter. The index is only a first step toward a more meaningful and sophisticated index which could be developed when more quantitative data on modernization becomes available.

Using a sample of counties drawn from those replying to the NACo/ICMA county functions survey, described in Chapter 6, the author developed county modernization scores for 302 counties. Since the NACo/ICMA survey returns were slightly higher from counties with the greatest population, the sample was drawn by population groups in a way that did not overweight the most populous counties. The county modernization index somewhat arbitrarily gives "1" point to a county for each of twenty modern functions which it provides; "5" points to a county having a county charter; and "5" points to a county having a council-administrator or council elected-executive form of government.

As Table 10-3 shows, the modernization score of a county increases as the population of the county rises. Counties in large and medium sized metropolitan areas had higher modernization scores than non-metropolitan counties. Highly urban counties had higher modernization scores than predominantly rural counties. Charter counties had higher scores than non-charter counties, as one would expect, since charter counties received a bonus of "5" points in the modernization index. After subtracting "5" points from the score of charter counties, the modernization score of these counties still exceeded that of non-charter counties. In a similar fashion, council-elected executive and council-administrator forms of county government had higher modernization scores than commission counties and would have higher scores even without their 5-point bonuses. Thus, the author's preliminary research indicates that the most modern county governments are: those in counties having populations of 100,000 or more people; those located in large and medium sized metropolitan areas; those at least 75% urban; and those with

Table 10-3

COUNTY MODERNIZATION SCORES OF 302 COUNTIES BY CATEGORY

| | Average Modernization Score | | Average Modernization Score |
|---|---|---|---|
| Population class | | Status of charter | |
| 250,000 or more people | 14.4 | Charter | 20.8 |
| 100,000 - 249,999 | 11.7 | Non-charter | 6.7 |
| 50,000 - 99,999 | 8.5 | | |
| 25,000 - 49,999 | 7.9 | Form of government | |
| 10,000 - 24,999 | 6.6 | Council elected- | |
| 5,000 - 9,999 | 4.6 | executive | 18.4 |
| 2,500 - 4,999 | 4.2 | Council-administrator | 14.1 |
| 0 - 2,499 | 3.0 | Commission | 5.5 |
| | | | |
| Department of Agriculture Classification | | Percent of urban population | |
| Large metro - core county | 11.5 | 75% - 100% urban | 12.0 |
| Large metro - fringe county | 10.1 | 50% - 74% urban | 7.5 |
| Medium metro | 11.3 | 25% - 49% urban | 7.1 |
| Small metro | 9.1 | 1% - 24% urban | 6.8 |
| Urbanized adjacent | 9.8 | 0% urban | 5.3 |
| Urbanized nonadjacent | 9.3 | | |
| Less urbanized adjacent | 6.5 | | |
| Less urbanized nonadjacent | 6.7 | Area | |
| Thinly populated adjacent | 5.6 | 0-199 square miles | 7.8 |
| Thinly populated non-adjacent | 4.2 | 200-399 square miles | 8.0 |
| | | 400-599 square miles | 7.2 |
| | | 600-799 square miles | 6.4 |
| | | 800-999 square miles | 5.4 |
| | | 1,000-1,499 sq. miles | 5.8 |
| | | 1,500-1,999 sq. miles | 8.3 |
| | | Over 2,000 sq. miles | 8.8 |

county charters and either council-elected executive or council-administrator forms of county government.

**An Agenda for Future Research in County Government.** The county modernization index, previously described, needs to be developed further by adding other factors which contribute to county modernization, such as the use of intergovernmental contracts and agreements, the use of the most current techniques in staff services such as budgeting, and achievements in program innovation. County officials should be polled to learn what criteria they would use to distinguish a modern county government from a traditional county.

A more sophisticated county modernization index could be used to determine the characteristics of the most modern county governments. Repeated annual calculation of the index would indicate the rate of county modernization. Furthermore, the relationship between the modernization of counties, program output, and the per capita cost of county functions needs to be more fully explored.[58] Identifying the most modern counties through an index would facilitate research on the factors which cause modernization. We need to know whether demographic factors (such as county populations) are mainly associated with county modernization or whether there are certain types of catalysts within the county government which tend to produce change. If the future of county government is dependent, to some extent, on county modernization, we need to know much more than we do now about what produces this modernization.

**Catalysts of County Modernization.** Preliminary research by the author indicates that there are four main catalysts for county modernization. Some of the impetus for modernization initially comes from citizen demands for new programs. As county governments add new programs and existing programs become more complex, county officials find that they need types of administrative leadership, patterns of intergovernmental relations, and types of staff assistance and program innovation, which were not previously needed. As the pressures mount, county officials may need the flexible types of authority found in county charters and also new forms of non-property taxation.

The vision of county officials and other county leaders undoubtedly provides the spark which ignites many county modernization plans. Sometimes this vision comes from a single county official who sees the need for a new county function, a county charter, or a strenghened form of county organization; and sometimes the vision comes from a board of county commissioners, a study commission, or a planning group.

A third catalyst for change comes from federal and state government sources. These include recommendations from national commissions (such as the Advisory Commission on Intergovernmental Relations) and state commissions on constitutional revision and local government. Even more important are changes in federal and state requirements which encourage (or require) counties to undertake new functions.

The final catalyst for modernization comes from state associations of counties and the National Association of Counties. One of the advantages of the American system of local government is that each county, city, and other local unit is free to experiment (within limits) with new programs and management techniques. The value of this experimentation would be lost unless some agency collected and analyzed information on innovative county programs and informed other county governments about these programs.

This service is provided on the national level by the National Association of Counties which annually gives achievement awards to county governments for innovative programs and informs other counties of the programs through its publication, *The Living Library.* The committees and staff of the National Association of Counties also provide the spark for change through recommendations which appear in the *American County Platform,* through studies which explore and recommend changes in county programs, and through technical assistance to individual counties. State associations of counties also provide their members with information on innovative county programs, technical assistance, and (in some cases) with reports and recommendations for change.

## CONCLUSION

American county governments have undergone substantial change in the sixty years since H.S. Gilbertson described the county as "the 'dark continent' of American politics."[59] Many of the evils pictured

by Gilbertson (such as the county alms house and the pocketing of fees by county officers) have been corrected.[60] Counties have assumed more than fifty new functions since Gilbertson's time, and the administration of traditional functions (such as welfare) has changed greatly. Sixty years ago, county home rule was a few years old, the county manager plan was just being proposed, and no county in the nation had an elected county executive. In sixty years, most of the reforms proposed by Gilbertson have become reality. Counties in at least fifteen states have adopted home rule charters, more than half of the people residing in counties live under a council-administrator or council-elected executive plan, most counties have planning organizations, and there have been a dozen city-county consolidations since World War II.

Despite the advances made by county government in the past sixty years, popular attitudes still reflect the views of some textbooks of the 1940s and 1950s. Many people have read that county government is "archaic," and they have little knowledge of county functions except those affecting their daily lives. County officials need to inform their constituents more effectively about county services in attractive informative booklets, such as those prepared by Nassau County (New York), Alameda County (California), and Montgomery County (Ohio). County agencies need more public feedback from public opinion surveys and other sources of public attitudes on county services.[61]

There needs to be more citizen participation in the decision-making processes of all units of local government including counties. Citizen participation can be encouraged through the scheduling of more public meetings in the evenings, use of more citizens' advisory committees, strict adherence to open meeting laws, and improved relations with the media. Meaningful citizen participation can also be stimulated through involving the public in setting goals for the county for a ten to twenty year period. The futures programs in Iowa, Minnesota, Washington, and other states have been successful in getting citizens to set economic, social, and governmental goals for change in their states.[62] The same process could be used by county governments to get their citizens to describe the type of future change (if any) they wish to see in their county, and these citizen views on the future of the county could be used as a guide for county goal-setting.

County governments have a priceless asset which many municipalities do not have, as Norman Beckman has pointed out. This asset is "what students of government would term 'adequate areal jurisdiction'—but what can better be described by the word 'space.' "[63] In single county metropolitan areas, it is possible for county government to become, if it is not already, the main unit of local government. County governments also have an important role in multicounty metropolitan areas. W. Brooke Graves and Mark H. Freeman have pointed out that "Even in those instances in which the metropolitan area spills over into two or more counties, the task of coordinating the efforts of a small number of counties is far simpler than that of coordinating the dozens or scores of

small local units to be found within most metropolitan areas."[64]

County government seems destined to gain more functions and increased importance in the next decade, and this trend will bring increased pressure for county modernization. A 1976 report of the Advisory Commission on Intergovernmental Relations states:

"In our considered judgment the county in many urban states will become a significantly more important unit of local government during the next decade. One-eighth of the municipalities plan to shift responsibility for a function(s) during the next two years to the county, and nearly one-half of the municipal respondents believe the transfers of functions to the county have increased the need for modernization of the county government. The structural reorganization and modernization of county governments will improve their capacity to provide services and thereby encourage municipalities to shift responsibility for functions and components of functions to the county."[65]

Counties have made substantial strides over the past sixty years and have the advantage of a larger area than any other unit of local government. However, the future of county government depends upon whether counties will be able to change further in organization, services, finance, and intergovernmental relationships to meet the changing needs of the next few decades. The rapidity with which counties can make needed changes will depend, in part, upon the flexibility and authority granted them by state constitutions and state laws. It will depend also upon the willingness of county officials to support necessary modernization and better public understanding of the need for change and the potential of county government.

## REFERENCES

1. Ralph R. Widner, "Future Possibilities for Local Governments in the U.S.", paper prepared for the Symposium on the Future of County Government in Boston, September 15, 1976, pp. 6, 7. The writer is indebted to Mr. Widner for some of the basic concepts expressed in this chapter.

2. U.S. Bureau of Census, *Current Population Reports, Series p. 25, No. 601, Projections of the Population of the U.S. 1975 to 2025*, (Washington: U.S. Government Printing Office, 1975), p. 11. The Series II (or middle) projection has been used here rather than the more extreme Series I and Series III projections.

3. Interview with Alastair McArthur, Coordinator of Intergovernmental Programs for Montgomery County (Maryland), in Boston, September 17, 1976.

4. Interview with Mr. Joseph E. Torrence, Director of Finance, Metropolitan Government of Nashville and Davidson County, in Boston, September 17, 1976.

5. Ralph Widner, p. A-1.

6. Ralph Widner, p. A-3, sees the major migration into the South. Alan Campbell pictures the migration as weakening the areas being abandoned and strengthening the South and Southwest. Alan Campbell, "The Macroeconomics of State and Local Governments", paper prepared for the Symposium on the Future of County Government, Boston, September 15, 1976, p. 14.

7. Alan Campbell, p. 14.

8. Ralph Widner, p. A-6.

9. The eight point program of Mr. Hayes, Chairman of the National Association of Counties' Steering Committee on Energy and Environment, is described further in *County News* (Washington) February 7, 1977.

10. Ralph Widner, p. 6.

11. Interview with Rio Blanco County (Colorado) Commissioner, William Brennan in Boston, September 15, 1976.

12. See National Association of Counties, *Controlling Boomtown Development, Sweetwater and Unita Counties, Wyoming* (Washington: National Association of Counties, 1976).

13. Interview with County Commissioner William Brennan in Boston, September 15, 1976.

14. Calvin L. Beale, *The Revival of Population Growth in Non-Metropolitan America* (Washington: Economic Research Service, U.S. Department of Agriculture, 1975), p. 6. Popula-

tion growth was 4.7% in non-metropolitan counties adjacent to metropolitan areas and 3.7% in counties not adjacent to metropolitan areas.

15. Ralph Widner, p. A-4. Calvin Beale, p. 9 states that the "decentralization trend in U.S. manufacturing has been a major factor in transforming the rural and small town economy, especially in the upland parts of the South."

16. Calvin Beale, p. 9, notes that there has been a spread of retirement settlements to the Ozarks, the Sierra Nevada foothills in California, the hill country and coastal plain of Texas, and the cutover region of the Upper Great Lakes.

17. Interview with Bernard Smith in Boston, September 16, 1976.

18. Ralph Widner, p. A-7.

19. Interview with Joseph Torrence in Boston, September 16, 1976. In 1977, Mr. Torrence retired and entered a consulting business.

20. Interview with Conrad Fowler in Boston, September 16, 1976.

21. Interview with Alastair McArthur in Boston, September 17, 1976.

22. Ibid.

23. For further information on this point see Alan Campbell, pp. 10-12.

24. Ibid., p. 11. This loss was incurred between 1972 and 1974.

25. The three options are described more fully by Alan Campbell, pp. 15-20. The increase in federal financing might include full federal government financing of welfare costs.

26. Ralph Widner, p. 7.

27. The idea was suggested by Alan Campbell, p. 16, in his description of a Minneapolis/St. Paul regional revenue sharing plan. In the plan, 40% of the non-residential tax base growth is shared on a formula basis among all jurisdictions in the region.

28. Ralph Widner, p. 4, states that "A lot of our local problems today are boundary problems; the capabilities of local governments do not match the scale of demands placed upon them or the financial resources available to them. There is little correlation any more between the functions of local government in many metropolitan areas and the territory and finances it commands."

29. Ibid., pp. 4, 5. Widner states that "the urban county,. . .may become a primary vehicle for services in the smaller metropolitan areas."

30. John DeGrove and Carolyn Lawrence, "Changing Patterns in County Government Service Delivery," paper prepared for the Symposium on the Future of County Government, Boston, September 15, 1976, p. 1.

31. Ibid., pp. 1, 2. They state that eventually most of these problems may need to be addressed on a multi-county basis, but sub-state regionalism is evolving slowly. In the meantime, they state, "much can, is and will be done at the county level to solve the problems of the 'spread city.'"

32. Advisory Commission on Intergovernmental Relations, *Governmental Functions and Processes: Local and Areawide* (Washington: Advisory Commission on Intergovernmental Relations, 1974), p. 7.

33. Ibid., pp. 19, 20.

34. Interview with Daniel C. Lynch, Douglas County (Nebraska) Commissioner, in Boston, September 16, 1976.

35. Ralph Widner, pp. 1, 2.

36. Ibid., p. 2.

37. Ibid., pp. 2, 6. One of Widner's suggestions was "to get the few cities that are in the business of financing welfare out of it as soon as possible."

38. See p. 174.

39. The CETA program was described further on pp. 178, 180.

40. Philip J. Rutledge, "The Future of County Government", paper prepared for the Symposium on the Future of County Government, in Boston, September 15, 1976, pp. 19-20.

41. Interview with Daniel Lynch, in Boston, September 16, 1976.

42. Interview with Neal Potter, Montgomery County (Maryland) Councilman, in Boston, September 16, 1976.

43. Ibid.

44. Francis B. Francois, "Counties and Intergovernmental Relationships Facing the Third Century," paper prepared for the Symposium on the Future of County Government, September 15, 1976, pp. 15, 16.

45. Interview with Daniel Lynch in Boston, September 16, 1976.

46. Interview with Joseph Torrence in Boston, September 16, 1976.

47. Interview with John Orrick in Boston, September 17, 1976.

48. According to Bernard Smith, the Iowa Legislature imposed a 9% limit on the amount that counties may raise property taxes. Bernard Smith, interview, September 16, 1976.

49. Commissioners of Hamilton County v. Mighels, 7 Ohio St. 110, 119. (1857). Moore v. Walker County, 185 So. 175, 177 (1938).

50. Moore v. Walker County, 236 Ala. 688, 690 (1938).

51. Idaho, *Constitution*, Article XVIII, Section 5.

52. Recognizing the problems of trying to cast all county governments in the same mold, some states, such as Wisconsin, have acted in recent years to eliminate these types of uniform provisions in their Constitutions.

53. Bureau of Government, University of Wisconsin, *County Government and the Problems of Urban Expansion* (Madison: University of Wisconsin, 1959), p. 14. This was written before the county uniformity provision was substantially changed.

54. The Dillon Rule was quoted at length on pp. 106, 107.

55. For further information on home rule constitutional provisions and on optional forms of county government, see National Association of Counties, *From America's Counties*

*Today* (Washington: National Association of Counties, 1973), pp. 52-58.

56. Dewey Knight has recommended that each state legislature pass a fiscal responsibility act which provides that no additional services will be required of local government by the state unless a source of revenue is provided. Dewey Knight, "The Future of County Finance," paper prepared for the Symposium on the Future of County Government, Boston, September 15, 1976, pp. 3, 4.

57. The twenty modern functions are: air pollution control, airports, alcohol and drug programs, consumer protection, building code enforcement, energy management, human resources planning, growth management, job training, land use planning, mass transit, noise control, parking, performing arts, public housing, recreation, sewage treatment, water supply, water pollution control, and work release programs.

58. The techniques could be somewhat similar to those used to measure the outputs of state welfare, education, and taxation policies. See particularly Thomas Dye, *Politics, Economics, and the Public: Policy Outcomes in the American States* (Chicago: Rand McNally, 1966) and Ira Sharkansky, *Spending in American States* (Chicago: Rand McNally, 1968).

59. The widely quoted phrase was used in the subtitle of Gilbertson's book. H.S. Gilbertson, *The County, The "Dark Continent" of American Politics* (New York: The National Short Ballot Organization, 1917).

60. Ibid., pp. 50, 86.

61. See Kenneth Webb and Harry P. Hatry, *Obtaining Citizen Feedback: The Application of Citizen Surveys to Local Governments* (Washington: The Urban Institute, 1973) for descriptions of how public opinion surveys can be used to improve local government services.

62. For further information on state and local futures programs, see Keith A. Bea and Cynthia E. Houston, *Citizen Futures Organizations: Group Profiles* (Washington: Library of Congress, 1976). State futures programs include: the Delaware, Idaho, and Massachusetts Tomorrow Programs, the Hawaii and Iowa 2000 programs, Alternatives for Washington, and the programs sponsored by commissions on Maine's and Minnesota's futures. There have been some local futures groups, such as Dimensions for Charlotte-Mecklenburg County (North Carolina) and Nashville (Tennessee) Citizen Goals 2000 Committee. The Nashville citizens' committee was appointed by the Mayor of the Metropolitan Government of Nashville and Davidson County to provide guidance for the future development of Nashville. Ibid., p. 63.

63. Norman Beckman, "Taking Account of Urban Counties," *American County Government* 30 (October, 1965):68.

64. W. Brooke Graves and Mark H. Freeman, *County Government: Origins, Development, Present Status, Future Prospects with Special Reference to West Virginia* (Washington: The Library of Congress Legislative Reference Service, 1962), p. 51.

65. Advisory Commission on Intergovernmental Relations, *Pragmatic Federalism: The Reassignment of Functional Responsibility* (Washington: Advisory Commission on Intergovernmental Relations, 1976), pp. 69, 70.

# Bibliography

Several excellent bibliographies on county government have been published in the last decade making a lengthy bibliography unnecessary in this volume. This brief listing of references is intended to be used by students and county officials seeking additional data rather than scholars compiling a comprehensive list of sources. The style of this bibliography, adapted from the one used in *The County Year Book*, is intended to facilitate a search of subjects and titles rather than a search by author.

Bibliographies

*American County Government.* By John C. Bollens in association with John R. Bayes and Kathryn L. Utter. Beverly Hills: Sage Publications, Inc., 1969. Includes a comprehensive and well-annotated bibliography on county government of more than 300 pages.

"Sources of Information." By Rosemary Weise. *The County Year Book, 1976.* Washington: National Association of Counties and International City Management Association, 1976, pp. 229-248. Contains a selective bibliography of books, handbooks, periodicals, and other publications of value to county officials.

Books on County Government in the United States (By date of publication)

*The County: The 'Dark' Continent of American Politics.* By H.S. Gilbertson. New York: The National Short Ballot Association, 1917. A classic that deserves to be read in full, not only for the descriptions of county shortcomings in the early 20th century, but also for the recommendations for county government in the future.

*County and Township Government in the United States.* By Kirk H. Porter. New York: The Macmillan Company, 1922.

*County Government and Administration.* By John A. Fairlie and Charles M. Kneier. New York: The Century Company, 1930. Describes the organization and functions of county government and county-state relations at the time.

*American County Government.* By Arthur Bromage. New York: Sears Publishing Company, 1933. Contains descriptions of county-state relationships, the county manager plan, county consolidation, and other topics.

*County Government Across the Nation.* By Paul W. Wager, ed. Chapel Hill: The University of North Carolina Press, 1950. Contains chapters on county government in each state with lengthy case studies which describe the organization, services, and finances of individual counties.

*County Government in America.* By Herbert S. Duncombe. Washington: National Association of Counties Research Foundation, 1966. Describes county government history, organization, services, finances, and intergovernmental relations and provides lengthy case studies on five counties.

*Guide to County Organization and Management.* Washington: National Association of Counties, 1968. Includes articles by thirty-eight authors on subjects such as county home rule, county governing boards, county reapportionment, personnel, budgeting, purchasing, data processing, record keeping, transportation, public welfare, health, parks and recreation, and county planning. The articles are intended to be a practical guide for improved county administration.

*American County Government.* By John C. Bollens in association with John R. Bayes and Kathryn L. Utter. Beverly Hills: Sage Publications, Inc., 1969. Begins with a lengthy essay on the literature of county government which reviews existing studies and presents an agenda for additional research. A second section suggests new research approaches to a study of county government, and the final section (more than three-quarters of the book) provides an extensive annotated bibliography.

*Metropolitics and the Urban County.* By Thomas P. Murphy. Washington: Washington National Press, Inc., 1970. A comprehensive case study of the transition of Jackson County (Kansas City), Missouri from boss rule to a modern, reform government. The opening and concluding chapters provide insight on metropolitan problems and politics in other areas of the nation.

*Profile of County Government.* By Advisory Commission on Intergovernmental Relations. Washington: U.S. Government Printing Office, 1972. Contains chapters on county reform, the structure and organization of county government, county services, county zoning and land use controls, and county-special district relationships. The report includes valuable statistical tables on county functions and county power over special districts.

*From America's Counties Today, 1973.* Washington: National Association of Counties, 1973. A fact book containing sections on county home rule, organization, programs, finances, and intergovernmental relations written by the NACo staff.

*Grass Roots Government: The County in American Politics.* By Susan W. Torrence. Washington: Robert B. Luce, Inc., 1974. Describes county services and their effect on the average citizen. The book also contains chapters on the politics of public decisions, the growth of public unions, the struggle for regional cooperation, and the impact of the federal government on counties.

*County Year Book.* Washington: National Association of Counties and International City Management Association, 1977. Includes extensive statistical studies on county governments and services as well as a listing of all counties and the names of their chief officials. Both the 1976 and 1975 *County Year Books* contain a number of articles on county trends, finances, employment, services, and administration.


Books and Handbooks on County Government in Selected States
(By state name)

To understand the functions, powers, organization, finances, and services of county government in a particular state, the best sources are state law and publications designed to assist county officials in performing their duties. The following have been published since 1970:

Alabama. *Manual for Alabama County Commissioners.* By James D. Thomas. University: Bureau of Public Administration, University of Alabama, 1975.

California. *California County Fact Book, 1975.* Sacramento: County Supervisors Association of California, 1975.

Florida. *Florida County Commissioners Manual.* Tallahassee: State Association of County Commissioners of Florida, 1972.

Georgia. *Guidebook to Georgia County Government.* Paul M. Hirsch, ed., Athens: Institute of Government, The University of Georgia, 1970.

266 • *Modern County Government*

Idaho. *Handbook for County Officials in Idaho.* By Michael S. Vollmer, Herbert S. Duncombe, and Katherine D. Pell. Moscow: Bureau of Public Affairs Research, University of Idaho, 1974.

Iowa. *Manual of Instructions for Newly Elected County Officials.* Des Moines: Iowa State Association of Counties, 1975.

Michigan. *Guide to Michigan County Government.* By Kenneth VerBurg. East Lansing: The Institute for Community Development and Services, Michigan State University, 1972. This is the most comprehensive of the state handbooks for county officials.

Minnesota. *Minnesota County Government.* St. Paul: Association of Minnesota Counties, 1975.

Mississippi. *A Manual for Mississippi County Supervisors.* 2nd Ed. By Dana B. Brammer. University: Bureau of Governmental Research, University of Mississippi, 1973.

Montana. *Manual for County Commissioners.* Missoula: University of Montana Law School, 1973. See also *Montana Counties on the Move.* By Jerry Holloran. Helena: Montana Association of Counties, 1974.

Nebraska. *Guide to Nebraska County Government.* By Willis D. Moreland. Lincoln: Nebraska Association of County Officials, 1975.

New Jersey. *County Governing Bodies in New Jersey.* By Harris I. Effross. New Brunswick: Rutgers University Press, 1975. Provides a comprehensive and well documented history of the development, reorganization, and reform of the New Jersey Boards of Chosen Freeholders from 1798 through 1974.

New Mexico. *The New Mexico County Commission.* By James I. Grieshop. Las Cruces: Cooperative Extension Service, New Mexico State University, 1974.

New York. *County Legislative Guide.* By Clark Hamlin. Ithaca: Local Government Program, Cornell University, 1975.

North Carolina. *County Government in North Carolina.* Revised Edition. Joseph S. Ferrell, ed. Chapel Hill: Institute of Government, University of North Carolina, 1975. The 24 articles included in this book provide comprehensive coverage of subjects such as county recreation, social services, records management, criminal justice planning, and other subjects.

South Carolina. *Guide to South Carolina County Government.* Columbia: South Carolina Association of Counties, 1975.

South Dakota. *South Dakota County Officials Handbook.* 4th Ed. Compiled by Ed J. Leahy. Vermillion: Governmental Research Bureau, University of South Dakota, 1975.

Utah. *Handbook of County Government in Utah.* Salt Lake City: Utah Association of Counties, 1973.

Virginia. *The Virginia Local Legislator: A Guide for Municipal Mayors and Councilmen and County Supervisors.* Charlottesville: Virginia Municipal League, Virginia Association of Counties, and the Institute of Government, University of Virginia, 1972.

Wyoming. *Handbook for Wyoming County Commissioners.* By John C. Miller and David Mullinax. Laramie: Institute of Business and Management Services, University of Wyoming, 1974.

Publications on Individual County Governments

To obtain detailed knowledge of county programs, structure, and finance, it is essential to study at least several counties in depth. The types of publications that would be most useful are:

Annual Financial and Audit Reports. Most county financial reports are useful only for a study of county finance, but some financial and audit reports contain program information. For example, the performance audit reports of the King County (Washington) Auditor contain useful information on the objectives, practices, and procedures of county departments.

Annual County Reports. Many of the larger counties issue annual reports describing the structure of county government and county programs. For example, Nassau County (New York) has a 50-page report containing an extensive description of county services and many photographs of county facilities.

Budgets. Most county budgets are financial plans that provide little program information. However, some of the larger counties, such as Montgomery County (Maryland), Fairfax County (Virginia), Westchester County (New York), and Nashville-Davidson County (Tennessee), have budgets which provide the public with useful descriptions of county programs.

Case Studies of County Politics. There are a few books on county politics. Among the best is *Metropolitics and the Urban County.* By Thomas P. Murphy. Washington: Washington National Press, 1970. Some excellent, short case studies of county politics have appeared in *The Washington Post* and the *Empire State Report.*

Case Studies of County Programs. The *Living Library,* published by the National Association of Counties, lists award winning case studies which may be purchased from NACo for the cost of photocopying and handling.

Comprehensive Plans. The comprehensive plans of most counties are invaluable sources of information about the geography, economy, population, and current land uses in individual counties. Many comprehensive plans, such as that of Weld County (Colorado), discuss the growth and and land use problems facing the county.

Departmental Reports. The most detailed descriptions of specific county programs may often be found in the annual reports of individual county departments. For example, one may find in the annual reports of the Allegheny County (Pennsylvania) Health Department detailed descriptions of the county's disease control, maternal and child health, water protection, air pollution control, and other programs.

League of Women Voters Reports. A number of local Leagues of Women Voters have produced studies that provide very good sources of information on county government.

Publications of the National Association of Counties (not previously listed)
(1735 New York Avenue, Washington, D.C. 20006)

*Achievement Award Case Studies.* Counties having an innovative program are encouraged by NACo to send in a description of the program and how it was established. These case studies are reviewed by the NACo staff, and if they find them sufficiently noteworthy, the county is given an achievement award. The award-winning case studies are described briefly in the *Living Library* and may be obtained from NACo by paying a small fee for photocopying.

*American County Platform.* The official statement of the National Association of Counties which is published annually after the mid-summer meeting of the Association. This publication of more than 100 pages describes the position of NACo on subjects such as home rule and regional affairs, community development, criminal justice, education, employment, environment and energy, health, and land use.

*Consolidation: Partial or Total.* Provides views of officials in 1973 from counties such as Duval (Florida), Dade (Florida), Marion (Indiana), and Davidson (Tennessee) on the question of how successful total or partial city-county consolidations have been.

*County News.* A weekly newspaper which contains articles on national legislation and administrative action affecting counties, innovative county programs, and other news of interest to county officials.

*National Survey of the Appointed Administrator in County Government.* Reports the results of an extensive survey in 1973 of appointed county administrators.

*NACo Fact Sheets.* Short, printed research reports which provide the latest information on a variety of subjects. For example, a January, 1977 sheet on elected county executives listed all the counties in the nation having an elected executive and the total population in each state governed under this form of government.

*New County Times.* A supplement to *County News* which provides in-depth coverage of specific county functions or issues. The supplements include articles by academicians, county officials, and others on topics such as regionalism, transportation, and community colleges.

Research Reports and Manuals on County Programs. The staff of the National Association of Counties has written more than 100 research reports of varying lengths in the past decade, and they are available from NACo in printed or duplicated forms. The reports include: statistical reports on county programs such as *County-Wide Law Enforcement.* By A. Anthony McCann (1975). There are case studies such as *Organizing and Reorganizing for Local Criminal Justice Planning: Five Examples.* By Duane Baltz (1975). Some reports provide information on innovative county programs such as *Special Report on County Criminal Justice Programs.* By Donald Murray (1974). Final reports on some NACo grants, such as *The Rural Human Resources Project* (1974), provide very useful information on county government. NACo publishes sets of manuals on traffic safety, solid waste management, county engineering, and other subjects which are also valuable for research on county government.

Symposium on the Future of County Government. A four volume set of papers prepared for the NACo Conference on the Future of County Government held in Boston on September 15-19, 1976.

## Other Sources

Advisory Commission on Intergovernmental Relations (ACIR), 726 Jackson Place, N.W., Washington, D.C. 20575. The reports of the Advisory Commission on Intergovernmental Relations are essential reading for students of county government and county officials. For studies of regionalism, sub-state districting, and local government reorganization, see particularly: *Regional Decision Making: New Strategies for Substate Districts* (1973); *Regional Governance: Promise and Performance* (1973); and *The Challenge of Local Government Reorganization*

(1974). For a description of transfers of functional responsibility from one unit of local government to another and criteria for the assignment of functions, see: *Governmental Functions and Processes: Local and Area-wide* (1974) and *Pragmatic Federalism: The Reassignment of Functional Responsibility* (1976). The Advisory Commission on Intergovernmental Relations has published many reports on local taxation, including: *The Property Tax in a Changing Environment* (1974) and *Local Revenue Diversification: Income, Sales Taxes and User Charges* (1974). The ACIR report *The States and Intergovernmental Aids* (1977) describes types of state aid and the impact of state aid systems on counties and other local units. In *Community Development: The Working of a Federal-Local Block Grant* (1977), the ACIR describes a block grant program affecting local government. There are also ACIR reports on criminal justice and other programs, such as: *State-Local Relations in the Criminal Justice System* (1971); *Making the Safe Streets Act Work* (1970); and *Intergovernmental Responsibilities for Water Supply and Sewage Disposal in Metropolitan Areas* (1962).

Census Bureau, Department of Commerce, Washington, D.C. 20233. The decennial census provides statistics on the characteristics of population by income, occupation, and many other groupings. To keep abreast of population trends of counties between census periods, see the PC series of census reports. The *City and County Data Book*, published by the U.S. Government Printing Office in 1973, contains extensive information on the economy, housing, labor force, trade, agriculture, income level, and population of each county. A census of governments is conducted every five years in years ending with "2" and "7". Among the major census reports of the 1972 Census of Governments were: *Volume 1, Government Organization; Volume 2, Taxable Property; Volume 3, Public Employment; Volume 4, Government Finances; and Volume 5, Local Government in Metropolitan Areas.* Report No. 3 of Volume 4, describing county government finance, is particularly useful.

International City Management Association, 1140 Connecticut Avenue, Washington, D.C. 20036. A co-publisher of *The County Year Book*, the ICMA publishes numerous source books valuable to local officials including: *Municipal Police Administration* (1971); *Local Government Personnel Administration* (1976); *Management Policies in Local Government Finance* (1975); *Urban Public Works Administration* (1976); and *Principles and Practices of Urban Planning* (1968).

Journal Articles. The scholarly publications in political science have contained surprisingly few articles on county government. Aside from *The County News* and *New County Times*, published by the National Association of Counties, the best source of short articles on county and local government is the *National Civic Review*, published by the National Municipal League. The most comprehensive article on county government appearing in the *American Political Science Review* was Clyde F. Snider "American County Government: A Mid-Century Review," 46: 74, March, 1952.

Monographs. Some monographs published by universities go beyond a description of county government in a state and provide useful sources on county government or county problems throughout the nation. See particularly *The Emerging Patterns of County Executives* by William H. Cape (Lawrence: Governmental Research Center, The University of Kansas, 1967); *City-County Consolidation: A Guide for Virginians* by S.J. Makielski (Charlottesville: Institute of Government, University of Virginia, 1971); *Effect of Law on County and Municipal Expenditures* by David Minge (Laramie: Wyoming Law Institute, University of Wyoming, 1975); and *Handbook of Montana Forms of Local Government* by James L. Lopach and Lauren S. McKinsey (Missoula: Bureau of Government Research, University of Montana, 1975).

Reports of Federal Agencies and Presidential Commissions. Federal agencies publish a number of excellent reports on economic, social, and other characteristics of counties and their populations. See particularly *Social and Economic Characteristics of the Population in Metro and Nonmetro Counties,* 1970 by Fred K. Hines, David L. Brown and John Zimmer (Washington: Economic Research Service, U.S. Department of Agriculture, 1975). The Office of Management and Budget has been the source of useful publications on intergovernmental relations, such as *Strengthening Public Management in the Intergovernmental System* (Washington: U.S. Government Printing Office, 1975). Presidential commissions have provided valuable reports in functional areas, such as *The Challenge of Crime in a Free Society* by The President's Commission on Law Enforcement and Administration of Justice (Washington: U.S. Government Printing Office, 1967). There are many other federal reports on specific functions of government of interest to county officials.

Textbooks on Local and Metropolitan Government. For a comprehensive description of county governments in the 1950s, see: *Government in Rural America* by Lane W. Lancaster (New York: D. Van Nostrand Company, Inc., 1952) and *Local Government in Rural America* by Clyde F. Snider (New York: Appleton-Century-Crofts, Inc., 1957). The urban county, city-county consolidation, and the politics of metropolitan reform are covered in books on metropolitan government, such as: *The Metropolis: Its People, Politics and Economic Life,* 2nd edition by John C. Bollens and Henry J. Schmandt (New York: Harper and Row, 1970) and *The American Metropolis,* 2nd ed. by Leonard E. Goodall and Donald P. Sprengel (Columbus: Charles E. Merrill Publishing Company, 1975). Some state and local government textbooks have a chapter on county government including *State and Local Government,* 3rd ed. by Russell W. Maddox and Robert F. Fuquay (New York: D. Van

Nostrand Company, 1975). Some books of readings on local government have chapters or articles on county government. See particularly, "County Government Is Reborn" by Bernard F. Hillenbrand in Joseph F. Zimmerman, ed., *Readings in State and Local Government* (New York: Holt, Rinehart and Winston, Inc., 1964).

Textbooks on Parties and Interest Groups. There has been surprisingly little written in textbooks on party and interest group organization at the county level. For references to books on county politics in particular states, see footnote 32 in chapter four of this volume. The most comprehensive description of the lobbying activities of the National Association of Counties and other public interest groups may be found in *When Governments Come to Washington* by Donald H. Haider (New York: The Free Press, 1974).

The Urban Institute, 2100 M Street, N.W., Washington, D.C. 20037. Among the many publications of the Urban Institute of value to county officials are: *Measuring the Effectiveness of Basic Municipal Services* (1974) and *The Fiscal Impact of Residential and Commercial Development: A Case Study* (1972).

# Index